£5.90

2nd

Edition

ALEXANDRE DUMAS

MICHAEL ROSS

ALEXANDRE DUMAS

David & Charles
Newton Abbot   London   North Pomfret (Vt)

British Library Cataloguing in Publication Data

Ross, Michael, b. *1905*
  Alexandre Dumas.
  1. Dumas, Alexandre, b. 1802 – Biography
  2. Authors, French – 19th century – Biography
  843'.7   PQ2230

  ISBN 0–7153–7758–2

Photoset by
Northern Phototypesetting Co, Bolton
and printed in Great Britain
by Redwood Burn Ltd, Trowbridge & Esher
for David & Charles (Publishers) Limited
Brunel House, Newton Abbot, Devon

Published in the United States of America
by David & Charles Inc
North Pomfret, Vermont 05053, USA

For Margot

Contents

Foreword

There have been few books in English written about Alexandre Dumas the great romancer. This may seem strange since the name of Dumas is probably as familiar to English readers as that of Charles Dickens and Walter Scott. There must be few people who have not heard of *The Three Musketeers* and their sequels or of *The Count of Monte-Cristo*. Even if they have not read the novels, they are familiar with the stories through the media of the cinema and television. On the other hand, it is probably true to say that apart from students of the French Romantic movement which followed the fall of the Napoleonic empire, there are few persons today who are familiar with even a small proportion of Dumas's vast output – an output which has never been equalled by any other author, not even Balzac. No one can claim to have read all Dumas's works. There exists no edition of his complete *oeuvre* even in France. Calmann-Lévy's comprehensive edition of 350 works is by no means complete. Despite Dumas's universal popularity, English translations comprise a mere fraction of the whole.

Dumas's own biography, as fascinating as any of his own romances, is even less well known. His own diffuse *Mes Mémoires* which include a wealth of material irrelevant to his own life, are supplemented by his travel books (few authors travelled more than he), but comprehensive biographies are rare in English. As far as I am aware the first to be written was *Alexandre Dumas* by Percy Fitzgerald, published in 1873. This is more of a Victorian curiosity than a reliable account, nor, of course does it include the great romancer's last days. Moreover it is extremely biased, but Fitzgerald's comparative analysis of the French and English theatre in the middle of the nineteenth century is a little gem of Victorian chauvinism and cannot fail to interest the social historian.

Of course it is palpably obvious that Dumas alone, without the assistance of collaborators, could not have written the five or six hundred novels, plays, travel books and vignettes attributed to him. What I have tried to emphasise is that many writers were happy to collaborate with him and that he usually paid them handsomely, and that it was often publishers and editors who insisted, against his own wishes, that credit for the work should be given to him, and to him alone. However, it must be admitted that he was not always entirely honest.

Of course he plagiarised (as so many great authors have done); and he made enemies as every successful man does, but he rarely bore a grudge for long and was quick to forgive. His duels were mere play acting. Maybe he was vulgar, but as the Goncourt brothers insist, he was essentially lovable and fascinating, how else could he have been accepted with such affection, not only by the leading artists, writers and musicians of his time, but also the 'upper crust' of the Faubourg Saint-Germain, the Royal princes and foreign nobility. For all his vulgarity, bombast and conceit, I have attempted to show that Dumas was not the dishonest charlatan as so many of his detractors tried to prove him to be.

Of his biographers, André Maurois in his excellent biography, *Les Trois Mousquetaires*, translated into English, shared my view, as did Professor Hemmings whose book *King of Romance* appeared as I was writing my own version. I am, however, not so much interested in analysing Dumas as an author, as Parigot has done, but in Dumas, scallywag though he may have been, as a man of infinite charm and one who would never intentionally hurt a fellow writer.

Michael Ross
Barnes 1980

Author's Note
The Comédie Française, also known as the Théâtre Français or Théâtre Royal, was originally founded by Louis XIV in 1680. The troupe played at a number of different houses, and eventually became established at the Théâtre Royal in the rue Richelieu, an annexe of the Palais Royal.

CHAPTER ONE

The General

The month is February, the year eighteen hundred and twelve. In four months' time Napoleon's Grande Armée will cross the Niemen on its disastrous invasion of Russia. However, there is still no hint of impending disaster in the little town of Villers-Cotterêts, which lies between Paris and the borders of Belgium.

Evening is descending on the vast forest which surrounds this little relay stage post. All is quiet among the bare oaks and beeches, it is even a little eerie; but for the ten-year-old boy who is purposively making his way through the twilit glades, the forest holds no fears. He is a true son of the woods — nonetheless, he is not altogether happy as he searches for his friend, Boudoux, the bird-snarer.

In a clearing in the forest there is a tumbledown hut which he seeks.

'Boudoux,' he calls. 'Boudoux, are you there? It is I, Alexandre. Alexandre Dumas.'

From the shadows of the hut emerges an extraordinary figure. Physically he seems composed of the refuse of creation. Quasimodo, the hunchback of Notre-Dame, would have seemed almost beautiful beside him. His face is scarred and furrowed and almost eaten away by smallpox. His nose is flattened like a gorilla's and his upper lip curves like a serpent's from ear to ear, which makes his mouth capable of accommodating a whole leg of mutton. His beard is scanty, red and coarse. Moreover, he is lame. He is indeed a strange contrast to the slender ten-year-old, with his fair curly hair falling to his shoulders, his dazzling white complexion, blue eyes and red sensitive lips.

'Oh, Boudoux, my friend, please help me; hide me for two or three days. I have run away from home.'

'Run away from home!'

'They want to make me a priest. I won't be a priest – I won't.'
Boudoux scratches his head and ponders for a moment.
'Have you a blanket?' he asks. 'No? Well then run back home and
fetch one – the February nights are cold — and leave a note for your
mother. You can stay with me two or three days. We'll go bird-snaring
in the ponds.'

Joyfully, the boy accepts. He slips back home, takes a blanket off his
bed and writes on a piece of paper: 'Do not be anxious about me,
mother dear, I have run away because I don't want to be a priest.'
Alexandre Dumas has crossed his Rubicon.

In the closing years of the eighteenth century the great forest of
Villers-Cotterêts was not so very different from its appearance today.
Then, as now, it was a hunter's paradise, abounding with wildfowl,
where deer roamed beneath the beeches and oaks, and wild boar
rooted for truffles. The little market town, from which the forest took
its name, had owed its prosperity to the dissolute Louis-Philippe, Duc
d'Orléans, Regent of France, who kept his licentious court in the
neighbouring château. Thirty-two inns had at one time flourished in
this staging post on the Soissons road, of which the Enseigne de l'Ecu
was by no means the least prosperous. The landlord of the Ecu,
Monsieur Claude Labouret, was a man of some consequence. Had he
not been major-domo to his Royal Highness? And was he not now, in
1789, commandant of the local national guard? In that year, as
revolutionary ideas were sweeping through France, this rich and
peaceful little town had had good reason to fear the 'pillagers' who
were said to be operating in the neighbourhood. At the request of the
officers of the civil militia, the government of Louis XVI was asked to
provide additional protection. In August, twenty troopers of the
Queen's Royal Dragoons, quartered at Soissons, were sent to Villers-
Cotterêts for this purpose. The cavalrymen in their smart uniforms
presented a noble and a reassuring sight as they drew up before the
royal château, but none was so splendid as the giant mulatto whose
presence dominated the detachment. Marie-Louise Elizabeth, the
pretty young daughter of Monsieur Labouret, refused to have any
other than this gallant dragoon billeted at the Ecu. Smilingly, her
father agreed. He had no reason to regret his choice. Marie-Louise
enthusiastically wrote to her friend Julie Fortin: 'The long awaited
dragoons arrived two days ago. Everywhere they have received a

warm welcome. My father applied for a coloured man who is one of the detachment. He is very nice and is called Dumas; he is the son of a large landowner in San Domingo. He is as tall as cousin Prévost, but his manners are much superior. I would have you know, my dear Julie, that he is a very fine figure of a man.'

The giant mulatto — 'the gentle giant'* as he was to become known — was soon adored by his hosts, and that there was some mystery surrounding his birth added to his attraction. Perhaps, as ex-major-domo to a royal duke, it was not without a certain snobbish satisfaction that Monsieur Labouret learnt that his guest's real name was Thomas-Alexandre Dumas Davy de la Pailleterie, the son of a marquis (in fact, a courtesy title) and a Haitian Negress, Marie-Cessette Dumas. For a rich planter to take a coloured woman to be his wife in civil law in those days was not unusual, and the offspring of such unions were often regarded with the same respect as any other person.† Was not the Chevalier de Saint-Georges, a man of mixed blood like Dumas, prominent in the world of fashion, a composer and a musketeer, and acknowledged by the English Prince Regent — the first gentleman in Europe — to be the 'most attractive coloured man living'? Whether the marquis had ever legally married Marie-Cessette is very much open to question. For an eighteenth-century nobleman to marry one of his slaves seems highly improbable, but that the marquis gave legal status to his son is incontestable though there is no evidence that he ever made him his heir nor left him lands or money. Thomas-Alexandre Dumas could perhaps have claimed his title, but when his father the marquis returned to Paris in 1780 and took as a second wife his housekeeper (Marie-Cessette had died in San Domingo in 1772), a coolness developed between father and son, with the result that the old marquis, never famous for his generosity, drew his purse strings together more tightly than ever. The son, now eighteen years of age, found that to live in Paris without money was a poor sort of life, while the alternative of living more or less as an exile in the ancestral castle in Normandy, bore no comparison to the exciting, colourful life of the Antilles. Moreover, he disliked his stepmother. He therefore decided to make a future for himself. He told his father he had made a resolution — to 'enter the service' as a private.

* 'Giant' seems today an exaggeration. Although his strength was stupendous, he was in fact only 5ft 9in tall – tall for that time.

† No certificate of marriage, however, has ever been found.

13

'Wonderful!' replied the marquis. 'But as I happen to be called the Marquis de la Pailleterie and as I am colonel and commissary-general of artillery, I don't intend that you should drag my name through the lowest ranks of the army.'

'Then you object to my enlisting?'

'Not at all, but you must enlist under an assumed name.'

'Fair enough,' said his son; 'I will enlist under the name of Dumas.'

'Very good.'*

And the marquis, who had never been a very affectionate father, turned his back on his son, leaving him to follow his own devices. So the young mulatto enlisted (2 June 1786), as agreed, under the name of Thomas-Alexandre Dumas in the Sixtieth (Queen's Dragoons) Regiment.

Thus an immortal name was born while that of Davy de la Pailleterie sank into obscurity. Two weeks later the old marquis died 'as became an old nobleman who did not wish to see the fall of the Bastile'.†

Marie-Louise was soon head-over-heels in love with her dusky guest, a love which was reciprocated. When the young couple confessed their intention of getting married, Claude Labouret gave them his blessing, but made only one stipulation: his son-in-law must first attain the rank of corporal.

Young Thomas-Alexandre was quick to embrace the new liberal ideas sweeping the country, but neither he nor the Labourets could foresee that the Revolution would also sweep aside the rules of promotion which had governed the French army for generations past, and that only two years subsequent to his meeting with Marie-Louise, the young trooper of dragoons would be gazetted lieutenant-colonel in the Légion franche des Americains, a cavalry unit recruited almost entirely from manumitted slaves. So it was that Thomas-Alexandre and Marie-Louise were married on 28 November 1792, just two months after the convention had declared France 'La République

---

* The above conversation (certainly apocryphal) is a direct translation from Dumas's own *Mémoires*. The majority of unascribed quotations from Dumas in the present book are taken from *Mes Mémoires*.

† ibid.

Une et Indivisible' and barely more than a month before Louis XVI was to lose his head on the scaffold. The young couple enjoyed only seventeen days of blissful honeymoon before the soldier-husband once more reported for duty, leaving his wife with child. The first years of the Revolution took place without Thomas-Alexandre having any great share in them. The national assembly was constituted, the Bastille fell, Mirabeau waxed great, thundered and died, while as a private soldier or non-commissioned officer, Thomas-Alexandre performed garrison duties in the country. But soon all was to change. Eight months after his marriage, Thomas-Alexandre Dumas was gazetted brigadier-general to the army of the north; on 3 September 1793 he was appointed general of division in the same army; and finally, only five days later, he was appointed general-in-chief of the army of the western Pyrenees. It had taken him twenty months, starting at the foot of the ladder as a common soldier, to reach one of the highest positions in the army. Three days after his new appointment, Madame Dumas gave birth to a daughter, Aimée-Alexandrine.

The General was only able to snatch a few days' leave to see his newly born babe before he was off again, this time to Bayonne, threatened by the Spanish. His reputation had preceded him. 'His strength was proverbial in the army,' his son tells us in his *Mémoires*.

> During exhibitions of strength with which the soldiers amused themselves from time to time, the General would sit on his horse under a beam, then seizing the beam in his small hands like those of a woman, he would then raise the horse, gripped tightly between his thighs, from off the ground. He could lift four army muskets by putting a finger in each barrel, crush a helmet with his hands, lift a massive gate off its hinges and hurl a mutinous soldier over a wall.

— in short, the very model for Porthos of *The Three Musketeers*. But Thomas-Alexandre was not only a man of great strength, he was also courageous and humane. As commander-in-chief of the army of the western Pyrenees he obstinately defied the *représentants du peuple* — those odious political 'commissars' who followed the armies and who held powers of life or death, even over generals — by protesting against the presence of the guillotine outside his headquarters. Despite insults from the more fanatical sansculottes, he had not only resolutely closed the shutters of his windows but had forbidden his officers and men

15

from watching what he regarded as a senseless and cruel spectacle. It was an act of great courage, one which earned him (derisively) the nickname of Monsieur de l'Humanité, and which might easily have cost him his head. Indeed, he was summoned by Collot d'Herbois to justify his conduct before the convention, but even the terrorist politicians at the convention failed to intimidate him, and although acquitted, he was relieved of his command in the south and appointed divisional commander in the Vendée. To engage in a civil war — Frenchman against Frenchman — was not at all to the liking of the General, more especially as it was conducted by an army of peasants against the government of the convention, whose terrorist policies he had already openly defied. It was a most invidious posting. On his arrival at Fontenay-le-Peuple (today, Fontenay-le-Comte) he took stock of the troops under his command — the dregs of the *canaille*, as a contemporary writer described them. His report to the committee of public safety contained enough damning criticism of the republican army 'to get him guillotined twenty times over. It was a miracle that he was not guillotined once!' His report was very similar to that of the *ci-devant* Duc de Biron, who, in the same year, was appointed republican commander-in-chief of the Armée des côtes de La Rochelle. Biron, however, less lucky than Dumas, was denounced as a traitor to the people and executed for telling the truth.*

General Dumas's report was equivalent to a resignation and (as his son was to write) 'deserving something stronger; but some good genius or other protected my father.' Instead of paying with his head for the terrible truths he had uttered, and which were even more damning than those pronounced by Biron, he was appointed general-in-chief of the army of the Alps to replace Kellermann.

Here the herculean general distinguished himself by the capture of the redoubt of Mont Cenis. With three hundred men equipped with home-made climbing irons and wearing white nightshirts and cotton nightcaps, the better to disguise their presence against the snowy background, he led his force up an almost vertical cliff, thought by the Piedmontese to be inaccessible. He reached the summit unobserved. Once arrived there the soldiers began to clamber up over the enemy stockade, but the general, 'thanks to his superhuman strength, found

---

* For the history of this horrific civil war, see my *Banners of the King: the War of the Vendée 1793–94*, Leo Cooper and Seeley Service, London 1975.

a simpler and less noisy plan – he seized each man by the seat of his trousers and coat-collar and threw him over the palisade'.

Once again, as at Bayonne, he was to defy the *représentants du peuple*, this time in the Alpine village of Saint Maurice, where he not only protested against the presence of the guillotine, but ordered it to be destroyed and its timbers to be used for firewood to warm his hands, as he put it. It was only his brilliant victory at Mont Cenis, together with the capture of Valsain and the securing of the Saint Bernard Pass, that saved his head.

It is no part of our story to follow in detail the career of General Thomas-Alexandre Dumas, but to understand his son a short summary is not out of place. After being recalled to Paris to stand trial for the second time (at which he was acquitted, thanks to Carnot), the General was offered various factitious postings. In protest at the treatment accorded to him, he tendered his resignation and withdrew to Villers-Cotterêts, happy to be beside his wife and daughter. His resignation, however, was not accepted; on the contrary, he was instructed by letter to report back immediately to the convention to receive urgent orders. The letter was dated 13 Vendémiaire, Year IV. Unfortunately General Dumas was not in Paris at that moment, but the twenty-six-year-old protégé of Barras, General Bonaparte, was. Thus is came about that it was the little Corsican and not Monsieur de l'Humanité who dispersed the rebel sections on the steps of St Roche with his famous whiff of grape-shot, and laid the foundations of his future glory.

Bonaparte, as all the world knows, was subsequently given command of the armies of Italy. Dumas, once commander-in-chief of the army of the Alps, was relegated to the rank of divisional commander and ordered to place himself at the disposal of the newly appointed commander-in-chief. He served under Bonaparte in the Italian campaign of 1796, and, by the arrest of an Austrian spy bearing dispatches from Marshal Alvintzy to Wurmser, who was besieged in Mantua, procured invaluable information which enabled Bonaparte to lay his plans for the famous battle of Rivoli. At the siege of Mantua, Dumas gallantly repulsed a desperate sortie made by Wurmser, and successfully defended La Favorita against an Austrian attack. But in Napoleon's official bulletin (drawn up by Berthier) describing this battle, he was reported as 'posted in observation', a non-recognition of his services which infuriated Dumas. The statement may have been technically correct, but it ignored the fact that Dumas had been continuously under fire and had had two horses killed under him. He immediately wrote to Napoleon:

> General,
> I hear that the swine *[ce cochon]* whom you commissioned to draw up a report of the battle of the 27th has represented that I was engaged only in observation during the battle.
> I hope he will never himself be called upon to undertake observations of that character, for I am quite sure that, if he were, he would shit his pants . . .

Naturally this letter made Dumas another enemy. It was decided to have Dumas transferred to Masséna's corps and subsequently to Joubert in the Tyrol. It was probably this imputation of Berthier's lack of courage, not to mention the vulgarity of the letter, that was subsequently to have disastrous results for the mulatto general.

Joubert had no grudge against Dumas and generously shared his command with him. It was in the Tyrolese campaign that the 'dusky giant' *(le géant noirâtre)* earned his sobriquet of 'the Horatius Cocles of the Tyrol' by his single-handed defence of the bridge of Clausen, where he received three wounds, one on the arm, another on the thigh and another which shattered his steel helmet. Besides these, his cloak was riddled by seven bullets and his horse was shot from under him. In 1797 the treaty of Campo Formio was signed and General Dumas was once more free to spend a well-deserved rest with his family, but all too soon he was off to the wars once more, this time to follow Bonaparte into Egypt. Whatever unpleasantness there may have existed between the two men had seemingly been forgotten. According to his son, Bonaparte received his Horatius Cocles, as he affectionately called him, with open arms, and for a while they were such fast friends that they made a pact that whichever of them had a son, the other would stand godfather. But this friendship was not to last long – indeed, Bonaparte was soon to bear his dusky general an implacable hatred for reasons which will soon become apparent. Despite this hatred, Thomas-Alexandre continued to serve his master with unswerving loyalty, a loyalty which Bonaparte certainly did not deserve. Thomas-Alexandre was a soldier first, personal animosities were secondary. He suppressed a riot in Cairo 'when mounted on a big dragoon charger, which he handled like a perfect horseman . . . he appeared to the Arabs like the Angel of Destruction with his flaming sword . . . He rode to the Great Mosque, where the rebel leaders had taken refuge. The doors were shattered by cannon . . . 'The Angel! the Angel!' cried the Arabs and surrendered in superstitious fear.'

At about this same time the General found a buried treasure in the house which he then occupied in Cairo, a treasure worth some two million francs, which the owner of the house, in his hurried flight, had not had time to carry off. At once Dumas wrote to Bonaparte who was desperately short of money with which to pay his already discontented troops:

> Citizen General, the leopard does not change his spots, the honest man does not change his conscience, I send you a treasure which I have just found . . . If I am killed, or if I die of melancholy, remember that I am a poor man and that I leave a wife and child in France.

To appreciate the significance of this letter — 'the leopard does not change his spots, the honest man does not change his conscience' — we must return to the early days of the Egyptian campaign. The gruelling march from Alexandria to Cairo, the intense heat of the desert, the lack of both food and water, led not only the troops, but senior officers and generals, to wonder why ever they had been sent to this outlandish country. Were they fighting for France or Napoleon, who was to call himself the 'man of destiny' and to claim, incorrectly, that his name, translated, meant 'lion of the desert'? It was at a meeting of generals, including Lannes and Murat, in Dumas's own tent, to which he had invited them to share some deliciously refreshing melons, that these opinions were openly expressed. Dumas, denounced by some person present at the meeting, was summoned before his commander-in-chief. At the ensuing confrontation, he openly admitted that he voiced the opinion of his brother officers, but denied that he was their ringleader. When Napoleon burst into one of his famous rages, Dumas tendered his resignation, which was accepted. The destruction of the French fleet by Nelson at Aboukir, which led to even more discontent and increasing homesickness among the troops, prevented Dumas's immediate departure from France. But although he continued to conduct himself with exemplary courage and loyalty, Napoleon was never to forgive him for what he regarded as treachery, although

Thomas-Alexandre was only voicing the opinion of almost the whole army.

Soon after the disastrous destruction of the French fleet, Dumas, together with General Manscourt (his own chief of staff) and the famous mineralogist Dolomieu and others, chartered a vessel, the *Belle Maltaise*, and set out for France, which he hoped to reach in about twelve days' time. It was two years, however, before he saw his homeland again. Violent storms had thrown the *Belle Maltaise* off course and drifting before the ship was forced to put in at the Neapolitan port of Taranto. The King of Naples and the Two Sicilies was hostile to France, and Dumas and his companions found themselves treated not as prisoners of war but as criminals and thrown into a prison in Brindisi without trial. Here the General was kept incommunicado for two long years. Why he was regarded as such a dangerous enemy to the Kingdom of the Two Sicilies is difficult to understand; why he was not shot outright instead of being the victim of attempts to dispose of him by arsenical poisoning is incomprehensible. During the twenty months of his captivity his health broke down completely, and when at last he was released he was partially paralysed, almost blind in one eye, deaf in one ear and a mere shadow of the man who had been known as the Horatius Cocles of the Tyrol and the Angel of Destruction with the flaming sword.

Great was the rejoicing, although mixed with distress, when the crippled giant returned to Villers-Cotterêts to lay aside his sword and settle down with his ever-faithful Marie-Louise and his baby daughter, Aimée-Alexandrine.

But beyond the confines of this sleepy country town, how much had happened during the General's absence! Bonaparte, foiled before Acre and left for six months without news from France, learnt unexpectedly* for the first time of the disastrous defeats suffered by France during his absence – the recapture of Mantua, the battle of Novi and the death of Joubert. Then, deserting his army in Egypt, Napoleon had secretly left for France. On 16 October 1799, he had overthrown the inept Directory and on the famous 18 Brumaire had

---

* Commodore Sir Sidney Smith, in command of the squadron blockading the town, had sent him copies of newspapers containing the news.

himself proclaimed First Consul. On 6 May he had set out for Italy, crossed the Saint Bernard Pass and on 14 June had defeated the Austrians at Marengo, the same day as Kléber, whom he had left in command of the army, was assassinated in Cairo.

On 18 February 1802 an armistice between France and the King of Naples had been signed and the crippled General Dumas was released in exchange for the Austrian General Mack. On 5 April Dumas reached the French headquarters in Florence. From here he wrote to Bonaparte giving a full account of his sufferings while a prisoner of the King of the Two Sicilies. A week later he wrote to the three consuls (and to Bonaparte personally) claiming a share of the indemnity exacted from the Neapolitan government. His son was later to write:

> But the clouds of Egypt which, according to Bonaparte, lasted only six hours, had crossed the Mediterranean, and were thickening over my father's head ... he was not long for this world and was soon to disembarrass Napoleon of one of those last Republican generals who had crossed Bonaparte on his path. Hoche had died by poison; Joubert had been killed at Novi; Kléber had been assassinated in Cairo; my father was now feeling the first attacks of a cancer in the stomach – the result of the arsenic which had been given him ... my father was not included in the division of the 500,000 francs granted as indemnity to the prisoners ...

However, in that year little seemed to have changed outwardly in the little town of Villers-Cotterêts, though the years of plenty were now past. There were no longer thirty-two inns doing a flourishing trade, no court to attract a host of visitors. Claude Labouret had been obliged to close his prosperous inn and take a modest but roomy house, 54 rue de Lormet, and live upon his savings. The General, whenever well enough, once more mounted his horse and hunted in the surrounding forest. Marie-Louise was again with child – a boy perhaps, the boy to whom Bonaparte had once promised to be godfather. With the advent of peace, with no more fear of mass recruitment, the country people were once again able to enjoy their innocent country pleasures in time-honoured fashion – Mardi Gras, Easter, and perhaps the most delightful of all, Whitsuntide, when the flowers of the forest were opening and there was dancing on the village green and country maids changed their sabots for buckled shoes and wore gay ribbons in their hair. It was then that from far and wide came the hucksters and pedlars of gossip as well as goods, itinerant *rôtissiers* and *pâtissiers*, tumblers and clowns and all sorts of side-shows, including one old man who had his booth upon his back, bent almost double under its weight, with his eyes fixed on the dusty road and his nose to the ground.

This booth contained all the paraphernalia for what we would call a Punch and Judy show, but in France was known as *polichinelle*. The French *polichinelle* was not the hump-backed, hook-nosed little fellow who for centuries had terrified, enthralled and delighted English children of all ages, but was none other than a mischievous prototype of Goethe's Faust – a sort of Til Eulenspiegel – who is finally carried off by the devil to whom he has sold his soul. But the wandering impresario who set up his booth on the village green of Villers-Cotterêts had an original touch of genius. His devil was no Mephistopheles, dressed in red, but was as black as the plumes on an undertaker's hearse, with a scarlet tongue and a scarlet tail, whom, for reasons best known to himself he had named 'Berlick'. Among the throng which gathered to laugh and shiver at the wickedness of the black puppet on that Whitsun of 1802 was Marie-Louise Elizabeth, who was expecting her second child. Marie-Louise gripped the arm of her neighbour as she watched with fascination the antics of the puppet and remarked that it was dangerous for a woman in her condition to be frightened by anything.

'My dear,' she said, 'I'm afraid my child will be a Berlick.'

The two women went back laughing to the little white house in the rue de Lormet, but the laughter of the mother-to-be was a trifle nervous.

At four-thirty on the morning of 23 July, Marie-Louise gave birth to a son. The midwife gasped with something approaching terror. The baby's face was so purple as to be almost black. *'Mon dieu!'* the mother whispered, 'I *have* given birth to a Berlick.'

So Berlick became the nickname of Alexandre Dumas, son and heir to the young republican general, Thomas-Alexandre Dumas Davy de la Pailleterie.

Delighted to have a son and heir, the half-pay general immediately wrote to Marshal Brune, his old comrade-in-arms who, like Napoleon, had promised to act as godfather to his first-born son:

My dear Brune, I am happy to tell you that my wife gave birth yesterday morning to a fine boy who weighs nine pounds and is eighteen inches long.

You see if he grows in the outer world as he has in the inner, he promises to reach a good size!

And then he added:

I have just reopened this letter to tell you that the little fellow has just pissed over the top of his head. A good augury, don't you think?

CHAPTER TWO

Childhood

The child Alexandre's first impressions were not of Villers-Cotterêts but of the grandiosely named Château des Fosses near the little town of Haramont to which the family moved shortly after his birth. The 'château' was in fact a small unpretentious house. The boy, the hero of our story (to whom I will in future refer to as Alexandre or as Dumas *tout court*), was one of those children born with an exceptionally retentive memory. Apart from his mother and his father, the household, as he recalls

> consisted of, 1st, a large black dog called Truffe, who had the privilege of being welcome everywhere as I habitually rode on his back; 2nd, a gardener named Pierre, who for my benefit used to lay in a stock of frogs and adders in the garden . . . 3rd, a negro, Hippolyte, my father's valet; 4th, a keeper, Mocquet by name.

Mocquet, in fact, had a profound influence on the future author, who regarded him 'with a species of veneration seeing that he had wonderful stories to tell me every evening, about ghosts, were-wolves and hunting exploits'.

At Les Fosses, General Dumas continued to hunt and shoot (whenever his health permitted him to do so) with his friends and neighbours, M Collard and M Deviolaine. M Collard, who lived in a delightful little château three miles from Villers-Cotterêts, was of aristocratic lineage, but during the Revolution he had dropped the name of de Montjouy, retaining only that of Collard. He was a man of great charm, always smiling and always ready to give a warm welcome to the little Dumas who regarded his château as a veritable palace. M Deviolaine, a cousin by marriage of the Dumas family, was a person of

24

great standing in the little town since he was inspector of forests of Villers-Cotterêts. He too had his (official) residence, which to the youthful eyes of Dumas also seemed palatial. It was surrounded by a delightful garden. But although M Deviolaine was at heart a kindly man, his rough exterior, 'like the bark of one of his own oaks', and his terrible temper terrified both his own numerous family and little Dumas. Dumas was to write of him: 'The strange thing was that his outburst never resulted in anything but a vast amount of clouds and flashes – of hailstones or thunderbolts there was nothing.' He wouldn't have hurt a fly. We shall have more to say of M Deviolaine later.

When kept indoors by ill-health, the General wrote letters to former comrades-in-arms, to the minister of war, to Bonaparte himself – pathetic letters in which he recounts his poverty, his ill-health, reminding them of his services, and asking for his arrears of pay. None of his letters was answered. In the summer of 1805, unable to afford the upkeep of Les Fosses, the family moved once again, this time to the little village of Antilly, but only for a brief period before returning to Villers-Cotterêts to live with 'Grandpa Labouret'. But now the General's health was deteriorating steadily. On the advice of a doctor who had some reputation in the neighbourhood, he was recommended to visit Paris to consult the well-known specialist Baron Corvisart.* For some time General Dumas had had the intention of visiting the capital in order to see Brune and Murat personally. He therefore willingly made the journey accompanied by his little son. Corvisart gave the General a regimen to follow, but little hope. Young Dumas was to remember this visit vividly all his life.

Murat had greeted his old friend coldly; Brune, warmly. Murat and Brune had lunched with the General and Alexandre. The meal concluded, the General called to his son, and putting Brune's sword between his legs and Murat's gorgeously plumed hat on his head, made him gallop round the dining table. The scene was pathetic. The General knew he was dying and knew, too, that despite the marshals' promises to intercede with Napoleon on his behalf, there was little that these men could do, either in the matter of back-pay (which amounted

* Jean Corvisart, Napoleon's favourite doctor; created baron in 1805.

to nearly nine thousand francs) or in helping his wife, should he die. Indeed, Napoleon's reply to Brune was to be: 'Never mention that man's name to me again,' and to turn his back on him.

On his return to Villers-Cotterêts the General seemed to lose all heart. He was unable to tolerate any noise. He sat alone at the window of his room brooding over Napoleon's injustice and despairing of being able to provide for his wife and children. In February 1806, after a final gallant effort to mount his horse, he was forced to bed. On the twenty-sixth the end came. After receiving absolution from the Abbé Grégoire, the General died at midnight in the arms of his beloved Marie-Louise. Earlier in the evening he had asked for little Alexandre, but was told he was in the care of his cousin Marianne, the locksmith's daughter.

'Don't disturb the poor child,' he said; 'he will be asleep.'

Young Alexandre sat watching and feeding his precocious imagination on the flames and sparks that came from the locksmith's forge. Then Marianne came and put him in the cot, facing her own bed. Both Marianne and young Alexandre were awakened at midnight by a loud knock on the door. In the glow from a night lamp the boy saw Marianne sitting up in bed, looking scared.

Both outer doors were locked. The boy got out of bed in his nightshirt.

'Alexandre, where are you going, child?" Marianne asked. Calmly, he turned to face her and said,

'I'm going to open the door to Papa, who is here to say goodbye to us.'

Marianne sprang from her bed and carried him, struggling in her arms, back to his cot, while he cried: 'Goodbye, Papa! Goodbye, Papa!'

The following morning little Alexandre was told that the good God had taken his father and that he would never see him again. The boy ran all the way home. He slipped into the gun room. Then, clad in his child's smock, he emerged carrying one of his father's fire-arms, a weapon larger than himself, and proceeded to climb the stairs, making such a clatter in that house of death that his mother came out onto the landing, surprised to see him there, her face wet with tears.

'Child!' she exclaimed. 'Where are you going?'

'I'm going to Heaven to kill God for taking Papa from us.'

Surprising words to come from the pretty, blue-eyed boy; the baby

26

with a purple, wrinkled face had grown into a little cupid with a gun in his arms instead of a sheaf of arrows, determined to avenge the death of his father. If Bonaparte himself had appeared in that doorway, doubtless the child would have tried to shoot him.

Gently loving hands wrested the gun away from him. The sad little boy, who was to become one of the most popular novelists of all time, walked slowly away under bare February trees into the vast forest of Villers-Cotterêts.

Although his father died when the boy was only three and a half, he never spoke or wrote of him except with veneration and love, as if of a man he had known intimately and long. Dumas, as already mentioned, had a remarkably retentive memory and it was the tales the General told him which were the source of his inspiration; it was the General who linked him with history. The General as a youth had met that old roué the Duc de Richelieu (who figures in several of his son's romances), and as a son of the Revolution the General had been familiar with the giants of the past. He had served at the side of Bonaparte; he had described to his son the Battle of the Pyramids, the taking of the redoubt of Mont Cenis, and many other brilliant exploits. To anyone familiar with Dumas's sequel to *The Three Musketeers, Vingt ans après*, it is possible to recognise in Raoul the young Dumas listening to his father:

'You have not forgotten the Bastion St Gervais, Athos, and the napkin which was made into a banner?' And d'Artagnan then related to Raoul the story of the Bastion, and Raoul thought he was listening to one of those deeds of arms belonging to the days of chivalry recounted by Tasso and Ariosto.

Combined with his veneration for his father, he retained all his life a love for the forests of Villers-Cotterêts. However much he was to love the glitter and glamour of Paris, he remained at heart a child of the woods.

The death of the General, who during his last years had possessed nothing but his half-pay allowance of 4,000 francs, left the family practically without provision. All that they possessed was some thirty acres of land in the village of Soucy, once the property of Alexandre's maternal grandfather. There was also a house and a splendid garden in the Place de la Fontaine, which was to revert to his mother some day, but the occupier died only in 1817, at the age of ninety-three. It was now Marie-Louise's turn to solicit help from her husband's former friends. She wrote to Brune, Murat, Augereau, Lannes and Jourdan to obtain a pension from Bonaparte, now crowned Napoleon, Emperor of the French. But hope was dissipated when the unfortunate widow received a letter from Jourdan stating that under the law of 8 Floréal, Year XI, no pensions could be granted to widows of soldiers except those killed in battle or who died within six months from wounds received. Jourdan concluded his letter by stating that the only means of success remaining to Madame Dumas was to present herself personally to the Emperor and solicit his kind offices.

Madame Dumas accordingly set out for Paris to present herself to his Majesty the Emperor, but the Emperor refused the audience she begged for, and she returned to Villers-Cotterêts, the poorer by the money she had expended on her journey.

CHAPTER THREE

Boyhood

What was now to become of little Alexandre? His mother wanted him to be a priest. She had been so proud of him at his first communion, wearing a blue coat with brass buttons over a white quilted waistcoat and snow-white cambric shirt and cravat, his eyes looking more intensely blue than ever, and his hair, which was to become a frizzy black mop later in life, as gold as the trimmings on the priestly vestments under the soft glow from the taper in his hand.

Alexandre was overcome by the music played by Hiraux on the church organ, nearly fainting in ecstasy, thinking that he had found religion, sobbing hysterically for days afterwards, but the Abbé Grégoire said drily – 'My boy, I would prefer that all this were less violent and more lasting.'

Hiraux was known in the town as Papa Hiraux, a musician of the Hoffman cut, wearing a maroon frock-coat and a wig which came away with his hat every time he raised it to a lady. This wig he only wore on Sundays and fête days. On ordinary days Papa Hiraux wore a black silk cap which he would pull down over his ears, an expression of intense pain showing on his thin, parchment features every time a pupil played a wrong note.

Among those pupils for a time was young Dumas (his sister Aimée Alexandrine, then at school in Paris, was an accomplished singer) but Alexandre did not share his sister's gifts. After three years of lessons he was still unable even to tune his violin. Honest Papa Hiraux felt obliged to tell Madame Dumas that it would be robbery to take any more of her money. Her son would never make a musician – music's loss was literature's gain.

Not unnaturally, Madame Dumas was disappointed. Despite her

straitened circumstances she wished her children to have the best possible education. The last thing she wanted for her son was that he should be a soldier. Even before 1812 there was hardly a woman, mother, wife, sister or sweetheart in the whole of France who did not execrate the very name Bonaparte, despite the fact that he had now declared himself emperor, and despite the fact that he referred to his soldiers as 'my children'. Madame Dumas had had too bitter an experience of *that*.

Then the problem seemed to be solved. A cousin, the Abbé Conseil, died, and in his will left a bursary to the Seminary of Soissons, some seventeen miles north-east of Villers-Cotterêts, so that one of his relatives might be trained for the priesthood. The future priest was to be Alexandre Dumas.

The plan failed due to Alexandre's own pigheadedness and sensitivity. At first, he listened to his mother's pleas and agreed to study for the Church. Madame Dumas was delighted.

Gathering his belongings together for the journey to Soissons, he observed that he had neither inkstand, nor a receptacle for his pens. How could one study to become a priest without a horn inkstand and a receptacle for pens?

Madame Dumas, good woman, saw the sense of her dutiful son's argument and gave him twelve *sous* to purchase what he needed. Monsieur Devaux, the shopkeeper, told the prospective seminarist that he would get him what he required by the same evening.

Unfortunately, or perhaps fortunately, for Mother Church, it so happened that one of Alexandre's cousins was in the shop when he returned, a witty, lively tomboy of a girl named Cecile.

She told her cousin that she was delighted at his decision and wished him every success in the career he had chosen.

'When you are ordained,' she said sweetly, 'you will be my spiritual adviser!'

That was enough for Alexandre. A great wit himself, he could never tolerate feminine barbs. He threw inkstand and pen-holder at the shopkeeper, put the twelve *sous* back into his pocket and hurried from the shop. With the money he bought a loaf of bread and sausage and escaped into the great forest, a priest-to-be on the run.

An appropriate start in life for a boy who had been nicknamed after the effigy of the devil in a Punch and Judy show! Three days later the prodigal returned home, contrite and a little fearful. But of course, after scolding him, his mother forgave him – as always.

The seminary disposed of, Alexandre attended the village school under the direction of the Abbé Grégoire, but he was an inattentive pupil and often played truant. He much preferred to company of Boudoux the bird-snarer, or that of the poacher Hanniquet, or old Mounier, a former fencing-master, now an inmate of the poor-house.* Sometimes to his great joy, the terrifying M Deviolaine, who in reality was a kindly man, invited him to his splendid house and later, when the boy was older, allowed him to accompany him (unbelievable privilege!) on hunting expeditions. M Collard, now his legal guardian, also often invited him to stay at his château of Villers-Hellon; Madame Darcourt, the intimate friend of Madame Dumas, who lived next door with her daughter, also made him welcome. Madame Darcourt was the possessor of a lavishly illustrated volume of the great natural-historian Buffon which was a continual source of fascination for the boy. While the women busied themselves chatting and sewing, Alexandre would withdraw into a corner, engrossed in his book. The result was that he learnt to read. *'How,'* Dumas recounts, 'I hardly know, but I can tell *why*. It was in order to make myself familiar with the habits and the instincts of the animals whose pictures I saw.' By the age when most children were still learning to spell, Dumas was reading everything he could lay hands on, even the gazettes. Monsieur Collard possessed a magnificent illustrated Bible which he also read with avidity. His mother encouraged unceasingly this desire for reading, while his sister, when on holiday from school, taught him to write. *Robinson Crusoe, The Arabian Nights* and an illustrated Mythology replaced Buffon and the Bible. He was to remember all his life everything he read of classical mythology and the *Arabian Nights*. Not a god or goddess, not a faun, dryad, or hero, but he knew their pedigree – and isn't *Monte-Cristo* no more than an updated version of Aladdin's cavern?

Alexandre in his *Mémoires* admits that his precocity in the accomplishment of reading made him unbearably conceited: 'I can still see myself ... taking part with the utmost gravity in the conversation of the grown-ups, giving them the benefit of my store of knowledge, sacred and profane ... I was not a favourite with the other children of the village. I was absurdly vain, proud and cocksure and

---

* The château of the former regent had been converted into an alms-house.

full of admiration for my own small self, and yet with all that, full of good inclinations.'

His other accomplishment was a beautiful penmanship though, unlike his contemporary Victor Hugo, he never attempted to draw. But although he was able to read and write and was unrivalled in penning the most elaborate colophons, curlicues, arabesques and exquisitely formed italic lettering, he was lamentably backward in his school studies. On the other hand, if a first-rate ignoramus, he was already at the age of ten a budding first-rate sportsman. Thanks to Mounier he was soon to be an expert with the foil, and under the eyes of Messieurs Deviolaine and Collard, he was to prove himself at an early age an exceptionally good marksman and, like his father, a fine horseman; he knew already the arts of snaring, poaching and woodcraft to perfection – knowledge which later he was to put to good purpose in his novel *Ange Pitou*.

For young Dumas the next two years passed uneventfully. Week succeeded week peacefully enough in Villers-Cotterêts. From time to time there came news of titanic events from far afield – victories for the French (or more correctly for Napoleon): Lutzen, Bautzen, Wurtchen, Austerlitz; then came the decline of the Emperor's star; disaster followed disaster: Moscow, Colmar, Besançon, Landau, Forbach, Leipzig. Dumas wrote:

we were about to witness what we had not witnessed either in 1792 or in 1793, that is, the invasion of France. Those who did not live at this period cannot conceive the depth of execration sounded in the hearts of mothers by the name of Napoleon. In truth, in 1813 and 1814, the old enthusiasm was extinct. It was not to France, the common mother – it was not to Liberty, that goddess of all, that mothers were making the sacrifice of their children – it was to the ambition, the egotism, the pride of one man.

Now began those terrible conscriptions. Thanks to the millions of men squandered in the valleys and on the mountains of Spain, in the snows and rivers of Russia, in the swamps of Saxony and in the sands of Poland – a generation of men between the ages of twenty and twenty-five had disappeared. Conscription began at the age of sixteen and men remained liable for service until they were forty. Every town, village and hamlet dreaded the arrival of the recruiting officer. Rich and poor, young and middle-aged, able and disabled alike were taken, and young as he was, Dumas's impressions of those terrible years remained ineffaceable. So that forty years later when writing *Conscience l'Innocent*, he was able to recapture those days as vividly as though recounting an event of yesterday.

More than once his mother clasped the twelve-year-old Alexandre to her breast: 'Oh, when I think that in four years you will be a soldier, and that *that man* will take you from me – me, from whom he has already taken and to whom he has never given – and will send you to be killed on some battlefield . . .'

Following Leipzig, defeat followed defeat. No one believed any longer in 'tactical withdrawal'. France was surrounded. The allies were everywhere. The boom of cannon from Château-Thierry could be heard in Villers-Cotterêts; Laon had been captured. Then one day it was learnt that Soissons had fallen and that the dreaded Cossacks would not be long in making their appearance in the peaceful streets of Villers-Cotterêts. Marshal Mortier's corps, with what remained of his young guard, had been ordered to defend the passage of the forest. That night the Marshal dined with Monsieur Deviolaine, who sent for Alexandre. The veteran soldier, the hero of so many battles, was old before his time. He took Alexandre on his knees and spoke to him of his father and of his godparent, Marshal Brune, now in disgrace. The dinner was gloomy, the evening doleful. The Marshal withdrew early, went to bed and fell asleep. Dumas recounts:

At midnight, we were awakened by gunshots. Fighting was going on in the parterre. The Marshal had been careless about his sentries, the enemy had captured his [gun] park and he himself, half dressed, had made his escape by Monsieur Deviolaine's back-door. In the morning the enemy had disappeared, taking with them our twelve pieces of artillery. The same day the Marshal fell back on Compiègne and the town remained left to itself.

Near Villers-Cotterêts was a vast, ancient, underground labyrinthine quarry. Here, with the ever-present danger of Cossacks suddenly descending on the town, the inhabitants staked out shelters for themselves. Nevertheless they were taken by surprise when, one wintry February morning, a wild troop of these dreaded horsemen from the steppes came thundering down the high street. The terror-fascinated Alexandre, who could not tear himself from the window, was left with an indelible vision of foam-flecked horses, pounding hoofs and fierce, bearded men armed with long lances. Then, as suddenly as they had appeared, the horsemen turned around and, still at full gallop, plunged back along the Soissons road, loosing off one random pistol-shot which killed a shopkeeper who had rashly opened his door.

The sudden descent of the Cossacks had terrified the townsfolk. Madame Dumas was determined at all costs to leave Villers-Cotterêts. But where was she to go? In fact, as her son tells us, she had not the slightest idea, 'only she fancied that, by change of place, she might conjure away the danger'. It was quite fortuitous that she and Alexandre went to Mesnil, a village close to Paris. But it soon became apparent that Mesnil lay right in the line of the enemy's advance. The Allies were already in Meaux-sur-Marne and their forward troops had penetrated as far as Bondy.

Madame Dumas now decided to return home, but on reaching Nanteuil it was learnt that Villers-Cotterêts was already occupied by Russian troops and rumour had it that Cossacks had found their way into the underground quarry and had perpetuated the most appalling atrocities. The little township of Crépy, however, which lies off the main road from Laon to Paris, though only a few miles from Villers-Cotterêts, might, due to its position, be overlooked by the enemy and provide Madame Dumas and her thirteen-year-old son with a refuge. Like Peronne, Crépy had so far remained, if not inviolable, at least inviolate.

So it was to Crépy that Alexandre and his mother made their way, there to be welcomed by family friends, Dr and Mme Millet. A detachment of imperial infantry and some two or three hundred hussars, cut off from the main army, had taken up position in the town. Scarcely had Mme Dumas and Alexandre settled down in the Millets' house on the fringe of Crépy than sentries from the infantry detachment, more alert than those of Mortier's corps, reported that a squadron of Prussian cavalry was approaching the town. Without hesitation the French troops prepared to engage the enemy. Alexandre, from the attic window of Dr Millet's house, was now about to witness, to use his own words, 'A spectacle both magnificent and terrible'. Not more than twenty paces from where he stood glued to the window, 'as close as the first row of boxes in the circus is to the stage, a combat in dire earnest – a combat life for life – was being fought'. There were charges and counter-charges, a mêlée of horses and the ring of steel on steel – then the French infantry advanced with the bayonet. The Prussians brought up reinforcements. The French were routed and dispersed . . . After all the turmoil came a great calm. The dust settled in the silent street, empty but for the bodies of dead and wounded. Dr Millet, once a military surgeon, was the first to leave his house to render help to those in need of his services.

Young Alexandre also helped, carrying basins of hot water while the surgeon washed and dressed wounds and the women prepared lint and bandages. One of the least seriously wounded of the Prussians told them that he and his companions belonged to a detachment of 3,000 men which had received orders to camp in the open as much as possible, as their commanders were always in fear of some nocturnal massacre if they trusted themselves to the towns. 'However, it will all be over soon,' added the wounded man, 'as Paris surrendered the day before yesterday.'

No one could believe him. Paris surrender? Never! But it was all too true. The allies had entered Paris on the night of 31 March/1 April. The senate had appointed a provisional government; on 2 April a decree of the senate had declared Napoleon to have forfeited his throne. Louis XVIII was named King of France.

A fortnight later Madame Dumas and Alexandre went back to Villers-Cotterêts.

Two or three days later, after a long conversation with Monsieur Collard (who was about to set out for Paris), Madame Dumas took her son on one side. With a serious air she said to him: 'Your grandfather, the Marquis de la Pailleterie, served Louis XVI just as your father served the republic. Now attend carefully to this, for probably your whole future will depend on the decision we are about to take. Will you call yourself Davy de la Pailleterie like your grandfather? In that case you are the grandson of the Marquis Davy de la Pailleterie, Gentleman of the Bedchamber to the Prince de Conti and Commissary-General of Artillery; that will get you a bursary, or else you can become one of the pages, and in any case you have a position ready made for you with the reigning family. If, however, you choose to call yourself Alexandre Dumas, *tout court*, as did your father, the republican general, every career before you is closed.'

Madame Dumas went on to say that M Collard was leaving for

Paris, that he knew Talleyrand and the Duc d'Orléans and a number of other influential persons about the new court.

'According as you decide for yourself, he will act,' said his mother.

Alexandre had no hesitation in replying. 'I'll call myself Alexandre Dumas and nothing else. I knew my father, who came to say goodbye to me at the moment of his death. What would he think if I should disown him and call myself after my grandfather whom I had never known?'

Madame Dumas was proud of her son and yet a little sad. When M Collard returned from Paris, he brought no hopes for Alexandre, only a licence for his mother to open a tobacco shop, a benefit usually reserved for widows of non-commissioned officers.

To provide for this event Madame Dumas had left the rue Lormet to take up residence in the Place de la Fontaine in the house of a M Lafarge, a coppersmith, who had let his first floor to her, and who had also promised to give up his shop should she require it. And so it was that the widow of the great republican general 'M de l'Humanité', the Horatius of the Tyrol, became the proprietress of a provincial store selling tobacco and salt.

M Lafarge's son, Auguste, was to have a very considerable influence over the impressionable Dumas. Auguste Lafarge, a handsome young man, was head clerk in a solicitor's office in Paris, but was anxious to set up his own practice. For this, however, he needed money. He had therefore returned to his family with all the attractions of Paris about him – a box-coat with numerous capes, as were fashionable at that time, a watch-chain hung with massive trinkets, skin-tight trousers and boots of the hussar fashion – with the object of captivating some wealthy heiress. No difficult matter, he thought, for one so versed in fascinating the fair sex in Paris.

Auguste, although somewhat conceited, was nevertheless a charming youth and something of an intellectual too. 'He had mingled with the literary world of the day; composed pretty sonnets, and as though born to riches, would take a gold piece from his pocket and throw it down in a lordly way in payment of any trifling purchase.' He was installed in the apartment which Madame Dumas had rented from his father. Dumas was most impressed by this young man of fashion, and despite the difference in ages, the two became fast friends, a friendship encouraged by Madame Dumas who, simple woman, held up Auguste as a model for her son to follow. Together they went bird-snaring with Boudoux, and when free from his lessons (which was often) Alexandre listened entranced to Auguste's stories of Paris, of the theatre and of the society of men of letters whom he claimed to know intimately. Alas for Auguste, the heiress whose hand he sought refused him; his attractions had failed. Before leaving for Paris, he produced an epigram – an epigram of eight lines, an epigram of revenge composed by a thwarted young man. Unfortunately Dumas does not quote the lines, but tells us that just as he was departing, Auguste sent the little verse to him and twenty other friends and that it caused an eight days' sensation in the small provincial town:

I confess that the sensation attaching to the name of an absent person bedazzled me. I became ambitious of this glory of making people talk about me in places where I was not . . . The verses of Auguste Lafarge were the first ray of light poured upon my life. He kindled in me ambitions still indefinite, a dream rather than a perception, an aspiration rather than a purpose.

CHAPTER FOUR

The Hundred Days

The tranquillity of Villers-Cotterêts was shattered when, on the morning of 7 March 1815, subscribers to the *Moniteur* read with astonishment an announcement written (in the usual governmental circumlocutory prose) to the effect that Napoleon Bonaparte had landed at Golfe-Juan at midday on 1 March and was advancing on Paris. The sympathies of Villers-Cotterêts were royalist rather than Bonapartist, so that the first impression produced by the news was one of hostility, rather than welcome. Being on the main road from Paris to Mezières, which passes through Soissons and Laon, and being thus one of the vital arteries which fed northern France, Villers-Cotterêts had numberless carriages, coaches and couriers passing through it. These carriages and couriers sometimes brought vital news which the newspapers did not publish, such as Napoleon's entry into Grenoble and Lyons. When on the evening of 21 March a courier came riding post-haste into the town, everyone ran to the post house, where the courier was changing horses, to hear the latest news.

'Well,' they asked him — 'well, what is it?'

'Well, gentlemen,' replied the courier, 'His Majesty the Emperor and King [of Elba] made his entry into the Tuileries at eight o'clock yesterday morning.'

The history of the hundred days, when Napoleon escaped from Elba, is well known. Dumas, like everyone else, realised that war was inevitable. On 25 March the allies had covenanted not to lay down arms until they had crushed Napoleon; on 30 March, England engaged to furnish the allies for three years with a hundred million francs; and on 26 May the emperors of Russia and Austria and the King of Prussia left Vienna to march on France. There was no hope of preserving peace.

At the beginning of June, French troops began to march through Villers-Cotterêts. Much as Dumas had come to hate the name Napoleon, he admits he could not feel anything but joy at seeing once more those time-honoured uniforms – those old cockades, hidden away in drum barrels, and brought to light again on the road from Elba to Paris – those flags, riddled by bullets of Austerlitz, Wagram and Borodino:

> Marvellous, too, was the sight presented to my eyes by all that Old Guard – a military type that has disappeared from these latter days – a type which was the animate embodiment of the ten Imperial years we had passed through – the living and glorious legend of France.
>
> In three days, thirty thousand men – thirty thousand giants passed through, firm, calm, sombre; not one but felt that a part of that grand Napoleonic edifice, cemented by his blood, rested its weight on his shoulders, and every one of them seemed to us proud of their burden, though we felt that they bent beneath it . . . They represented the purest blood of France, twenty years of struggle against the whole of Europe . . .

Then it was announced in the papers that Napoleon was leaving Paris on 12 June to join the army and would pass through Villers-Cotterêts at about seven or eight o'clock. At six Dumas was waiting at the end of the rue de Largny, but quickly realised that to obtain the best view of the Emperor would be at the relay posting house. He ran off as fast as his legs could carry him:

> I reached the stage post and saw dashing towards me, like an avalanche, three carriages at headlong speed, drawn by steaming horses, and with postilions in full livery, powdered and laced.
>
> Everyone rushed for the Emperor's carriage . . . He was seated far back on the right-hand side, dressed in his green uniform with white facings and wearing the star of the Legion of Honour. His pale, sickly face, which seemed massively set in a block of ivory, inclined slightly forward over his breast. On his left was seated his brother Jerome.

Dumas, who claims to have been first on the scene, tells us he overheard the following exchange:

> 'Where are we?' said the Emperor.
> 'At Villers-Cotterêts, Sire,' said a voice.
> 'Six leagues from Soissons, isn't it?' he replied.
> 'Yes, Sire, six leagues from Soissons,'
> 'Get on quickly.'

And he fell back into that kind of drowsiness from which the momentary halt of the carriage had aroused him ... Meanwhile new horses had been put between the traces; fresh postilions were in the saddles; those who had just unharnessed were waving their hats and shouting 'Vive l'Empereur!' The whips cracked; the Emperor made a slight inclination of the head by way of acknowledgement; the carriages set off at full gallop and disappeared at the end of the Soissons road. The mighty vision had vanished.

The first news that filtered through was optimistic – the passage of the Sambre had been forced, Charleroi had been taken, the battles of Ligny and Quatre Bras had been fought and won. Four days passed without any further news. Then, suddenly, on 20 June, ten or twelve exhausted Polish cavalrymen, wounded and tattered, rode into the town. At first, what they had to tell was not believed: the French army was not in retreat, it was in rout. At four o'clock in the afternoon the English had been defeated, but at six o'clock Blücher, with 40,000 men, had arrived in the nick of time, and had decided the battle in favour of the enemy – a battle as decisive as ever fought.

Then, at seven o'clock in the evening, a mud-bespattered courier arrived, his horse quivering in every limb and ready to drop with fatigue. Alexandre, agog for further news, was among the first to crowd around the horseman, but the man refused to answer any questions – either he knew nothing or would say nothing. After ordering four horses for a carriage which was following, he leapt into his saddle and was off again. Here is how Dumas describes what followed:

The four horses are taken from the stable, harnessed and await the carriage. A dull rumbling, rapidly drawing nearer, tells us of its approach. We see it appearing at the end of the street: it draws up at the door.

The post-master comes forward and stands bewildered. At the same moment I clutch him by the skirts of his coat.

'Is it he – is it -- the Emperor?'

'Yes.'

Yes it was the Emperor – in the same position as I had seen him before, in a similar carriage, with one aide-de-camp beside him and another facing him ... It is exactly the same man – pale, sickly, impassive; only the head droops a little more over the chest. Is it mere bodily exhaustion? Is it anguish at having played for the World – and lost? ...

'Where are we?' he asked.

'At Villers-Cotterêts, Sire.'

'Go on.'

> And as on the former occasion, after putting a question in almost identical terms, he gave the same orders and started off as rapidly . . .

Although we know how prone Dumas was to dramatise himself, there is no reason not to believe that on this occasion he is telling the truth; for, so profoundly did the two glimpses of the Emperor affect him, that he describes these events almost in the very same words in three of his works: *Les Bords du Rhin*, *La Villa Palmieri*, and *Conscience l'Innocent*.

If the veracity of the Polish hussars* had been questioned, the Emperor's second journey through Villers-Cotterêts dispelled any doubts as to the defeat at Waterloo. The extent of the disaster, however, was not brought home to the simple townsfolk of Villers-Cotterêts until the morning of 22 June, four days after the battle, when the main body of the defeated army began to filter through the town.

For three days a hideous procession passed under the windows of the tobacco shop in the Place de la Fontaine. First came those who had escaped from the carnage safe and sound or with only slight wounds. But how different from the thirty thousand giants, 'calm, proud and sombre', who had passed by only some ten days previously. These fugitives from the battlefield were mingled indiscriminately, marching without order, without drums, almost without arms. Next came those who were wounded more severely, but could still march or keep on horseback. Last came those who could neither march nor sit on a horse, poor creatures with arms carried off, legs broken, gaping wounds in their bodies, lying in carts, ill-bandaged or not bandaged at all. As Dumas tells us – and so vivid is his account that one can feel that this happened only yesterday and not over a century and a half ago – the poor creatures still lifted themselves up, waving some blood-stained rag, to shout, if ever so faintly '*Vive l'Empereur*', sometimes to fall back dead:

> Where were these men being taken? Why intensify their agony by this exposure to a blazing June sun, by the absence of every kind of dressing for their wounds? Was it that there were so many of them that all the towns between Waterloo and us were encumbered with them?

* They had first been suspected of being German spies and had been temporarily confined to the town gaol.

41

Ah! It is thus we see – far from the blare of trumpets, far from the roll of drums, far from the smoke of cannon and flash of musketry – 'tis thus we see that war is not only hideous, but also mad and insensate!

At last the carts, bearing their hideous burdens, became less frequent and then ceased altogether. Then began the passage of those corps which Jerome, the young brother of the Emperor, the inexperienced soldier whom Napoleon had placed on the throne of Westphalia, had miraculously rallied under the cliff walls of Laon.* Every regiment was reduced to two-thirds; only fifteen of the two hundred Mamelukes who had so proudly ridden into battle with their wide red trousers, their turbans and curved scimitars, returned, the rest had been killed or dispersed.

After a short interval of calm, came the visitors. Six thousand Prussians and an English regiment marched into the market square to the sound of bugles, fifes and drums. Two British officers – 'fine young fellows, with capital appetites', as Dumas describes them – were for a short while billeted on Madame Dumas. As neither officer spoke French and Alexandre spoke no English, a strange conversation was carried on between one of the officers and the French youth in schoolboy Latin. They drank a glass of wine together, 'and for the rest of the day we understood each other – more or less', as Alexandre recounts.

Soon everything resumed its normal course and in Villers-Cotterêts, far removed from all disturbances, isolated in the middle of its great forest, it might have seemed that no great earth-shaking events had ever taken place – some people may have had an evil dream, that was all. Alexandre, now a handsome lad of fifteen, spent much of his time in the company of MM Collard and Deviolaine, hunting in the forest, or with Boudoux and Mocquet and other foresters. His life was centred on the forest. But all these hunting expeditions, however pleasant, offered no kind of future to a youth whose patrimony, despite all Madame Dumas's economies, was melting away at an alarming speed. It was essential for him to find employment. So it was that Madame Dumas approached Maître Mennesson, the lawyer, who

---

* Under the command of Marshal Soult.

had so long looked after the affairs of the Dumas family. Maître Mennesson, after a little hesitation, agreed to take Alexandre into his employ in the capacity of third clerk – or, as some unkind persons were to say, as errand-boy. Although loath to give up his independence, Alexandre acquiesced to this arrangement. After all, had not his friend, the elegant Auguste Lafarge, started life as an attorney's clerk – Lafarge, who was now reputed to be making his way so brilliantly and successfully?

Madame Dumas was delighted that her son so willingly followed her wishes.

Alexandre's apprenticeship to the law was by no means unpleasant. Maître Mennesson was a good fellow at heart. A disciple of Voltaire and a republican, he had always maintained a great admiration for the unfortunate republican General Dumas, who had been so cruelly treated.

The title of 'errand-boy', which Alexandre had found so humiliating at first, proved to be the most agreeable part of a clerk's work. Maître Mennesson used to execute deeds for peasants in the neighbouring villages and it was part of Alexandre's duty to take these deeds for signature, whenever (which was often) the peasants found it inconvenient to come in person to the notary's office. Receiving notice the day before of the journey he was to undertake, Alexandre took appropriate measures. If it was the shooting season, he brought with him his gun; if it was the close season, he set out the previous evening to spread lime twigs over all the ponds that lay on his route. Thus, in the first case, he seldom returned home without a brace of rabbits or a hare; in the second, a bagful of birds, all welcome additions to the family larder.

At Whitsuntide that year a ball was held in the town. The Abbé Grégoire's niece, Laura, and her friend, Vittoria, said to be Spanish, were coming from Paris for the occasion. The news of their visit was announced to Alexandre by the Abbé himself, who insisted that he should dine with him and the young ladies before attending the ball. It is true that young Dumas had learnt to dance, but he had never yet held a young lady in his arms. He had been taught how to dance with only a chair as partner! He was overwhelmed with shyness. He was still, after all, only a country bumpkin.

Whitsunday arrived, and Alexandre, in his bright blue coat and nankeen breeches, was presented to the two charming young ladies. Mlle Laura was fair, tall and slender; Vittoria, on the other hand, was pale and plump, 'with eyes which possessed a velvety softness' and a 'fully developed figure and bosom'. After the company had risen from the Abbé's hospitable table, it was suggested that before the ball opened, the young people should take a walk – the time-honoured promenade. Alexandre offered his arm to Laura while the handsome Vittoria followed, a few steps behind, accompanied by the little old hunchbacked sister of the Abbé. The two young Parisiennes, dressed in the height of fashion, were the cynosure of all eyes. Alexandre was acutely embarrassed. His costume, though excellent for a child at his first communion in 1816, was somewhat eccentric for a young man making his first steps into society in 1818. Knee breeches were then only worn by the inveterately old-fashioned. To add to his embarrassment, a young dandy from Paris, who for the last two or three years had been employed at the château, happened to meet the little party, and taking a look at Dumas through his quizzing glass, remarked audibly, 'Ah! There's Dumas going to his first communion again, only he hasn't got a taper this time.'

'Who was that?' asked the girls.

'Oh, a fellow called Miaud,' replied Alexandre. 'Just a clerk employed at the poor house.'

'Really,' said Laura, 'from his dress I would have taken him for a Parisian.'

His dress! The poor boy blushed to the roots of his hair. So a man was judged by his dress. 'It was a sudden flash that illuminated my ignorance,' wrote Dumas forty years later.

But worse was still to come. The avenue terminated in an enormously wide ditch or 'ha-ha'. The moment had arrived, thought Alexandre, to regain his somewhat lost superiority.

'You see that ditch over there,' he said. 'I can jump it, I bet Miaud couldn't – it's fourteen feet wide.'

'And quite right too,' replied Laura. 'What good would it do him?'

Alexandre was appalled at her apathy – but perhaps her apathy came from incredulity. 'You shall see,' said Alexandre, and taking a running jump, landed on the far side. As he came to the ground with a bend of the knees, there came an ominous *ke-rr-ak* and he felt a draught of cold air. He had split his breeches.

With no explanation, or by-your-leave, he rushed home to his mother who quickly made the necessary repairs, while he swallowed a glass of home-made cider; then back as fast as his legs could carry him to the dance hall. Dancing had already started. The girls found him 'delicious' and 'amusing'; as for Alexandre, he found the experience of holding a young woman in his arms positively intoxicating, and although his previous partner in the waltz had only been a chair, he found to his delight that he danced extremely well.

But beneath all the girls' compliments he sensed a sort of mocking raillery. He was 'a mere plaything of no importance', he tells us:

> I had in the space of ten minutes grown quite old. It was not bashfulness this time, but real pain that I felt – no mere flush rising to my forehead but a sharp gnawing that drew the blood from my heart. I was entering into the second circle of human life . . . All my child-life had vanished, just as at an earthquake, villages, towns and mountains, lakes and rivers vanish away . . . The one positive incontestable reality was that for the last quarter of an hour, I was in love. With no person yet – simply Love . . .

Overnight, the country bumpkin, who lived only for hunting and shooting, had entered on the first steps to manhood.

A few days later the two Parisiennes left Villers-Cotterêts. Alexandre was never to see them again. But now his senses were awakened. Most of his young friends had sweethearts – he would follow their example:

> Almost all the girls in Villers-Cotterêts had some more or less serious affair on hand. For some reason we in Villers-Cotterêts had the English custom of free and easy associations between the sexes which I have never seen in any other French town . . .
>
> While I waited patiently for one of these affairs to break up, I went to every party and took part in all the walks and dances. It was an excellent apprenticeship, and after six weeks or so an engagement between a boy named Richou and Adèle Dalvin was broken off by the boy's father.
>
> I had learned much during my six weeks of watching others, and this time I was not involved with a sarcastic and exacting Parisian girl who knew the world much better than I. Adèle was even shyer than I and mistook my pretended courage for the genuine. This gave me great assurance. Now I was the attacker and I soon realized that only by long and patient wooing could I break down Adèle's obstinate resistance. Thus began my study of the delicious struggle of love which asks unceasingly and is not discouraged by an eternity of refusal – a study that has lasted throughout my life.

In the summer we all met at eight o'clock. If the weather was fine, the park invited us. In winter or or bad weather we met at the home of Adèle's friend, where her mother and aunt surrendered the two front rooms to us . . . in the front rooms we chatted, squeezed against each other, two to a chair, and repeated the same stories we had told the night before. On Sundays we met at three and walked and danced until midnight. And then there were fêtes in neighbouring villages to which we went in happy bands – and returned in silent pairs.

This was the first and perhaps the only completely pure love of the many loves of Alexandre's long life. Not that it did not end in the inevitable seduction. It was the inevitable consequence of a young, healthy, good-looking country boy and girl being thrown together at the most impressionable time of their lives. Not that Adèle succumbed to his charms easily – indeed, it was a whole year and a half before she finally surrendered. Alexandre would slip out of his window and by devious well-known paths make his way to the little garden house in which Adèle's mother had given her permission to sleep. Poor Adèle, how could she resist the persistent wooing of this village Romeo? In summertime they walked together in the great forest, and what more natural than to make love on the sun-dappled grass beneath the oak trees, with blue skies above, glimpsed through interlacing branches?

It is not surprising that the pretty milliner finally fell for the charms of Alexandre. He was no longer the gawky boy of a few months back. He now took a pride in his appearance and, with the slender means at his disposal, strove to emulate Miaud in elegance. In the last year he had grown 'as tall as a bean pole', nor was he unconscious of the fact that he was an exceptionally attractive youth. His nose was straight, his hair was still fair and curling, his complexion was radiant and his eyes a sparkling blue. Only his thick, red, sensual lips were a reminder of his coloured grandmother. He was no longer an object of gibes – on the contrary, the youth of the town now regarded him with a certain respect. His mother might keep a humble tobacconist shop, but she was also the widow of a distinguished general; Monsieur Deviolaine, the leading citizen of the town, was her relative and friend, while the aristocratic Monsieur Collard was not only a friend, but Alexandre's guardian; the Abbé Grégoire and Maître Mennesson both held her in the greatest respect. But it must be confessed that at the age of eighteen, Dumas was not the polished sophisticate that he would have liked to be. There were many rough corners still to be made smooth.

46

Into this happy, carefree life of 1818–19 there now stepped Adolphe de Leuven who, more than any other, was unconsciously to shape the destiny of the young Dumas. If Adèle had awakened him to love, it was de Leuven who awakened in him a love of literature.

Adolphe de Leuven was the son of Count Ribbing de Leuven, who had been exiled from Sweden for complicity in the murder of King Gustavus III. The count had sought refuge first in France and Switzerland (where, it was said, he became the lover of Madame de Staël) and later in Belgium; and after Waterloo he had once again returned to France. Monsieur Collard was an old and intimate friend and it was at the home of the latter that Dumas first met the young viscount.

Adolphe de Leuvens, an aristocrat to his fingertips, was as polished, artistic and well-educated as Dumas was ingenuous and untutored; but from their very first encounter, the two young men were drawn together.

Adolphe, young as he was – he was not yet twenty – had observed, read and travelled much. He spoke without affectation of the great men and women he had met. Dumas listened open-mouthed to his new-found friend. Adolphe, appalled at the young provincial's ignorance, both scholastic and literary, decided to take him in hand. It was not the Abbé Grégoire's fault that Dumas was an ignoramus. When it came to routine learning, the future author of over four hundred works might have made a less patient man than the Abbé tear his hair out by the roots. Grammar, arithmetic, Latin and, strangely enough, history – he disliked them all. Although he had learned to read at an early age, he knew nothing of Shakespeare, of Goethe, Schiller, Scott, and little of the French classics. True, thanks to Maître Mennesson, he had dipped into Voltaire, but his notions of great literature were derived from minor writers such as Bertin Parny and Demoustiers, particularly the latter, who as a native of Villers-Cotterêts was regarded locally as a great figure. But of Beranger, Eugene Scribe and Chenier he had never read a word. Yet it was this ignorant youth who was to formulate the idea of a national theatre and obtain international celebrity – a celebrity almost unequalled by any other writer of the nineteenth century.

Although it was Adolphe de Leuven who was to play the predominant role in the formation of Dumas's destiny, there was a second influence who now entered his life. This was a certain Amadée de la Ponce, a young Parisian of independent means, a former officer of hussars, who for some reason or another had decided to rusticate in Villers-Cotterêts. De la Ponce, who spoke Italian and German as fluently as his native tongue, offered to teach these languages to young Dumas, with whom he had become on friendly terms almost at their first meeting. One of the books from which Dumas learnt Italian was a romance by Ugo Foscolo entitled *Lettere di Jacopo Ortis*, which he later translated. This book (to quote Dumas's own words) gave him 'a glimpse – an intuition of romance which until then was completely unknown to me'.

After two months Dumas was able to speak Italian fairly correctly – German came not so easily, but, if unable to speak German, he was soon able to read Goethe and Schiller in the original. It was de la Ponce who said to him: 'There is something else in life besides pleasure, love, sport, dancing and all the wild dreams of youth! There is Work: Learn to Work – that is the way to fulfilment!' If any pupil took a lesson to heart, it was Dumas.

CHAPTER FIVE

The Clerk with Literary Aspirations

At this time a change occurred in Maître Mennesson's office, as much to the advantage of Dumas's literary education as it was to the disadvantage of his legal training. Miguet, the head clerk, a real dry-as-dust character, was replaced by a young man named Paillet. Paillet was wealthy (his family owned a fine estate near Villers-Cotterêts) and, although some eight years Dumas's senior, he had long been on friendly terms with our hero and now as chief clerk treated him with indulgence. The days when Dumas had been merely an errand-boy had passed and for some time now, under Miguet's strict eye, he had been obliged to spend more and more time at his desk, engaged in drawing up deeds of conveyance, bills of sale, marriage settlements and other such humdrum tasks. Now, under Paillet, he had much more freedom and was able to devote himself to his studies of Italian and French, to shooting and hunting, and clandestine meetings with Adèle.

With Paillet he visited Soissons to see a performance of *Hamlet* given by a touring company of students from the Conservatoire. Although it was not Shakespeare's *Hamlet*, but a very indifferent adaptation by Durçis, Dumas was nevertheless thrilled and hastily wrote to ask his friend Fourcade,* now in Paris, to obtain for him a copy of the play. This time he received a true translation of Shakespeare's tragedy and, if we are to believe him, learnt the whole of Hamlet's lines by heart. If we discount a visit to the Comédie-Française with his father at the age of three, this was his first experience of the theatre.

---

* Fourcade had formerly been employed in M Mennesson's office as second clerk.

In his *Mémoires* he wrote: '*Hamlet* was the first dramatic work that impressed me — an impression of deep and inexplicable sensations, indefinite longings, mysterious flashes, by the light of which I saw nothing as yet but chaos.' In fact it was from this moment that Dumas might be said to have embarked on a literary career. It was now that, in collaboration with his sophisticated young friend, de Leuven, he wrote three one-act melodramatic vaudevilles — *Les Abencerrages,** *Le Major de Strasbourg* and *Le Dîner d'Amis* — none of which, however, was original, for all three were thefts from other writers.

Thus passed tranquilly enough the years 1820–21. Then there arrived Monsieur Arnault, a well-known playwright, to tell the young *vicomte* that he was come to take him to Paris to join his father, who, no longer a proscribed exile, was a guest of the Arnault household. The parting between the young men was sad, but Adolfe promised to write at length and often; and with his portfolio crammed with manuscripts, he left for the capital, assuring Dumas that 'he would see what the theatres would yield to the "open sesame" of their three melodramas'.

It was about this time, too, that Dumas was to experience his first heartbreak. In July 1822 he went to spend some weeks with his sister and her husband at Dreux. On his return in September he learnt that Adèle was shortly to be married to a wealthy man twice her age. The eyes of Adèle had suddenly been opened to the fact that her whole future (she was now twenty years of age) was being compromised by a young man who could never make her reparation. She had come to the realisation that for the past three years she had been living in a fool's paradise: the gay and carefree girl had suddenly become a serious young woman. The irresponsible Dumas found her attitude difficult to understand. He tried to see her, but she shut herself away from him. By chance, he did see her once more. It was her wedding day and he was hunting in the forest when he saw the bridal procession pass by. With the passing of the procession and the fading of the music, first love faded too. Thirty years later he was to turn this incident to dramatic account in his *Meneurs de Loups*.

---

* Abencerrages (Ben Serragh), a noble Moorish family which came to Spain in the eighth century. Their struggles with the family of the Zegris and their tragic destruction in the palace of the Alhambra in the time of Abu Hassan (1466–84), the last but one of the kings of Granada, became legendary. Châteaubriand based his romance *Les Aventures du Dernier des Abencerrages* on the legend, a romance which provided Cherubini with the libretto for an opera.

It was shortly after this last glimpse of Adèle that Dumas changed his employment and became articled as second or third clerk (he could not remember which) to Maître Lefevre, a solicitor at Crépy, the same small town where as a young boy he had witnessed that 'spectacle both magnificent and terrible', when French and Prussians had fought a battle to the death in the street beneath his window. Dumas soon realised that despite his new master's outwardly severe demeanour, the apparently straight-laced lawyer enjoyed the gay life of Paris. Indeed, Maître Lefevre often made sudden unexpected visits to the capital, absenting himself for three or four days at a time, a habit which was to have no small influence on his young clerk. In the meanwhile, despite his promises, Adolfe's letters were not only few, but far between, and those he wrote were discouraging. Theatre managers, it seemed, were blind to the talents of the two youthful geniuses; one and all had turned down their masterpieces. I have mentioned only three of the vaudeville melodramas with which Dumas opened his dramatic career, but in these formative years he had also written other works – *Pèlerinage à Ermenonville* (a bad pastiche of Demoustier, as Dumas was the first to admit),* and a three-act melodrama, *Ivanhoe,* based on Walter Scott's romance, both of which he sent to de Leuven. The future, which had seemed so rosy (*la vie en rose*) when Adolphe had departed for Paris with a portfolio crammed full of manuscripts, now assumed a different complexion. Paillet, who had renounced the career of lawyer and now, thanks to his family, was the owner of a small estate all of his own, was sympathetic when young Dumas told him of his disappointment. Together they conceived the idea of making a sudden and truant expedition to Paris during one of Maître Lefevre's absences. But to achieve this plan there were obstacles. Although Paillet came of a wealthy family and even owned his own few acres of land, he was unable to lay his hand on ready cash; as for Dumas, he had none. His mother had already sold the small property she possessed and was now almost entirely dependent on the income she derived from her tobacconist shop, together with the salary her son received as an attorney's clerk. But such obstacles were not sufficient to deter the two young men from visiting Paris. Although Adolphe de Leuven's letters had been discouraging, the very fact that his correspondence revealed

---

* This never saw the light of day, since a contrite de Leuven confessed to having lost it.

51

that he had the entrée to so many distinguished figures in the literary and theatrical world, inspired our hero to renew his friendship with the young *vicomte* and meet these stars with whom both de Leuven and Lafarge claimed to be on such intimate terms. Living in M Arnault's house, and as his guest, Adolphe had in fact now obtained a closer view of a world into which his friendship with Talma had already partly introduced him, a world of which he had previously boasted.

Dumas and Paillet put their heads together. Paillet had twenty-eight francs; Dumas had seven. Paillet, however, was the owner of a horse; together they would take turns to ride, and with Dumas's fowling-piece they would between them poach their way to Paris, giving their spoils to the innkeepers *en route* in return for lodgings – a splendid idea which paid dividends.

After successfully outwitting a number of gamekeepers, the two young men entered Paris on a November evening with four hares, twelve partridges and two quail – at market value, thirty francs' worth of game. As the most suitable hotel in which to stay, Paillet had chosen the Hôtel des Vieux Augustins, where his family was known to the proprietor. Not wishing to admit that he had no money, he explained to the landlord that he had laid a wager with some Englishman to the effect that he and Monsieur Dumas could stay in Paris and return without spending a penny; consequently, in order to win the bet, he desired to treat with mine host for a load of game. The landlord thought the whole thing a great joke and agreed in return for the game to provide the young travellers with board and lodging for two days and two nights, including forage for the horse. Everything amicably settled, the travellers were treated to a generous supper and retired to bed.

Dumas was awake at seven o'clock the following morning. No sooner dressed than he set out for rue Pigalle where de Leuven was living. It was yet scarcely dawn, and Dumas, unfamiliar with Paris, was soon lost in a maze of streets, suddenly to find himself in the Palais Royal. Half the shops here were still shut, but it was with a thrill of excitement that he saw before him the Théâtre Français (today the Comédie-Française) and a bill which read:

TOMORROW, MONDAY
SYLLA
A Tragedy in Five Acts in verse
by M de Jouy
the part of Sylla will be played
by M TALMA

At all costs he was determined to attend the opening performance,* but perhaps in view of his impecunious situation it were better if de Leuven obtained him complimentary passes.

It was not until nine o'clock that he finally reached his destination — rue Pigalle. Adolphe was sound asleep. It was only with difficulty that Dumas roused his friend. 'Wake up,' he said, 'wake up, dress yourself and come along to Talma's.' Somewhat reluctantly, Adolphe rose and dressed.

'What in heaven's name! Have you become a millionaire to make this journey to Paris?' What was all this fuss about? Talma? Why did he want to see Talma? Dumas was shocked. Did his friend and collaborator not know that the great tragedian was that very evening making a first-night appearance at the Théâtre Français?

Dumas's first impression of the famous tragedian was one of disillusion. He was very short-sighted and his hair close-cut. When the young men made their entrance, Talma was at his toilet, naked except for a large towel wrapped round his waist. Under the conditions, his appearance was far from poetical. Shy and embarrassed, Dumas hung back, but Adolphe, whose boasts of knowing the great man had not been in the least exaggerated, had no hesitation in requesting the actor for two complimentary tickets. Talma, seizing one end of his towel and drawing it over his shoulder like a toga, half revealing his chest, took up a pen and signed two free passes. There was, Dumas tells us, something 'truly majestic' in his movement, which made him 'tremble at the very sight'. When de Leaven brought forward the timid lad from Villers-Cotterêts and introduced him as a budding poet, the son of General Dumas (whom Talma had once met at the house of the Chevalier de Saint-George), the most greatly admired actor immediately extended a welcoming hand. Dumas in his *Mémoires* tells us that he felt he had 'touched the hand of a god'.

---

* In fact it was not the opening night: the play had been running for a week.

For young Alexandre the day passed only too slowly. Like any provincial he spent the day visiting the sights of Paris – Notre-Dame, the Jardin des Plantes, and even passing the guards to view the Tuileries. The day seemed endless. At last the hour arrived when he was to meet Adolphe de Leuven at an arranged rendezvous – the Café du Roi, at the corner of the rue de Richelieu and the rue Saint-Honoré:

> I reached the rendezvous before Adolphe, and entering the café I seated myself at a table. Having calculated what would cost me the least to take, I concluded that a *petit verre* would be the thing; and as, to have the right of waiting, you must call for something, I called for a glass of brandy (I may say I have never been able to drink a drop of that abominable liquor; however, though obliged to order it, I was not obliged to drink it).
>
> Scarcely had I taken my seat, when I observed one of the *habitués* (and that he was so I judged from the fact that I saw absolutely nothing on the table in front of him) rise up and advance towards me. It was Lafarge one step further on the road to poverty – Lafarge with a coat shiny at the elbows, and trousers shiny at the knees.

Lafarge, the dandy with the box-coat with its profusion of capes, the aspiring playwright, the reputedly brilliant lawyer, had certainly fallen on bad times; nevertheless, he adopted a patronizing attitude towards the youth from the country. He pointed out the many celebrities seated at the neighbouring tables – all known to him – many of whom were writing; there was Rochefort the famous journalist, there was Theaulon, the dramatist, composing a five-act play in verse.

'What!' exclaimed Dumas, 'Writing verses in a café?'

'To begin with, *mon cher*, this is not a café' said Lafarge; 'it is a kind of literary club; all the people you see here are authors or journalists.'

To which Dumas replied, 'I have never seen a café where they consume so little and write so much.' A *mot* which greatly amused Lafarge. But intriguing as was the atmosphere of the Café du Roi, time was pressing.

At last, the door of the café was flung open and Adolphe arrived, just in time to escort his friend to the theatre as the curtain was rising. No one remembers de Jouy or *Sylla* today. Its popularity in 1823 lay in the fact that the plot, departing from historical accuracy, in many ways represented the last days of the fallen Emperor Napoleon and his abdication. Talma, in his role of Sylla, was the incarnation of the ivory-faced emperor whom Dumas as a boy had seen pass through Villers-Cotterêts on his return from the field of Waterloo.

Dumas, who had never seen any such performance in his life, was enthralled.

The curtain fell to thunders of applause. The performance over, Adolphe proposed that they should visit the tragedian in his dressing room. Adolphe, very much at his ease, pushed open the door. The room was crowded: Dumas remained on the threshold very humble and abashed.

'Talma,' said Adolphe, *'nous voici* – we have come to thank you.' Talma, still wearing his toga from which he had just cast off the imperial purple, peered round. 'Come in, come in,' he said, catching sight of Dumas. 'Well, Monsieur le poète,' he added, 'are you satisfied?'

'I am more than that, *monsieur*; I am wonderstruck,' replied our hero. Talma was graciousness itself and offered him a pass for the following Thursday when he was appearing in *Regulus*, a tragedy by Lucien Arnault.

'Impossible, I must go back to the country.'

'What are you doing in the country?'

'I scarcely dare tell you – I am a notary's clerk.'

'You need not despair on that account!' said Talma, 'Corneille was an attorney's clerk.' Then, turning to the assembled company, 'Gentlemen,' he said, 'let me present you a future Corneille.'

Dumas blushed up to the eyes.

'Touch me on the forehead,' he said to Talma; 'it will bring me luck!'

'Well, so be it, Alexandre Dumas, I baptise thee Poet, in the name of Shakespeare, of Corneille and of Schiller!'

So much for Dumas's account of his meeting with Talma. As usual it is difficult to know truth from fiction. It must not be forgotten that Dumas wrote of this meeting forty years after the events he records. Nor must it be forgotten that at the time of writing Dumas was already famous, and that since he was writing his memoirs in serial form at so much a line, he was unable to resist the temptation of padding out his reminiscences, nor was he able to resist every opportunity for exaggeration.

It was not until the following Wednesday that Dumas and Paillet arrived back in Crépy, laden with two hares and six partridges which they had saved from the previous day. In the market-place the truants parted company – Paillet to return to Villers-Cotterêts, Dumas to creep into M Lefevre's house by the back entrance and to hasten to his room and change his clothes. Through the window he called to the servant Pierre to ask if there was any news of his master. It was with a sinking heart that he learnt that Maître Lefevre had returned the previous night. Hoping against hope that his absence had gone unremarked, he slipped behind his desk and settled down to work. The hour for dinner arrived. In those patriarchal days, masters and apprentices, lawyers and their clerks, sat down to table together in a friendly relationship. But that night the atmosphere was far from one of conviviality. The meal concluded, Maître Lefevre beckoned to Dumas. His two colleagues tactfully absented themselves. After scratching his left foot with his right hand, a nervous habit he had whenever he had to make an important pronouncement, Maître Lefevre took a pinch of snuff, and then turning to Dumas, asked:

'Monsieur Dumas, do you know anything of mechanics?'

'In theory, no sir,' replied our hero, 'in practice, yes.'

'Very well then, Monsieur Dumas, you know that for a machine to function efficiently, none of its wheels must cease working. I am the mechanic in charge of the machine and you are one of its wheels . . .'

The hint was obvious. 'However,' added the lawyer, 'this warning is only meant as provisional.' 'You are very good, sir,' replied Dumas, 'for my part, I prefer to take it as formal.'

His mind was already made up. His future lay in Paris. Poor Madame Dumas. Never had she been so destitute, but Alexandre, who in his old age was to admit that he had never known the meaning of despair, even in the blackest moments, was determined to leave his provincial home and dusty files for the glamour of the theatre, the glitter of cafés and the society of men of letters.

He succeeded in selling some Piranesi engravings which had belonged to his father and which had long been gathering dust in the attic; he raised a further substantial sum of money playing billiards with old Cartier, who kept the posting house inn. Cartier, who refused to acknowledge that Dumas was the better player, consistently doubled the stakes. Not having ready cash, Cartier paid his losses in rounds of drink. At the end of five hours' play, Dumas, who drank neither spirits nor coffee, had won *six hundred glasses of absinthe*. Expressed in money this represented ninety francs, enough to pay his coach fare to Paris a dozen times over. Next he visited a M Danré, a family friend, who was on familiar terms with General Maximilien-Sebastien Foy, a one-time companion-in-arms of General Dumas. General Foy had not only distinguished himself in the French campaign in Spain, but had also fought at Waterloo. Since 1819 he had been elected to his *département* as a liberal member of the *chambre des députés*, and although not an eloquent speaker, had earned himself a reputation as an honest man and spokesman for the people. A letter of introduction to him from M Danré could prove extremely useful.

M Danré had no hesitation in providing the necessary introduction, and furthermore promised (not altogether willingly) to assure Madame Dumas that no harm could come to her son in Paris. Precisely by what means the young man with no qualifications was to earn a living remains a mystery; Dumas had no doubts, however, that a brilliant future lay before him. In his *Mémoires* Dumas tells of an incident which occurred when he was a mere babe-in-arms. Despite his phenomenal memory, this is surely an example of Dumas's irresistible urge to dramatise himself, just as he did in his account of his meeting with Talma. It is palpably impossible for a child of two to have recollected word-for-word the following conversation:

'You remember when I was two years old, what that fortune-teller you consulted predicted about my future,' he said to his tearful mother when M Danré called on her with reassuring words.

'What did she say?' asked Danré.

'Her words were,' said Dumas: 'I cannot tell you, Madame, what your son will become; only through clouds and lightning flashes like a traveller who crosses high mountains. I see him obtaining to a position which few men attain . . . I will not say that he commands nations, but I can see that he is speaking of them. Your son belongs – although I cannot give any precise indications of his destiny – to that class of men we call RULERS. Not a King but something similar – something more enviable perhaps. Not all Kings have crowns on their heads or sceptres in their hands.'

'So much the better,' observed his mother. 'I have never envied the lot of Madame Bonaparte.' Then, turning to M Danré, 'But I would like to ask you whence he gets all these ideas?'

'Gets them indeed! They are part of his destiny . . . They are part of his convictions.'

And so, it was that the fond and tearful mother agreed against her natural inclination to part with her wilful son.

CHAPTER SIX

Marshals and Generals

It was at half-past five on a Sunday morning in May 1823 that Dumas descended from the diligence and made his way to the Hôtel des Vieux Augustins. Though physically and emotionally exhausted (his parting from his mother had been most painful), he could scarcely sleep. At nine o'clock he was already dressed and eager to set out for the de Leuven residence, in the rue Pigalle.

Sunday in Paris appeared to him like a city of the dead. All shops were closed. The streets were empty except for a few churchgoers. Dumas's ebullient spirits sank as he made his way through the seemingly deserted city, past shuttered shops and near-empty cafés. He almost wished himself back in Villers-Cotterêts. He seemed to forget that it was still only early morning and a Sunday.

Once in the de Leuven home however, among friends, his normal high spirits returned. The Count was already up and about, amusing himself in his garden, 'by offering a morsel of sugar to a rose' as Dumas recounts. Monsieur de Leuven gave him a warm welcome and allowed him the hospitality of his house.* 'There's sure to be some attic vacant,' he said. 'You'll have to arrange things with the rats, but I believe you to be quite capable of coping with them. Now go and fix things up with Adolphe – get along with you.'

Adolphe, as usual, was still in bed, but his excuse was that he had been working until the early hours on a play, *La Pauvre Fille*, which was to be ready in five or six days' time for an official reading. When will I ever reach that point? thought Dumas to himself. But in the meanwhile practical affairs came first.

* It is to be presumed that the Count had either rented or bought the house from M Arnault. In his *Mémoires*, Dumas does not make this clear.

He still possessed a letter to his father from the Duke of Belluna (Marshal Victor), now minister of war, in which the Marshal thanked the General for services rendered in Italy and promised to lend him his assistance should he ever require it. Perhaps he might extend his promise to the General's son. There were other letters too, from Sebastiani and Jourdan. In his innocence Dumas was convinced that these former comrades of his distinguished father would welcome him with open arms and find him employment in one of the ministries. He penned a carefully worded letter to Marshal Victor, requesting an interview. Adolphe, more worldly-wise than Dumas, advised his friend not to rely too much on Victor, and to waste no time in paying his respects to Jourdan and Sebastiani. On the very next day he presented himself at the doors of the marshals.* His first visit was to Jourdan. Since he had made no appointment, he was agreeably surprised that he was admitted without delay. It became immediately apparent that Jourdan, on hearing from his major-domo that a Monsieur Alexandre Dumas was requesting an interview, had jumped to the conclusion that the reports he had received of the General's death, fifteen years previously, had been false. At the sight of the young Alexandre, his face fell. He had never even known that his old friend had had a son; and try as he might to establish his identity, Dumas was dismissed as an impertinent imposter. He next called on Sebastiani, who had always been very close to his father, and to whom he owed a debt of gratitude for putting him on the first rungs of the ladder to future honours and glory. Now, as a junior minister of the crown, he had become pompous and condescending. Dumas found the general pacing up and down a *salon*, dictating to four secretaries seated at the four corners of the room, each of whom offered their august superior, as he passed, a pinch of snuff from a gold *tabatière* placed beside their inkpots and quills for this very purpose. True, Sebastiani acknowledged Dumas to be his father's son, but his welcome was cold. He hinted that he might be able to offer him a very humble position as clerk but he was already overstaffed. Dumas declined the offer – he, the son of a distinguished general, a general who, in his opinion, was far greater than Sebastiani, albeit now a count, had ever been – he, Alexandre Dumas, was not prepared to sit at a desk offering snuff to this pompous old fellow. After a mere ten

* Dumas refers to them as marshals. In fact, Sebastiani was only created marshal in 1840.

minutes' interview Sebastiani gave him a cold handshake and bade him adieu.

Forty-eight hours had passed since he had written to the Duke of Belluna requesting an interview, and still there was no reply. Not a little disappointed, he began to leaf through the *Almanach de 25,000 addresses*, with no very clear idea in his head of what he was seeking. Quite by chance his eye fell on the name of General Verdier, a man he remembered his mother having mentioned with respect, and who had served in Egypt under his father. Twice his father's friends had cold-shouldered him; third time lucky, perhaps. Dumas lost no time in hastening to number 6 Faubourg Montmartre, where the general lived, a mere ten minutes walk distant. He was surprised to find no fine mansion like those of Jourdan and Sebastiani, but a simple tenement house. Here there were no lackeys or Suisses to guard their masters from importunate visitors, just an elderly concierge. 'General Verdier, if you please?' inquired Dumas. 'Fourth floor. The little door on the left,' replied the concierge. Scarcely believing his ears, Dumas climbed the steep stairs to the fourth floor. True enough, there was the small door on the left, furnished with a simple bell-pull. With beating heart, he rang.

The man who opened the door was about sixty years of age; he wore a cap trimmed with astrakhan, a green frogged jacket and moleskin trousers – in his left hand he held a small palette charged with colours, and a paint brush.

Dumas could not believe that this strange little man was the general, and he was acutely embarrassed when the painter explained that, despite all appearances to the contrary, he was indeed General Verdier. Politely the soldier -painter inquired what he could do for his young visitor. Abashed, Alexandre explained that he had come to Paris to find work, that he was the son of General Dumas and that he had relied on the patronage of his father's former comrades-in-arms, Jourdan, Sebastiani and Victor (to whom he had written, soliciting an interview and who had not even bothered to reply), only to be shown the door. He had often heard his father mention the name of Verdier as a good friend – perhaps he could help? Verdier remembered his father well – 'the bravest and handsomest man in the army'; but as for counting on *his* patronage, alas, he was the last man in the world on whom to rely. He had been treated almost as shabbily as his old friend General Dumas, and had not been given a pension.

Indeed, Verdier was almost penniless. 'Don't rely on any of these men,' he said. 'Go early tomorrow morning to see General Foy. He is sure to help you . . .'

That evening Dumas dined at a cheap restaurant as Verdier's guest, and, thanks to Adolphe de Leuven, who had obtained two passes for a performance by Talma, he was able to repay the old soldier's kindness by inviting him to the theatre.

General Foy now remained his only hope. At ten o'clock on Tuesday morning, he presented himself with some nervousness at 64 rue de Mont-Blanc, the home of the soldier-deputy.

No sooner had he announced himself as M Alexandre Dumas, the bearer of a letter from M Danré, than he was shown into the general's study. Dumas saw before him a small, slender man with thinning grey hair. He was standing at a tall writing-table, working on his *History of the Peninsular War*. The room was littered with maps, open books, copies of speeches and documents of all sorts. This interview, probably the most important of all Dumas's life, is best described by himself.

All of a tremble, I advanced into the room. Turning to me the General asked, 'Would you be the son of the General Dumas who commanded the Army of the Alps?'

'Yes, General.'

'They tell me that Bonaparte treated him very badly and that this treatment was extended to his widow.'

'He left us destitute.'

'Can I be of help in any way?'

'I admit, General, that you are more or less my last hope.'

'How so?'

'Please be so good as to acquaint yourself with the contents of this letter from M Danré' I said . . . Foy unsealed the letter and began to read . . .

'Oh, General,' I cried out in an accent which must have greatly impressed him, 'I am completely lacking in education, and what is so shaming, I only realise it now for the first time. But I'll make up for it, I promise you . . .

'Meanwhile, have you any means of supporting yourself?'

'Absolutely none, General,' I replied, overwhelmed by my ignorance.

The General looked at me with an air of pity. 'Never mind,' he said, 'I won't abandon you . . .'

'Give me your address,' said the General, 'I will consider what can be done for you.' . . . I began to write while the General looked over my shoulder. I had no sooner written my name, then he exclaimed:

'We are saved!'

'How so?'

61

'You write a capital hand.'

I dropped my head, I could no longer bear the load of my shame. 'A capital hand!' That's all I possessed. One day I might be perhaps a copying clerk – this was my future. I would have gladly cut off my right hand.

General Foy continued, without paying too much attention to my inner feeling. 'Listen,' he said to me, 'today I am dining at the Palais Royal, I will talk to the Duc d'Orléans of you. I'll tell him that he must take you into his office – you, the son of a Republican General. Sit down there,' he continued, indicating a vacant desk, 'and write a petition in your best handwriting.'

When I had finished, the General took my petition, read it, and scribbled a few lines in the margin. I was humiliated to note that his handwriting was as good as my own. Then he folded the petition and placed it in his pocket and, holding out his hand in token of adieu, he invited me to breakfast with him on the following day.

General Foy was as good as his word. He had obtained a position for Dumas as supernumerary clerk (ie on probation) in the secretariat of the Duc d'Orléans at a salary of twelve hundred francs per annum. He was to start work on the following Monday under a M Oudard. Dumas could scarcely believe his ears – this was a fortune. He threw his arms round the good General's neck and embraced him. Foy began to laugh:

'You are an excellent fellow at heart,' he said, 'but don't forget your promise: *study*.'

'Ah, yes, General, I promise. I am going to live by my penmanship, but one day I will live by my pen.'

'Come then, take up your pen now and write to your mother.'

Dumas protested; he preferred to announce the news in person. Today was Tuesday; he would spend Wednesday, Thursday, Friday and Saturday with her and return on Sunday in time to report at his office on Monday. 'But you'll ruin yourself on coach fares,' protested the General. It was Dumas's turn to laugh – 'I have an account with the post master' – and went on to tell the story of his five-hour-long game of billiards with old Cartier.

Breakfast finished, and once more thanking the General, he rushed off to tell the de Leuven family his good news.

Refusing dinner with his hospitable friends, Dumas took the four o'clock coach for Villers-Cotterêts and arrived home at one o'clock in the morning. He rushed into his mother's room to awake her, shouting, 'Victory, victory!' The next morning the whole town was aware of the wonderful news. He was lionised and received everywhere with open arms. The very ones who had predicted to his mother that her worthless son would never be anything but a good-for-nothing were the first to say that they had never doubted his ability; they had always said that one day young Alexandre would be a somebody and were now delighted that their predictions had been realised. What utter humbug, thought Dumas. He was already beginning to learn something of the world.

On his return to Paris on the following Sunday to take up his appointment, Dumas's first necessity was to find suitable lodgings. The Hôtel des Vieux Augustins was far too expensive, nor did he wish to impose himself on the always hospitable de Leuven household. On the very day of his return, 'after going up and down many staircases, [he] found a room which possessed the luxury of an alcove . . . the walls covered with a yellow paper at twelve *sous* a roll'. It was on the fourth floor of number 1 Place des Italiens [now Place Boieldieu], a little square facing the Opera Comique. The rent was reasonable: ten francs a month. He didn't bother to haggle with the concierge, but agreed to take it on the spot. In his ignorance he vastly over-tipped the caretaker but it was money well spent, since *madame la concierge* agreed in return to act as his housekeeper, keep his room neat and tidy, and run little errands for him. His furniture, he told her, would be arriving in a few days' time.

Once he had found suitable accommodation, he was determined to make himself better acquainted with the capital. Paris on a Sunday, he found, was not the city of the dead he had imagined it to be when he made his call on the de Leuven household earlier in 1823. As yet unfamiliar with the city, he restricted himself to strolling along the boulevards – not the boulevards of Hausmann with which we are familiar today, but boulevards which were on the whole narrower and into which debouched an infinite number of *petites ruelles*, little streets dating from former centuries, immortalised in the etchings of Charles Meryon. The Boulevard Saint-Germain, the rue Saint-Honoré and the Marais still boasted their *grands hôtels particuliers*; the Champs-Elysées was a fashionable promenade, while the boulevards des Capucines and Italiens were renowned for their theatres and fashionable cafés. In many respects however, the capital still remained a medieval city. The very names of its streets are evocative of a former age – rue des Mauvais Garcons, rue des Francs Bourgeois, rue des Chanoines, rue de la Sourdières . . . In the centre of the city, the Louvre, the Tuileries, the Palais Royal, the Palais de Justice, the Place de la Concorde and the newly constructed rue de Rivoli were the real glories of Paris. Napoleon had entrusted the architects Percier and Fontaine with many grandiose schemes – neo-classical in conception (the Arc de Triomphe, the Arc du Carrousel and the façade of the Eglise de la Madeleine* are but a few examples), but in 1823 many were as yet not completed, or were never to be built at all.

Strolling aimlessly along, Dumas found himself outside the Café de la Porte Saint Honoré. Glancing through the windows, he suddenly caught sight of a familiar face, that of Hiraux, the son of the good old man who had once tried to make a musician of him. Though somewhat older than Dumas, the two had been boyhood friends and it was with pleasure that the lonely Alexandre pushed open the door of the café to greet his old companion. The pleasure was mutual, and even more gratifying to Dumas himself when Hiraux revealed himself to be the proprietor of the place and invited Alexandre to dine at his expense. While dinner was being prepared, he placed all the newspapers of the establishment at his young friend's disposal. As his dinner was costing him nothing, Dumas decided to spend the money thus saved on a visit to the theatre. Guided by Hiraux, he glanced through all the advertisements and finally decided to visit the Théâtre de la Porte Saint-Martin where Mlle Dorval and M Philippe, both famous in their day, were performing in a revival of *Le Vampire*, an absurd but popular melodrama.

Dumas in his *Mémoires* devotes four entire chapters to this, his first regular visit to a Parisian theatre. Gulled into buying a place in the queue, he was under the impression that he had bought himself a ticket for the pit. Taunted as a gate-crasher, laughed at because of his old-fashioned dress and greeted with guffaws of laughter when he removed his hat to reveal no longer fair curling locks, but a mop of already darkening frizzy hair, Dumas, usually so gentle-mannered, struck one of the bullies, and, always the gentleman, gave his name and address, adding that he would be pleased to vindicate the insult on the following morning between eight and ten o'clock. The very idea of challenging one of his tormentors to a duel made him even more ridiculous in the sight of these ill-mannered oafs, who all began to

* The Madeleine was to have been created 'a temple to the armies'.

64

shout, 'Throw him out!' A few moments later he found himself alone in the street. Although shaken by his experience, he was still determined to see the play. With some difficulty he procured another ticket (one at the price of three) this time in the orchestra stalls. Here, in much more respectable society, he found himself seated next to a gentleman who, before the rise of the curtain, was deeply engrossed in a book with the curious title of *Le Pâtissier François*, with a long subtitle which included the words [I translate] *Directions to prepare every kind of egg for Fast Days and others, in more than sixty different ways, published in Amsterdam by Louis and Daniel ELZEVIER, 1665.*

'Pardon me, *monsieur*,' said Dumas, somewhat astonished at his own audacity in addressing a stranger, 'but I could not refrain from reading the title of your book. Are you so very fond of eggs?' The gentleman, surprised, turned to his young neighbour. 'I believe you addressed me?' he said politely. Dumas, encouraged by the kindly manner of the gentleman, repeated his question, explaining that he had an uncle, a *curé*, a great gourmand who had once laid a wager that he could eat one hundred eggs at a sitting, but certainly did not know sixty different recipes and would be most interested to acquire the book. The kindly gentleman explained that what he was reading was an Elzevier edition of priceless value and almost unprocurable. Naturally Dumas had never heard of Elzevier and was fascinated by what his new acquaintance told him of bibliophiles and rare books and much else. The oafs in the pit who had insulted him, he was told by his kindly neighbour, were no more than members of a *claque* (hired applauders), a practice initiated by the Emperor Nero. Certainly, his challenge would never be followed up. Their conversation was only interrupted by the rise of the curtain, but was resumed during the intervals. It soon became obvious that his new acquaintance disliked the play, and criticised audibly not only the 'book', but the performance. There were cries of 'hush!' all around. The performance came to a halt as attempts were made to evict this importunate critic. 'I saw this play some years ago,' he told Dumas. 'I thought it bad at the time; now I find it even worse.' Finally the critic was forcibly evicted by the police for causing a public nuisance.

This incident would not be worth mentioning but for its sequel, which was to have such a great influence on Dumas's career. Dumas did not share his neighbour's opinion of the play. He found Mlle

Dorval, whom he was to know so well in later years, magnificent as the heroine, and the plot by no means absurd. What he did not realise at the time was that he was witnessing one of the first attempts in 'romanticism', something hitherto quite unknown in the French theatre. The plot, however absurd, had to it a fantastic side which pleased his imagination and planted in his mind the germ of *Don Juan de Marana*, which did not see the light of day until eleven years later. Nor did he realise that his neighbour was a well-known figure in the literary world.

The following morning, Dumas was awake early, but as predicted by his friend of the previous night, no one came to demand satisfaction for the blow he had delivered. Nevertheless, he was by this time aware that there was (as he puts it) something *de trop* about his person and his garments. Therefore, before leaving for the office, he had his hair cut short – in fact too short, so that, to use his own words, he resembled a shorn seal – and his coat, which was at least a foot too long, he had delivered to a tailor for necessary alterations.

On his arrival at the Palais Royal, M Oudard, the *chef de bureau*, greeted Dumas in the most friendly manner, telling him that he had been particularly recommended to him by two persons. Dumas was puzzled. Two persons? General Foy? Yes, but who was the second? To his great surprise, M Oudard told him that his second sponsor was none other than M Deviolaine – M Deviolaine, who had so often reproached him for his idleness, for wasting his time, for poaching with undesirable characters, for writing trumpery verses and third-rate plays; this same M Deviolaine had actually recommended him for a clerkship in the secretariat of the Duc d'Orléans!

M Deviolaine was now superintendent of forests, not only of Villers-Cotterêts, but of all the vast acres belonging to the House of Orléans, and had his office in the Palais Royal. Dumas, at Oudard's bidding, hurried off to thank his cousin. Deviolaine greeted the young man in his usual gruff manner – a manner which belied his natural generosity and fundamental good nature. Once again he warned Dumas not to waste his time scribbling bad verse and threatened to claim him from M de Broval (the director general), lock him up in one of his own offices and make life a burden for him should he ever do so. Dumas protested that it was to write that he had come to Paris, and nothing would deter him. But instead of kicking him out of the room as he threatened, M Deviolaine concluded the interview by saying, 'Come, come, embrace me,' adding 'Want any money – eh, rascal?' Dumas politely refused. 'Then come and dine with us whenever you like . . . but now get out, you are wasting my time.'

Dumas withdrew, while M Deviolaine, still growling in his usual way, bent his head over the report on which he was engaged.

Dumas's work during his first probationary weeks was apparently exemplary; he even enjoyed it. This was largely due to his immediate superior, a M Lassagne, a handsome man of about thirty-five. Lassagne was intelligent and well-informed. An intimate friend of all the great vaudevillists of the time, he found relaxation from bureaucratic life, which he detested, in literary activities. He wrote witty *chansons*, contributed articles to popular newspapers, and collaborated in some of the most delightful vaudevilles of the operatic theatres. This was exactly the superior Dumas required. Forty years later he was to write:

> he made me love the time I passed at my desk, because he was always at hand ready to explain things to me – to teach me something new about the life on which I was just entering – about the world, to which I was an utter stranger – and about literature, foreign and national, of which, in 1823, I was almost equally ignorant.

Dumas was a willing learner, despite the fact that much of his work was extremely dull. He developed the facility of making exquisite copies of documents (the actual contents of which he never absorbed) and developed the fine art of folding his finished products, and of making and sealing envelopes, each task to be executed in a different way according to the rank of the recipient, from kings to commoners. In fact, when eventually he gave in his resignation in 1831, the royal duke, by that time King Louis-Philippe, gave a sigh of regret and accorded the highest tribute that Dumas was ever to receive from his most Christian Majesty: 'Deuce take it! What a pity he's going. He was the best sealer of letters I have ever known.'

It was very shortly after his arrival, while Ernest, the second clerk, was instructing him in this delicate task of folding and sealing letters, that Lassagne, who at that moment was perusing the newspapers, suddenly exclaimed:

'Hah! That's the man all over.'

'What d'you mean?' asked Dumas.

Instead of replying, Lassagne read out aloud:

A scene which recalls the episode of La Fontaine at the first presentation of *Le Florentin* occurred yesterday evening at the third performance of *Le Vampire*. Our learned bibliophile, Charles Nodier, was ejected from the Porte Saint-Martin theatre because he interrupted the performance by hissing. Charles Nodier* is one of the anonymous authors of *Le Vampire*.

So it was the famous Nodier with whom Dumas had spent such an agreeable evening! He could now claim acquaintance with one of the leading critics and literary figures of Paris, whose soirées at the Bibliothèque de l'Arsenal were already famous. Of course Dumas had heard of Nodier, but knew nothing of his writings. It was the ever-helpful Lassagne who enlightened him and recommended him to read such charming tales as *Trilby la Fée aux Miettes, Histoire du chien de Brisquet, Jean Sbogar* . . .

At the first opportunity, Dumas acquired a copy of the latter. 'The reading of this book began to shake my faith in Pigault-Lebrune [a moralistic novelist whom Dumas had hitherto much admired],' Dumas was to write. If Adolphe de Leuven and Amadeé de la Ponce laid the foundations to Dumas's literary future, it was certainly Lassagne who was the first to build upon them. 'What France is looking for now is the *historical novel*,' he told his young friend. 'But,' replied Dumas, 'the history of France is so dull and tedious.'

'Indeed, how d'you know that?'

'I've been told so.'

'Poor boy, read it for yourself,' replied Lassagne, 'and then you will change your mind.'

Thus, in some ten words, Lassagne opened a road which was to lead Dumas to a fame, as yet undimmed.

About a month after his installation in the secretariat, M Oudard sent for Dumas; he wished to see him in his private office. Since both the Chevalier de Broval, the director general, and M Oudard had already complimented him on his diligence and the quality of his work, it was with no qualms that he obeyed the summons.

* Nodier, who is usually described as an elderly man, was in fact only thirty-six at the time.

Oudard greeted him with a solemn face. The Duc d'Orléans, he told Dumas, had just requested the services of a copying clerk who could transcribe quickly and accurately a document which he was preparing for his legal adviser; above all he needed a man of discretion; the document was not to become the public property of the whole office.

'I thought of you, as you write quickly and well,' said M Oudard. 'It will be a chance for introducing yourself to the Duke – I will take you to his room.'

It was a very nervous young man who was shown into the royal presence, but the Duke soon put him at his ease; directed him to a desk and gave him a long document of fifty pages in his own hand to transcribe. This time Dumas did not copy automatically but read the document carefully from end to end. It concerned a case, too long to describe here, which at the time was to be a *cause célèbre*. It had to do with a certain Maria-Stella Petronella, Baroness Sternberg, who laid claim to the rank and fortune of the Duc d'Orléans, which she asserted to be rightfully hers. It was a document in confutation of this claim which Dumas was summoned to transcribe.*

Dumas completed the work at eleven o'clock at night. The Duke was highly satisfied; his only criticism being Dumas's almost total lack of punctuation. As Dumas himself admits, 'throughout my whole life I put in punctuation stops to my own feelings, or rather, I put none at all'.

Three weeks later M Oudard informed Dumas that his probationary days were over and that he had been placed on the permanent list at a salary of 1,200 francs a year, soon to be raised to eighteen hundred. His financial position was further improved by the production at the Ambigu of a verse comedy, *La Chasse et l'Amour*,† a mediocre piece which he had written in collaboration with de Leuven and James Rousseau, an experienced writer.

---

* The contessa's case, with all the royal cards stacked against her, was inevitably lost. From Dumas's own description of the case, Maria Petronella was no mere adventuress, but had good grounds to believe that she was a legitimate heiress of the Orléans branch of the royal family.

† Following *La Chasse et l'Amour* he wrote another comedy, *La Noce et l'Enterrement* in collaboration with Lassagne, a work of no consequence (although it ran for forty nights), and a number of poems, including a lengthy *Elegie* written on the death of General Foy. In addition to these, he tried his hand at the short story and published three tales at his own cost. He sold only four copies but had the honour of receiving a favourable notice in the *Figaro*, by the young republican critic Arago, who was to play a prominent role in the three day revolution.

Dumas in his *Mémoires* gives an amusing account of how his collaborators sat up all night to work with him on this play, while they consumed vast quantities of wine and hot punch in the process. Rousseau invariably got drunk and had to be escorted home and propped up on the pavement outside his lodgings, to awake in the morning to find a few coppers in his hat. Passers-by had taken him for a beggar. In fact Rousseau was by no means a pauper and if out of funds, never failed to obtain advances from M Porcher, a wealthy patron of the arts who was always prepared to give financial assistance to writers in need. It was Rousseau who introduced Dumas to Porcher, who at their very first meeting advanced the budding young playwright 300 francs on the strength of his participation in the writing of *La Chasse et l'Amour*. Porcher hardly ever failed to help Dumas whenever our author was in financial straits, which was nearly always.

Mediocre as *La Chasse et l'Amour* was, it nevertheless earned Dumas three hundred francs – the equivalent of three months' salary. This windfall arrived just in time, for the young author had now embarked on a love affair with a sentimental young dressmaker eight years his senior.

Catharine Labay (or Lebay) occupied a small apartment opposite to that of Dumas. Here she had a work room which she ran very competently with the help of a few girls. According to contempary accounts, she was fair-haired and plump, with a light complexion and a serious disposition. She was a native of Rouen, where she claimed to have married and then left a half-mad husband. Every biographer of Dumas, with the exception of Maurois, seems to have accepted this as the truth; but in fact no such union ever existed and the 'madman' was entirely fictitous. Later, when Catharine Labay acknowledged Alexandre Dumas *fils* as her child, she had, in order to make the declaration valid, to confess that she was unmarried.

Dumas's courtship and ultimate seduction of Catharine was a whirlwind affair compared with his courtship of Adèle Dalvin. Dumas in 1823 was an extremely occupied young man, for he read extensively, and although his official hours of work at the secretariat were only from ten in the morning until five in the afternoon, he was also obliged every other week to return to his desk from seven o'clock until ten or eleven at night 'to make up the pouch', that is to say, to send off the day's mail and evening newspapers to Neuilly, where the

Duc d'Orléans was in residence. This done, he was obliged to remain in or near his office until Monseigneur's instructions for the following day should reach him. This enforced confinement or close proximity to his office often precluded him from visiting the theatre, except to make the occasional visit to the Comédie-Française then known as the Théâtre Français which was in the precincts of the offices of the Palais Royal. This was excellent when Talma or Mlle Mars were performing, but the occasions when he was able to see these artists perform were few and far between, especially as M Oudard, who had the privilege of distributing tickets gratis every week, usually reserved these evenings for himself. But Dumas's enforced idleness was by no means wasted. Lassagne had drawn up for him an excellent programme of reading, from Aeschylus to Schiller, taking in Plautus and Molière on the way and, more important, Walter Scott and Byron. In the idle hours of the night, deprived of the company of Catharine and unable to visit the theatre, he spent his time reading. Lassagne had said to him: 'The neo-classical tragedies of our day will soon be forgotten. More venturesome writers will emerge. See that you are one of them!'

Only Sundays remained free to him. On these days of leisure Dumas took Catharine Labay for walks in the woods of Meudon. Inevitably, in the shade of the trees or in some dark grotto, they made love. Was Dumas truly in love with Catharine? Almost certainly not. One wonders whether Dumas throughout his whole life ever knew what true love meant, except in the case of his mother, to whom he remained devoted until her death. The little dressmaker had many good qualities – common sense, a love of hard work, loyalty and even charm, but Dumas, even when she told him that she was with child by him, made no mention of marriage – nor perhaps did she expect it of him. She was entirely uneducated and had no presentable relatives; besides, had she not led him to believe that she was already a married woman? Whether Dumas knew this to be a lie or not, he was determined to keep himself available for adventures of a more intoxicating kind.

When, on 27 July 1824, Catharine gave birth to a fine boy who was given the name of Alexandre, the third of the name, her lover, on the score of economy, was already sharing her lodgings. But now arose the question of his mother, to whom he had not dared mention either his liaison or his paternity. Madame Dumas had found the separation

71

from her son overlong, and fearing that she had not long to live, now suggested that she should sell her business and join him. Her son readily acquiesced* and took an apartment for her at number 23 Faubourg Saint-Denis, at a rental of three hundred and fifty francs a year. So Dumas, now an established assistant clerk at the age of twenty-two, had two *ménages* to maintain. The small success of *La Chasse et l'Amour* and *La Noce et l'Enterrement* had convinced him that if only he could get rid of 'the pouch' he could find time to write a masterpiece, but he was sensible enough to realise that to succeed he had to devote as much time as possible to reading the works of the masters recommended to him by Lassagne. It was shortly before the arrival of his mother in Paris that he made the acquaintance of a young doctor named Thibaut. As Thibaut lived only a hundred yards from the Palais Royal it was easy for Dumas to slip round to his rooms while waiting for the messenger to return from Neuilly.

Like Lassagne, Thibaut undertook to improve Dumas's education. In the mornings, between six and seven, he sometimes accompanied the doctor to the Charité hospital where he learnt a little of pathology and anatomy, though he never overcame his repugnance at the sight of operations and corpses. From these visits Dumas acquired a certain amount of medical knowledge, which he more than once put to use in his novels. We have his word for it that when writing *Amaury*, a novel which appeared in serial form in the newspaper *La Presse* in 1844, he traced the phases of lung disease, from which his heroine, Madeleine, was suffering, with such accuracy that one day he had the honour of a visit from the Comte de Noailles, who had come to request him to stop the publication of his novel. The count's daughter and son-in-law, both of whom were suffering from tuberculosis, had recognised in Madeleine's illness the symptoms of their own complaint; and both eagerly awaited every morning the arrival of their serial, to know whether the heroine was to die or recover.

As Madeleine in the story was already condemned by the author to die, publication was broken off. To put the two sufferers at ease, Dumas improvised a happy ending which he sent to them in manuscript. Although this restored their hopes, it unfortunately did

---

* Dumas's *Mémoires* make no mention of Catharine, but do mention the birth of his son. He also claims that it was he who was the first to suggest that his mother should come and join him in Paris.

not restore their health. The serial was not resumed until both were dead.

It was to Thibaut also that he owed his knowledge of poisons, a knowledge of which he made use twenty years later when he described the poisons employed by Madame de Villefort in *Le Comte de Monte-Cristo*.

A further change now occurred in Dumas's fortunes. It will be recollected that on joining the secretariat he had been warned not to dabble in literature. For this reason he had preserved anonymity when writing *La Chasse et l'Amour*; his name had not appeared either on programmes or play bills. Shortly before the production of *La Noce*, the report had somehow got abroad that Lassagne and he were collaborating. M Oudard had sent for Lassagne, who was reprimanded for giving Dumas a taste for literature which he maintained was bound to ruin the career of the young man. M Oudard had made Lassagne promise not only to write no more plays with Dumas, but also to take no further steps in putting the final touches to the one on which they had already embarked. This was a terrible blow to Dumas, who had borrowed three hundred francs from Porcher against future takings from *La Noce et l'Enterrement*.

Dumas immediately requested an interview with M Oudard.

'It is no concern of mine,' said the *chef de bureau*. 'I am simply transmitting to you the remarks of the director general.'

'I thought that M de Broval affected to be a patron of literature!' protested Dumas.

'Literature – perhaps so, but do you call *La Chasse et l'Amour* and *La Noce et l'Enterrement* literature?'

We only have Dumas's word that this interview ever took place, but even if embroidered and Dumas emerges as a dauntless opponent of bureaucracy, there is probably some truth in this account. After some further verbal exchanges, Dumas tells us that Oudard demanded with some asperity:

'So you are absolutely determined to continue with literature?' To which Dumas replied, 'Yes *monsieur*, both by necessity and vocation.'

'Very well then,' replied Oudard, 'let your literature be like that of M Delavigne, and instead of blaming you, we will encourage you.'

Casimir Delavigne, who held a highly paid position as librarian to the Duc d'Orléans, was a member of the academy and a respected writer of exceptionally dull 'classical' plays. The very idea of writing like M Delavigne seemed to young Alexandre so preposterous that he was prompted to reply that if he did not believe that in the future he would not produce something *different* from M Delavigne, he would give his sacred word never more to engage in literature.

The following day, and indeed for several days afterwards, the 'blasphemy' of which he was considered guilty spread throughout the corridors of the Palais Royal. It was regarded as the greatest joke, but one employee, in the accountant's office, a newcomer from the previous day, whom no one as yet knew, found nothing amusing in the situation.

'Why don't you laugh?' his colleagues quizzed him.

'Because I see nothing to laugh about.'

'What! Nothing to laugh about in saying he would do better than M Delavigne?'

'He did not say he would do better, he said he would do something *different*.'

'It's all the same.'

'No, it's by no means all the same.'

'Do you know Dumas, then?'

'Yes, and it is just because I know him that I promise you he will do something – what, I cannot say, but I promise that this something will astonish all the world – excepting me.'

The employee who had just entered the accounts department the day before was Dumas's old friend, the former hussar officer, Amadée de la Ponce, who had taught him Italian and German.

The account of Dumas's interview with M Oudard was written more than thirty years later, when Dumas was already famous. It seems highly improbable, however, that a junior clerk of twenty-two would have spoken to the head of his department in such lofty terms without receiving a serious reprimand, or even being dismissed. 'I bowed to him and left the room.' No, it is too good to be true. In fact, Dumas was not dismissed; on the contrary, he tells us that when a vacancy occurred he was appointed to the *bureau de secours*, (what today might be the department of social security) , a job which, although it did not carry the same prestige as that of a clerk in the secretariat of his Royal Highness the Duke,* was higher paid; at last he was free from the duties of superintending the dispatch of the 'pouch'.† His evenings were now free and he had the satisfaction of learning that *La Noce et l'Enterrement* had been accepted for performance at the Porte Saint-Martin.

It is difficult to separate the true from the false; indeed, it is sometimes difficult to follow chronologically Dumas's early career if one depends on his memoirs. André Maurois, for example, in his biography, *Les Trois Dumas,* dismisses entirely the interview between Dumas and Oudard as recounted above, and ascribes Dumas's freedom from routine office hours to his transfer from the secretariat and his appointment with the forestry commission under M Deviolaine. What is certain is that by 1827 Dumas had fully resolved to follow a literary career, although he had realised, after the productions of *La Chasse et l'Amour* and *La Noce et l'Enterrement,* his lack of experience.

> In my secret heart I shared to some extent M Oudard's opinion concerning my last two productions and for that reason I had not put my name to either of them, whereas by an instinct which did not deceive me, I had affixed it on my *Ode to the Death of General Foy* . . .

Even if this account of his interview with Oudard is pure fiction, it is certainly true that he 'carried on his education every day'. He became absorbed in Byron (whose name was on everyone's lips at the time), Fenimore Cooper (then resident in Paris) and particularly in Walter Scott and Schiller. Still uncertain of his own powers, he sought collaboration with Frédéric Soulié. Soulié was two years his elder and just twenty-five when they first became acquainted. Although Soulié had not met with any literary success, he was a man of decided ideas, something of a cynic, and 'could hold an opinion against the world'.

'His was one of the post powerful literary characters of the epoch, and one of the most vigorous temperaments I have known,' Dumas wrote. Soulié was what Herder (one of the initiators of *Sturm und Drang*) was to Schiller. He died, like so many of the Romantics, before his time, leaving behind him a mass of poems, tales, dramas and novels

---

* It was only since the accession to the throne of Charles X in 1824 that the Duc d'Orléans had been addressed as his Royal Highness, a title which Louis XVIII had resolutely opposed.

† Later in his *Mémoires*, Dumas relates that he was not free from the 'pouch' until 1829; that is, three years hence.

of which only *Mémoires du Diable* and a few *contes* are remembered today. As Dumas puts it: 'Il avait essayé un peu de tout, et il lui était resté un peu de tout ce qu'il avait essayé.'

Walter Scott, to whose works Dumas had been introduced by de Leuven while still in Villers-Cotterêts, was very much in fashion at the time. A version of *Kenilworth* had lately been performed with much success at the Porte Saint-Martin, and another of *Quentin Durward* was in preparation at the Français. Dumas decided to collaborate with Soulié on a drama to be called *Les Puritains d'Ecosse*, based on Scott's *Old Mortality*. To begin with, Soulié was enthusiastic; he was particularly fascinated by the characters of John Balfour of Burley, and of Bothwell. But for all their enthusiasm, collaboration between the youthful dramatists was impossible: their temperaments clashed, or as Dumas expressed it, 'Our two organisations, standing out each of them in relief, found no means in either case of toning down their excrescences.'

After two or three months of fruitless labour, they were still wrangling and had got no further than when they started. These months, however, had not been wasted. Soulié's brusque criticisms of men and things, their altercations and exchange of ideas, helped Dumas to find himself: 'I felt new forces springing to birth within me and like a blind man when sight is restored to him, it seemed to me that every day, little by little, my vision was covering a wider horizon.'

Still determined to write, he wrote a verse tragedy – *Les Gracques* (*The Gracchi*). 'I gave it its due,' he wrote in *Comment je devins Auteur dramatique*, 'by burning it.' This was followed by a verse translation of Schiller's *Fiesco*, not for financial gain, but for his own edification. The story of the Fieschi is pure Dumas, a story set in the sixteenth century. Giovanni Luigi de Fieschi, a member of one of the most illustrious houses of Genoa, attained a tragic historical celebrity in connection with a conspiracy of which he was the leader. Andrea Doria, the famous admiral, sprung from a family hereditarily at feud with the Fieschi, having expelled the forces of François I from the State, had restored a republican form of government and had effectively held in check the ambition of the nobles. Count Fieschi organised a plot for the overthrow of Doria and the establishment of an oligarchic government. Instigated by the approval of France and

Rome, Fieschi enrolled a formidable array of accomplices, his three brothers among the foremost. Three galleys were fully equipped, under the pretext of an expedition against the Turks, and all being in readiness, the attempt to sieze the city was fixed for 2 January 1547. Doria, despite repeating warnings, refused to ascribe treacherous designs to Fieschi. Complete success seemed at first to crown the conspirators. The gates of the city were forced, the fleet captured, and Doria put to flight. At this critical moment Fieschi had only to appear and become dictator of the city state, but he was nowhere to be found. Stepping from one galley to another in the darkness of the night, he had stumbled and fallen into the murky waters of the harbour. His cries went unheard. Borne down by his ponderous armour, he had perished miserably in the muddy depths below. With Fieschi's death the conspiracy collapsed and Genoa remained a republic.

It is not difficult to see how such a story would appeal to Dumas, and how influenced he was to be by Schiller. 'Of all dramatic writers, Schiller was the one who influenced him most, and time and again Dumas's unfailing memory helped'; but, true though this is, it was Shakespeare who was the first to 'release the springs of his dramatic genius'.*

* André Maurois, *Les Trois Dumas*.

CHAPTER SEVEN

The Shakespearian Players and the Romantic Revolution

In September 1827 there burst upon Paris the revelation of the English players. True, in 1822, another company had tried the experiment of performing Shakespeare in English at the Porte Saint-Martin, but the time was not yet ripe; only seven years previously Waterloo had been fought and lost. The English performers were pelted with apples and oranges and hissed off the stage. But five years later the intellectual climate had entirely changed; now the English players were received with unparalleled enthusiasm. Dumas, who had now taken up residence with his mother, though not neglecting Catharine, borrowed two hundred francs from Porcher; one hundred and fifty to be put aside for household expenses and the other fifty to be devoted to seeing the English players, who had been invited to perform at the Odéon.

Earlier in 1827, under the patronage of the Duke of Devonshire, Mlle Georges had played *Semaramis* and *Merope* in London with the greatest success, and it was this double triumph that had suggested to the director of the Odéon the idea of making arrangements with an English company to perform Shakespeare and Sheridan *(The Rivals)*. Shakespeare was virtually unknown except in adaptations. Apart from those already mentioned, Lemercier had made a tragedy with *Richard III* and Liadière another, based on the story of Jane Shore (which was not Shakespeare at all) and *Macbeth*. There was talk of Soulié's *Juliette* and Alfred de Vigny's *Othello*.

Decidedly the wind blew from the west and heralded the literary revolution.

Nor was this all. At the Porte Saint-Martin a work had lately been performed the dénouement of which, borrowed from Werner's *Twenty-fourth of February*, marked a revolution both by its cast and by its execution – this was *Trente ans ou la Vie d'un Joueur* by Victor Ducange and Goubaux. Besides the dramatic importance of this work, two eminent artists had revealed themselves in it – Frédérick Lemaître and Marie Dorval.

In his *Mémoires*, Dumas writes:

> Everyone knows *Trente ans*, everyone has seen it performed by the two artists I have named. But not everyone has seen it played amid the feverish excitement of its first representations – a fever which raged in all alike, actors as well as spectators ... Thus it was that the English players found the Parisian public in a white heat of excitement and calling loudly for fresh emotional experiences to follow up those that were just past.

The success of the English actors was phenomenal. The violence of their performance produced first astonishment, then enthusiasm. Kemble and Harriet Smithson could not have realised what an extraordinary impact their first performance was to have on the French public; and perhaps, in particular, on two impressionable young men – Dumas and Hector Berlioz. After *Hamlet*, Dumas, quite beside himself, left the theatre with a new world opened before him; after *Romeo*, an even more transported Berlioz, moved to the depths and hopelessly in love with Harriet Smithson, wrote his *Symphonie Fantastique* – surely the very essence of romanticism expressed in musical terms. Five years later he married 'Juliet' and in 1839 wrote his *Romeo et Juliette*, a landmark in musical history.

Dumas made frequent reference to those fateful Shakespearian performances:

> It is difficult to express what I felt from the moment that the curtain rose; the effect of that dialogue of which I had not understood a word, it is true, but which was made clear by the acting of the speakers; the naturalness of gesture which interpreted simply and truthfully the thought and word; that easy negligence of pose which made an audience forget they were witnessing a play because the actors forgot that they were playing to an audience – all this added to the poetry which is so intrinsically Shakespeare's, overturned all my ideas of the theatre, and as through a mist I perceived far off the towering peaks of the undiscovered heights.'*

---

* *Voyage en Suisse*. In his *Mémoires*, however, Dumas writes: 'Already, at this time, I knew Shakespeare almost by heart ... but stage plays are to be seen and not read.'

Théophile Gautier in his *Histoire du Romanticisme* spoke for all the young Romantics – authors, poets, painters and musicians alike – who wished to break away from the shackles of convention and classicism which had been imposed upon them for so long, which neither a great revolution nor the Napoleonic *épopée* had failed to shatter, when he wrote: 'Our imagination was fired by these foreign masterpieces, so rich in colour, so unfettered and powerful of fancy. The enthusiasm they inspired was a kind of delirium. It seemed that poetry had been rediscovered, and so, in fact, it had been.'

Dumas was completely bowled over by the playing of Kemble, Kean and Macready and the lovely Miss Smithson: 'For the first time, I saw in the theatre real passions felt by women and men of real flesh and blood.' He knew now what he wanted to do: 'to paint with a free brush; to bring upon the stage that physical violence which the classic writers had left in the wings'. But what subject was he to choose? The idea of a great dramatic tragedy occurred to him as if by accident. Shortly before the English players closed their phemonenal success, Dumas visited the *Salon*, the great annual exhibition of paintings and sculpture. Here a woman sculptor, a Mademoiselle de Faveau, now long forgotten, exhibited two small bas-reliefs which attracted great attention. The first of these represented a scene from Walter Scott's *The Abbot*; the second, *The Murder of Mondaleschi*. Dumas was greatly impressed by both works. He had read *The Abbot* and recognised the subject matter, but who was Mondaleschi? Afraid of showing his ignorance, he inquired of no one, but it being a Sunday and his free day, he decided to visit his friend Soulié with whom he had once attempted to collaborate. Soulié was the owner of a fine library (unlike so many young Romantics, he was a man of substance who had inherited a thriving timber business), and from him Dumas borrowed a copy of *La Biographie Universelle*. Here he read the articles on Mondaleschi and Queen Christina. He learnt that Mondaleschi, the lover of the Queen of Sweden, and jealous of the rising star of another Italian, Sentenelli, had written a number of abusive and imprudent letters, and had been put to death by his rival in the Galerie des Cerfs in the Palace of Fontainebleau at the instigation of the infuriated queen. Here to hand was the raw material for a drama worthy of Shakespeare!

Dumas again asked Soulié to collaborate with him, but the latter dryly refused. He was, he said, writing a drama on the same subject

General Alexandre Dumas.

ALEX · DUMAS ·

Dumas as a young man shortly before his first success with *Antony*. Achille
Deveria, 1829 (c).

himself. Finally it was decided that each should try his luck. This was unkind of Soulié, who knew that Dumas was bound to his office desk and had not the leisure to devote his whole time to writing; nevertheless, thanks to his boundless energy, Dumas prepared himself for the task by an arduous study of the works of Shakespeare, Molière, Corneille, Calderon, Goethe and Schiller, and 'blocked out' his plot, writing mostly in bed.

While thus engaged, he received notice to the effect that there was no further work for him in the *bureau de secours* and that he was assigned to the department of archives. This was a disgrace, Dumas tells us, brought about by his incorrigible refusal to give up a literary career. The new job was in fact a complete sinecure, presided over by a charming eighty-year-old gentleman, M Bichet, who still wore his hair with a queue and was invariably dressed in the fashion of 1788. After five days, Dumas had completed all the work assigned to him. Old Bichet, who had taken a fancy to him, while his other superiors, M Parseval de Grandmaison (who was so absent-minded that he was apt to forget his own name) and old M Pieyre who himself wrote odes, had no objection whatsoever to Dumas occupying his desk, although there was absolutely no work for him to do. They even encouraged him to continue writing *Christine*. This verse drama in five acts was almost completed, when the blow fell.

After two months of peace and encouragement in his humble archives department, Dumas received notification from the secretariat, that because his place was a sinecure, it had been suppressed, and he was ordered to report to the forest service department under the jurisdiction of M Deviolaine. Almost immediately, Dumas was in trouble. He refused to sit in a room occupied by five or six other clerks, whose idle chatter distracted him from his real vocation – that of a man of letters. He claimed for himself a little corner, separated by a thin partition from a compartment in which the office-boy kept the ink bottles and stationery. There then ensued a farcical storm in a teacup. Dumas was accused by his fellow clerks of regarding himself too superior to work with them; the office-boy complained and had his hat knocked off for his pains by the furious young playwright; the *chef de bureau* came down from the director's sanctum, bringing with him a verbal order, the purport of which was to recall to his place the undisciplined employee who had for one moment dared aspire to a desk of his own, or, as he put it, 'leave the ranks'. This order was immediately transmitted to the sub-chief, who transmitted it to the clerks in the big room, who transmitted it to the office boy. There was general jubilation throughout the department. A comrade was about to be humiliated, and if he did not bear his humiliation meekly, he would lose his place.

All this occurred in the absence of M Deviolaine, and consequently Dumas had not heard the last of the affair. Deprived of his privacy, he resolved to return home to his mother to await the arrival of his crusty but good-hearted relative. Poor Madame Dumas was in despair. Her wilful son, however, was adamant in his resolve to be left undisturbed, and continued to work furiously to complete *Christine*. He asked Porcher for an advance on the play, but when Porcher, quite naturally, said 'get it accepted first and then we will see', he wrote a note to Deviolaine requesting an interview as soon as he should return. Three days later Deviolaine summoned Dumas to his office. The long and short of it was that after telling the pigheaded young man that he only retained his services for his mother's sake, M Deviolaine finally capitulated. Dumas was allowed to retain his cubbyhole and work in peace.

Now freed from all detailed supervision, he found it possible to get through his office work at high speed, thanks to the rapidity with which he could write in his admirable hand, and devote a few hours a day to the completion of his play.

Hardly had he completed the famous line, *'Eh bien, j'en ai pitié, mon père ... Qu'on l'achève'*, where, as he puts it, he felt 'as embarrassed as a poor girl when she has given birth to an illegitimate child', the question arose: what was to be done with it? He had set his sights high; nothing less than the Théâtre Français, the august stronghold of the academicians and the classic grand style, was good enough for him. But how was he to breach the walls? If only Talma had still been alive, he might have reminded the great actor of their meeting when he baptised him in the names of Shakespeare, Corneille and Schiller, but Talma had died in 1826. Dumas later wrote, 'I possessed in those days that self-assurance which belongs to inexperience and supreme self-satisfaction. It has needed many successes to cure me of that *amour propre*.' Self-assurance he certainly possessed. That he, a modest clerk of twenty-six years with a salary barely sufficient to support his family commitments, a young man with little or no formal education and with no patronage, should have even considered submitting a verse tragedy in five acts to the Théâtre Français is almost incredible. But Dumas was no ordinary young man.

Dumas first approached M Arnault to request an introduction, but M Arnault, after reading a few lines, had cast the play aside. He next turned to M Oudard, who made the implausible excuse that he had no influence. These rebuffs were not sufficient to deter young Dumas. It will be recollected that the secretariat of the Duc d'Orléans was entitled to receive free passes for the Théâtre Français. These twenty-five passes were delivered each month to the office of the Palais Royal by the prompter of that illustrious playhouse, a man named Garnier. It was from this man that Dumas now sought advice. He stopped him on his way to carry out his monthly duty and inquired of him what he should do in order to be granted the honour of being allowed to read a play to the committee. He was told that the manuscript must be deposited with the 'examiner', but that there was already an accumulation of several thousand plays and that he might have to wait for years before receiving a reply. There was, however, a way of shortening formalities, provided he knew Baron Taylor.

Baron Taylor, an Englishman born in Brussels, naturalised a Frenchman and holding a commission in the French army, had become at the age of thirty-six, through the patronage of Charles X (by whom he had been ennobled) Commissaire du Roi aupreś de la Théâtre Comédie-Française. The appointment, though frowned upon by the classicists, was by no means a bad one. Taylor was, among other things, a painter, and had designed stage settings and costumes; he had also produced a number of comedies and, in collaboration with Nodier, had translated an English play. Charles X had appointed him to the Théâtre-Français with the purpose of bringing a little order into that establishment. Though many of the classical actors disapproved of him – even his English name was an offence – his administration, in the opinion of impartial critics, was honest and liberal-minded, and he did much to establish the Romantic school in France.

It was Lassagne who suggested to Dumas that he should ask Nodier for an introduction to the all-powerful Baron Taylor. Nodier, the eccentric bibliophile, whose acquaintance it will be remembered Dumas had made during a performance of *The Vampire* at the Porte Saint-Martin in 1823, was an intimate friend of the Baron. Dumas protested that Nodier would never remember him, but was nevertheless persuaded to write. The reply was not long delayed and took the form of a note from Taylor himself, making an appointment for seven o'clock in the morning. At the hour fixed, Dumas presented himself at the apartment of the *commissaire du roi*. An old servant-woman opened the door to him:

'Ah! *monsieur*,' she exclaimed, 'you are indeed doing the Baron a service; he is longing to see you. Come in.'

Dumas hastened into the sitting room and found Taylor in his bath; close beside him sat a gentleman who was reading him a tragedy. It was obvious that the unfortunate Taylor, imprisoned in his bath, was only too anxious to get rid of this importunate visitor. Despite the *commissaire*'s remonstrances, the playwright insisted on his right to read his play to the bitter end. Taylor resignedly sank back into his bath and motioned Dumas to wait for him in the bedroom. The reading of the play concluded, the Baron succeeded in dismissing his unwelcome visitor, and now shivering with cold, retired to bed. Dumas, in describing this farcical scene, wrote:

'Alas, *monsieur*,' I said to him. 'I have come at a very inopportune moment, and I fear you will hardly be disposed to hear me – at least with the indulgence I have need of.'

'Oh, not at all, that does not apply to you,' Taylor replied, 'as I know nothing about your work yet; but you may imagine what torture it is to listen every blessed day to things like that man's.'

'What! every day?'

[Taylor then showed Dumas the formidable schedule of his day's work.]

Monsieur le Baron, 'I hazarded timidly, 'perhaps you would rather I came again some other day?'

'Oh no, on no account,' said Taylor, 'now that we are here.'

'Very well, I said, I will read you one act only, and if that fatigues or worries you, you must stop me.'

'Excellent,' murmured Taylor, 'you have more compassion than your confrères. Come, that's a good sign. Read on, I am listening to you.'

And so it was that Dumas read *Christine*, timidly at first but with growing confidence as Taylor urged him to continue. No sooner was the reading accomplished than the Baron sprang from his bed.

'You shall come to the Français with me.'

'Good heavens! whatever for?'

'To take your turn for a reading as soon as possible.'

'What! You really mean I am to read it before the committee?'

'Yes, and not later than Saturday next . . .'

Dumas did read *Christine* before the committee, not on Saturday, but on the following Thursday. *Christine* was listened to with much approbation, and when the votes were taken, it was received with 'acclamation', subject to certain revisions by one of the advisers of the house. Dumas was too excited to pay much attention to the words 'subject to revision'. He left the theatre scarcely knowing what he was doing and flew towards the rue St Denis. Heedless of carriages and horses, he dashed across the road, tripped and fell into an open gutter, and on arrival at his mother's house discovered that his manuscript had dropped from his pocket. But this was of little consequence to him; he had the whole play in his head, it was simply a matter of rewriting. He burst into his mother's room. The poor lady, who did not usually see her son until five o'clock, uttered an exclamation of surprise. 'Received by acclamation!' shouted Dumas, and then began to sing and dance round the little room. His mother thought he had taken leave of his senses (he had not dared tell her previously that he was to read his play to the committee, in case it was turned down).

'But what will M Fossier say?' she demanded. Fossier was the clerk in charge of his office.

'Let him say what he likes. If he doesn't like it, I'll send him packing.'

'My poor child, it is *you* he'll send packing – you will be turned out.'

'So much the better, mother; I shall have more time for rehearsals.'

'But if your play fails and you lose your place, what's to become of us?'

'I shall write another play which will be a success.'

'In the meanwhile we must live.'

'What the devil! In seven or eight days time we receive our bonuses.'

'But while waiting for your bonus, which you haven't yet touched, you'd better go back to your office, where so far they know nothing; and don't boast to anybody about what's happened.'

Although M Deviolaine had given him the day off, Dumas conceded that his mother was right. It was half-past two and he had plenty of time to finish the official day's work. On his return to his office he found a pile of papers on his desk, but by six o'clock the work of copying was completed neatly and without a mistake. The remainder of the evening and night was spent rewriting *Christine* from memory.

The great day was 30 April 1828. On the following morning he reported to his office. The office-boy was the first to greet him. 'So you have been writing a tragedy,' he said maliciously, and showed him a newspaper. True enough there was small paragraph which read:

> Today the Théâtre Français accepted by acclamation a five-act tragedy written in verse by a young man who so far has written nothing.
> This young man is on the administrative staff of M le Duc d'Orléans, who smoothed away all difficulties for him and who strongly recommended him to the 'reading committee'.

Dumas, in his *Mémoires*, wrote, 'All distorted as this was, there was some foundation for the statement.' A rather ambiguous remark. True, Taylor, the *commissaire du roi*, had smoothed away difficulties; but what had the Duke himself done? Soon the news was all over the administrative offices. At two o'clock M Deviolaine arrived and immediately sent for Dumas. 'So it was to play pranks like this that you asked for leave of absence?' he demanded in his usual crusty manner. When Dumas asked politely if his work had suffered in consequence, Deviolaine replied that that was not the point; did he not realise that the actors were making a mock of him, and so on and on. It was in the middle of this conversation that the office-boy knocked on the door and entered. 'Excuse me, Monsieur Deviolaine,' he said, 'there is a *comédien* asking for M Dumas,' laying stress on the word *comédien*.

'A *comédien*! What *comédien*?' asked Deviolaine.

'M Firmin of the Comédie-Française.'

'Yes,' replied Dumas casually, 'he is playing the part of Mondaleschi; Mlle Mars, that of Christine . . .'

This was too much for poor Deviolaine, who threw up his arms in mock despair. 'Clear out!' he said. 'Mlle Mars putting herself out for you indeed! I can't believe it.'

Dumas took the opportunity of slipping out of the room.

Firmin had called to take him to see Picard, who had been charged by the Théâtre Royal with the task of 'going over' Dumas's piece. The choice of Picard was ridiculous. Picard, a little hunchback, with a pointed nose, the author of a hundred comedies, although an academician, was devoid both of talent and generosity of mind. Such a man could scarcely be expected to feel anything but horror at so violent and audacious a drama as *Christine*. When, a week later, Firmin and Dumas called on him to hear his verdict, Picard, after politely inquiring after his visitors' health, addressed Dumas with a charming smile:

'My dear sir, I sincerely hope that you have the means of earning your livelihood.'

'*Monsieur,*' replied Dumas, 'I am a junior clerk in the service of Monsieur le Duc d'Orléans at a salary of fifteen hundred francs a year.'

'Good. The best advice I can give you, my dear young man, is to go back to your office stool.'

A crestfallen Dumas was unable to believe in this summary verdict. How could anyone read *Christine* without seeing that the author had something in him? He appealed to Baron Taylor who, all sympathy, submitted the manuscript for Nodier's opinion. On the very next day, Taylor was able to show Dumas a note in Nodier's own hand on the first page of the manuscript. It read: 'It is my true and honest opinion that *Christine* is one of the most remarkable works I have read for twenty years.'

To quote Maurois: 'Was this a sound judgement? The verse was nothing like so good as that of the young poets who were Dumas's contemporaries. Victor Hugo, born in the same year, 1802, had a power, a gift of words and a virtuosity far superior to Dumas's mere animal high spirits . . . [But Dumas] knew, as though by instinct, how to construct a play, and how to appeal to the feelings of an audience.'

In consequence of Nodier's opinion the actors were called to a second reading on the following Sunday, and it was decided that the manuscript should be submitted to a second judge, a man named Samson, whose tastes were not so utterly opposed to the new style, and whose suggestions (beneficial as they later turned out to be) led to a complete remodelling of the piece.

Everything now seemed to be going well but, as matters turned out, the play was not after all to be performed at the Théâtre-Français. Why? For a combination of reasons. To begin with, ever since the death of Talma, Mademoiselle Mars had reigned there as queen. She had now turned fifty but still reserved the best parts for herself, with a special partiality for the roles of *ingénues*. Her miraculous appearance of youthfulness and her perfect diction gave her an authority which nothing could shake. Where casting was concerned, her word was law. She had made her reputation in classical roles – Marivaux, not Shakespeare, was her natural element. She was quite incapable of portraying the passions and emotions of a Desdemona, a Lady Macbeth or the madness of Ophelia, much less the heroines envisaged by Dumas and the Romantic school.

One day shortly after the acceptance, subject to corrections, of *Christine*, she visited Dumas in his dusty little cubbyhole in the Palais Royal. Assuming her most gracious air, she criticised the casting of the play and objected to certain lines she would have to speak; she wished them to be deleted. Dumas refused. The result was that rehearsals were unnecessarily protracted. Worse still, Firmin now in turn began to find fault with the lines apportioned to him in the part of Mondaleschi, while the actor who was to play the role of Sentenelli resigned from the Français to join the company of the Odéon.

It will be recollected that Soulié was also writing a *Christine*. This had now been accepted by the Odéon. Furthermore, yet another *Christine* had been written by a M Brault, a man already on his death bed, who was not only an academician and former prefect, but who had powerful backing. It was only natural after so much wrangling over Dumas's production that priority should be given to this dying old gentleman and that Dumas's play should be shelved indefinitely. To produce three versions of *Christine* at the same time would have been farcical. In his disappointment, Dumas did not see at the time that this was providential, for when in its revised form it was eventually produced at the Odéon on 30 March 1830, with Mlle Georges in the title role, the play was vastly improved.

The acceptance of M Brault's version of *Christine* in place of his own came to Dumas as a bitter blow, although in his *Mémoires* Dumas claims that on the solicitations of Brault's son and the Duc de Decazes he willingly allowed the dying poet to have his play produced before his own, 'since it would be a consolation to the poor man to see his play produced before he died'. But what was to happen to Dumas now? He had looked to the production of *Christine* for what was literally his daily bread; moreover, when the bonus fee of which he had spoken to his mother arrived, his share was fifty francs less than that of his fellow colleagues – a reduction which was meant as a warning 'to behave himself properly'. Dumas's salary from the secretariat was by no means sufficient to maintain two establishments and now, with an ever growing circle of literary friends, it was barely enough to meet his own immediate personal needs. Although he still attempted to support Catharine and his little son, his love for her had considerably cooled. The larger the world which he now began to frequent, the more dowdy seemed the little apartment in the Place des Italiens. His love affair with the little seamstress ran through all the time-old stages – scenes of jealousy, estrangement, coolness, boredom and, on Dumas's part, infidelities. She was not in the least interested in his literary ambitions. Incompatibility of temperament and want of mutual interests led to inevitable estrangement, despite the fact that she never ceased to love him. Her only ambition was to see Alexandre rise step by step in the civil service to become eventually, if not head of his department, at least chief clerk. Dumas, however, the born optimist, was convinced that he would one day make his fortune by his pen, not by his penmanship.

Garnier, the prompter who had advised him to submit *Christine* to Baron Taylor, now gave the young author a piece of advice: 'Write another play and give the principal part to Mlle Mars. Avoid giving her long lines. Be careful not to cross her in any way, and you will be certain of a production.'

'But, my dear Garnier,' said Dumas, 'one writes only the sort of verse one is capable of writing . . . As a matter of fact, I am planning to write a drama in prose.'

'So much the better.'

'I'll try to dig up a subject . . .'

Just as chance had led him to the bas-relief in the Salon which had inspired *Christine*, so now it gave him the plot for *Henri III et sa Cour*. One day the odious office-boy, who shared the cupboard with him in which paper and ink bottles were kept, had locked the door and had left the building on some errand, pocketing the key. Having run out of paper and still having a few more reports to copy, Dumas went to the office of the accounts department in search of a fresh supply of stationery. Quite by chance he caught sight of a large volume by the historian Anquetil lying open on a table. Glancing casually at the open page, he read of an incident that occurred during the reign of Henri III. The Duc de Guise, Henri le Balafré, aware that his wife,

91

Catharine de Clèves, was deceiving him with one of the King's minions – a certain Paul de Caussade, Comte de Saint-Megrin – decided to give a lesson to his duchess, despite the fact that he cared little about her infidelity.

One day at dawn, the Duke entered his wife's room (so the story ran), holding a dagger in one hand and a potion in the other. 'Decide, *madame*,' he said in a tone of fury, 'whether you wish to die by dagger or by poison.' She wept and begged him to pardon her; but to no avail – he forced her to drink the potion. Falling on her knees, she commended her soul to God. At the end of an hour – an hour of anguish, awaiting death – the Duke entered the room, serene of countenance, and informed his wife that the 'poison' she had drunk was nothing more than an excellent soup. No doubt this lesson made her more circumspect in future.

Here was a really marvellous scene! But who was this Duc de Guise and who was Saint-Megrin? Once more Dumas had recourse to the *Biographie Universelle*. This provided him with a number of details and referred him to the *Mémoires de l'Estoile*. The invaluable *Biographie Universelle* informed him that Pierre Taisan de l'Estoile (1546–1611) had been the famous chronicler of the reigns of the homosexual Henri III and the far from homosexual Henri IV, *le vert galant*. Dumas borrowed the book and found it fascinating. From it he learnt that Saint-Megrin, first gentleman of the royal chamber, had been assassinated by order of the Duc de Guise to teach him what happened to those who made love to princesses. Not bad, thought Dumas, but perhaps a little commonplace; certainly not enough material here on which to build a drama. He continued reading. He came across an admirable passage which would provide just the added spice to make a really gripping play. The fact that it concerned another personage of the same period, Bussy d'Amboise (1549–79), was of no consequence. After all, Dumas was writing a play, not a history book.

This young Bussy, he read, the lover of Françoise de Chambes, Comtesse de Montsoreau, had received a note written in her own hand asking him to visit her on a specified night during the absence of her husband. This she had written in obedience to her husband's orders and, in order to save her life, had agreed to be found, if not exactly *in flagrante delicto*, in a compromising situation by the jealous Count who would thus find an excuse to kill Bussy. At midnight the count, accompanied by several friends, all armed, burst into his wife's bedroom and murdered the unfortunate lover.

With this passage relating to Bussy, combined with the assassination of Saint-Megrin and memoirs of Walter Scott and Schiller, Dumas had the necessary materials for a play. He had to work up a few period details, but this presented no problems. He was to say later that this was one of the best-constructed plays he had ever written. In two months the work was completed. But 'two months' must be qualified.

Dumas tells us later that before actually writing a play there was always a long period of gestation. Once he had the germ of a plot in his head he would tell his friends the story over and over again, elaborating on his theme, or deleting this and that until the whole play was clear in his mind. During the writing of *Henri III*, he visited Villers-Cotterêts on a hunting expedition and told the plot of his play to old friends and acquaintances, always with slight variations. He tells us that his *Mademoiselle de Belle-Isle* and the *Juif errant* (which he regarded as one of his best novels) went through a gestatory period of nearly five years before he committed these works to paper. His only fear, he wrote, was that he might die before his inspiration saw the light of day.

CHAPTER EIGHT

Henri III et sa Cour

Once *Henri III et sa Cour* was completed, he hurried off to read it to Mme Waldor. Mélanie Waldor was the daughter of a M de Villenave, one of Dumas's new-found literary friends. Charles de Villenave, one-time editor of the *Quotidienne*, then manager of the *Journal des Curés* and founder of the *Mémorial Religieux*, professor of history of literature and translator of Virgil and Ovid, was above all an assiduous collector of rare books, autographs, prints and drawings. Ever since Dumas had given the old gentleman a letter signed 'Buonaparte', that is to say, signed by the first consul in the original Italian form of the name, ie with a 'u' – a real treasure for M de Villenave (for such form of signature was rare), Dumas had been a welcome guest of the Villenave family. He had first met M Villenave at one of the famous soirées held in his house by his daughter, Mélanie. These parties were attended by every one in the literary world except M Villenave himself who, leaving his daughter's guests to enjoy declaiming their latest masterpieces, retired to bed early.

The Villenave family consisted of M Villenave himself, his wife, their son Théodore, and Mélanie, married to a Belgian, a Captain Waldor, now a naturalised Frenchman and an officer in the Sixth Light Infantry, whom she did not love and who was nearly always absent on garrison duty in some provincial town. Mélanie was the woman to whom Dumas now turned when he found that Catharine Labay was no longer sufficient for him. The affair with Mélanie was beyond doubt the most important in Dumas's life. She was the only woman among the many with whom he had affairs to inspire a work. The liaison lasted three years, or perhaps it would be more correct to say that their relationship was severed after three years, since before half that time had passed, Dumas, just as in his affair with Catharine, had exhausted its emotions. There were the usual scenes of jealousy and reproaches on her part, infidelities on his. She was the one to suffer.

This first reading of *Henri III* was given before an informal audience. 'The play,' writes Dumas, 'produced a great effect, but first, *Henri III*, they said, was too *risqué* for a first work. I need not say that dear old M Villenave found all these new attempts quite monstrous and declared them to be aberrations of the human intellect'. Encouraged by the success of this first informal reading, Dumas arranged for another meeting. Several journals had first been started by young contemporaries of Dumas in opposition to the reactionary *Constitutionnel*, the *Courier de Paris* and the *Journal des Débats*, which reserved all its favour for Victor Hugo. Such new journals were the *Figaro* and the *Sylphe*, edited by Nestor Roquepan, Louis Desnoyers and a dozen or so other bold champions of the new literature. It was these young enthusiasts whom Dumas now invited to a second reading, including Lassagne from the secretariat, Firmin from the Comédie-Française, and his old friend de la Ponce. The play was greeted with enthusiasm by all. 'In *Christine* you were only partly right; in *Henry III* you were altogether right,' Lassagne told him.

Firmin arranged for an early reading to the committee of the Theâtre Royal – Firmin, Baron Taylor, Michelet, Samson, Mlles Leverd and Mars, and, for added lustre, the great Béranger himself, who was considered at that time to be the greatest poet of the day, immensely popular with the public and whose liberal views and anti-royalist lampoons were soon to get him into trouble with the censor and lead to his imprisonment. The piece was received with acclaim, this time without demands for alterations. The roles were distributed and the date for the first performance fixed and published in the journals. Dumas, now much more confident of success than he had been when *Christine* had first been presented to the committee, invited his mother to attend. It seemed that he already had a presentiment that she might not be alive to see the opening night.

All now seemed set fair, with the exception of the usual wrangles with the temperamental Mlle Mars regarding casting, and a set-to with an extremely influential journalist who thrived on scandal and who had stigmatised the play, asserting that the first duty of the Theâtre Royal was to present plays to which families could bring their innocent offspring and answer such questions as 'what does that mean?' without embarrassment. To explain to a child the meaning of a homosexual king and his catamites would be impossible. This scandal-monger could usually be silenced by a discreet bribe. This Dumas refused to do, but forced the miserable creature to make a formal retraction in his newspaper on the following day. It is difficult to believe that this journalist (Dumas does not mention his name) possessed the influence that he undoubtedly had, but it was certainly true that Mlle Mars paid him regularly to assure that he did not give her bad notices and that he regularly received a stipend from the Théâtre Français, the Odéon, the Opéra and the Opéra-Comique. 'He sold his pen to praise, to attack and even to keep silent.'

As in the case of *Christine*, the newspapers had made haste to announce the acceptance of *Henri III*, and as with *Christine* there had been much talk in the secretariat. At first nothing was said to Dumas, but after Firmin had several times requested the author's presence at the theatre to settle some point connected with scenery, casting and other details, it was noted that his desk was as often vacated as it was occupied. It was not altogether, therefore, to Dumas's surprise that one morning he was summoned into the presence of M de Broval. The director-general was awaiting him with a stern face which boded a storm. Dumas was reminded of his interview at Crépy with the notary, Maître Lefevre, and his discourse upon the well-organised machine and the insignificant little wheel which failed to perform its function. M de Broval, in soft-spoken tones, explained without preamble that literature and bureaucracy were incompatible; neither could exist beside the other; he therefore invited Dumas to choose between the two.

The moment had come for Dumas to use great discretion. He allowed M de Broval to round off his mellifluous phrases, and when he had finished, the young dramatist replied: 'Monsieur le Baron, I gather from what you have said that you leave me to choose between my situation as clerk and my vocation as a man of letters.'

'That is so, M Dumas,' replied de Broval . . .

'In that case', replied Dumas, 'I require that my dismissal, verbal or in writing, should be signified to me directly by M le Duc d'Orléans himself. Otherwise I will neither resign my place nor accept my notice. As for my salary of 125 francs a month, which you, M le Baron, have given me to understand is an exorbitant drain on his Royal Highness's purse, I am willing to give that up this very moment.'

'What! What!' exclaimed M de Broval in amazement; 'and your mother, sir, and yourself, how will you live?'

'That *monsieur*, is my concern,' replied Dumas. Thereupon the young playwright bowed and withdrew.

The next day the payment of his salary was suspended, but worse still was the fact that he did not even receive the gratuity due to him for nine months' work. According to Dumas, it was his Royal Highness, the Duke himself, who had written opposite his name '*Supprimer les gratifications de M Alexandre Dumas qui s'occupe de littérature.*' I find this hard to believe in view of the Duke's generous gesture a few days later. Whatever the truth of the matter, Dumas was penniless. What was he to do for money? Fortunately, Beranger, who was on the most friendly terms with Lafitte, the great banker, arranged for his young friend to meet the financier. Lafitte was not immediately willing to accommodate him with a loan, but finally, on Béranger's recommendation, agreed to advance him three thousand francs without interest. The only security he demanded was that a manuscript copy of *Henri III* should be placed in his strong room. The sum represented two years' salary!

Dumas hurried home to his mother with the money in his pocket. The poor woman did not know whether to weep with joy or cry with grief. She had had many talks with Madame Deviolaine, her neighbour, and already knew that Alexandre had been dismissed from the bureaux of the Palais Royal. What would happen if his play failed or was not produced, as had happened to *Christine*? How could he ever pay back the three thousand francs he had borrowed? How were they to live?

But Dumas, the eternal optimist, had no such misgivings. He threw himself heart and soul into rehearsals. It was while superintending one such final rehearsal that M Deviolaine's servant burst onto the stage to tell him that while leaving the apartment of M Deviolaine, close to his own home, his mother had fallen down the stairs and been discovered unconscious. By the time Dumas had rushed to the Deviolaines' apartment, his mother had been laid out on a couch. It was obvious that the old lady had suffered a severe stroke, and although she had recovered consciousness, she was only able to articulate a few words – the whole of her left side was paralysed.

The next two or three days were torture for Dumas, torn between grief, fearing every moment that his mother might die, hardly daring to leave her bedside, and at the same time supervising the production of his first drama: for all concerned, *Henri III* had to be a success. There was one way of making certain of the resounding reception he so desperately desired – to invite the Duc d'Orléans to the première. Despite the snub he had received /(or claims to have received) from the Duke regarding his bursary, he decided to approach his Royal Highness. Here again, it is difficult to believe that Dumas's account of his interview with the Duke is entirely accurate. According to our hero, the Duke made no objection to receiving his very junior employee.

'For a year or two now, Your Highness has been told that I am a headstrong and conceited fool [Dumas claims to have said]. You have, *monseigneur*, without listening to me, given your approval to those who accuse me . . . Tomorrow the case will be tried before the public. Be present at the trial, *monseigneur* – that is the favour I come to beg of you.'

The Duke, after some demur, explained that this was impossible, as he had 'thirty princesses and princes coming to dine'. Not to be put off, Dumas suggested that the Duke put forward his dinner by one hour and he would arrange for *Henri III* to be put back and that all his guests could then attend the performance. 'Very well,' replied the Duke, 'go and tell Taylor that if the Comédie-Française agrees to put back the performance by an hour, I will attend it and for that purpose will retain the whole circle. Are you satisfied? Now run along with you and good luck.'

This story has been discounted by many biographers of Dumas as pure fiction, but reference to the *Journal de Débats* of that date (12 February 1829) clearly shows that the whole of the circle was occupied by the Duke and his aristocratic guests. The house was packed. Dumas himself occupied a small box almost on the stage. His sister had a box on the first tier, in which she gave hospitality to Boulanger, de Vigny and Victor Hugo. So full was the house that they had applied to Dumas as a last resource; this was the first time that Dumas had met de Vigny and Hugo. Every other place in the house had been sold for the past week, a box fetching the enormous price of twenty louis!

From his box Dumas commanded an excellent view of the house. The first circle was crowded with princes and princesses, the gentlemen resplendent with the orders of five or six nations, the ladies

Je déclare sur mon honneur, et sur mon
Insouciance littéraire – que la Dame
aux Camélias, interdite par cette
stupide institution qu'on appelle
la Censure est une pièce essentielle-
-ment morale. et J'ai le droit
D'avoir une Opinion en morale
moi qui ai écrit 700 Volumes
qui peuvent entrer dans une
Bibliothèque de séminaire, ou
dans un couvent de jeunes filles

Paris 4 Octobre 1851

Al Dumas

An example of Dumas's beautiful handwriting that obtained for him his first job.

Alexandre Dumas père at the age of forty.

The 'Palace' of Monte Cristo.

glittering with diamonds. The whole aristocracy was massed in the first and second tiers, all the Romantics – Musset, Sainte-Beuve, Nodier and Baron Taylor – and lesser lights, leading journalists and politicians were present, nor had Dumas forgotten to obtain complimentary tickets for his former collaborators, Adolphe de Leuven, Rousseau and Lassagne. Nor was Catharine Labay forgotten; she was given a seat with strict instructions to bring the five-year-old Alexandre with her. Dumas was determined that his son should have theatre in his blood. Monsieur Deviolaine also attended the performance,* as did the Baron de Broval, not to mention junior employees and the dear old gentlemen in the archives department.

The first act was listened to with sympathy, although as Dumas admits, it is 'long, cold and tedious', but the closing words of the Duc de Guise, 'Saint Paul! Find me the same men who murdered Dugast!' were warmly applauded and stimulated both the public and the actors. At the fall of the curtain, Dumas rushed off to see how his mother was. The poor old lady was quietly sleeping. Her son gave her a gentle kiss, then once again dashed off to the theatre. The second act met with approval, if not enthusiasm, while the third, the one in which the Duc de Guise forces his wife to make an assignation with St Megrin, evoked cries of enthusiasm and thunders of applause.

Apart from the often farcical melodramas to be seen in the theatres of the '*boulevard de crime*' nothing so realistic had ever been seen on the French stage, least of all at the Francais. From the beginning of the fourth act until the end of the last scene, it was clear that *Henri III et sa Cour* was a triumphant success. When the curtain fell and Firmin brought forward Dumas, pandemonium broke loose. There were shouts from his Romantic colleagues: '*A bas Lemercier! A bas Arnault! The tyranny is broken!*' He could see Hugo, Vigny, Gautier, Nodier and even the dandy Musset all mad with excitement. Mélanie Waldor in her box was weeping, while Malibran, 'the tragedy queen', who had only been able to find a seat in the third row, leaning as far out of her box as she could, was clinging with both hands to a pillar to keep herself from falling. The Duc d'Orléans himself rose to his feet to applaud, an example followed by his retinue of princes and princesses.

---

* Although he missed much of it due to an attack of diarrhoea, he was still interested enough to return for the last act and come back again on the following Monday. Dumas, who met him in the corridor as the poor man rushed to the toilet, was at first under the impression that his crusty relative was leaving in disgust.

That same evening, returning home, Dumas found a letter from Baron de Broval, who only a few days previously had dismissed his junior clerk with ignominy. It read:

> I cannot retire for the night, my dear young friend, without letting you know how much I am delighted with your grand success, and offering my heartfelt congratulations to you and, in especial, to your excellent mother, on whose account you have experienced more anxiety than on your own. It was an anxiety which we – my colleagues and myself – also shared keenly, and now we rejoice in a triumph so justly earned by the co-operation of conspicuous talent with filial affection. I feel well assured that the crown you have won, and the future of the fame which your genius opens to you will leave you sensible to the expression of a friendship as sincere as that which I am happy to entertain for you.
>
> Baron de Broval
11 February 1829

No doubt, as Dumas settled down on the mattress which he had laid beside his mother's bed, he thought back to the time when he had returned to Villers-Cotterêts from Paris with a job in his pocket, and how all those who had predicted that he would always be a ne'er-do-well were the first to say that they had always known that he would be a credit to his mother. There is nothing like success to make friends – and enemies.

CHAPTER NINE

Theatrical Success

Few people have seen a change pass over their life as rapid as that which passed over that of Dumas during the four hours occupied by ʼ the performance of *Henri III*. Completely unknown in the evening, he was, for good or ill, the talk of all Paris on the following morning. He awoke to find himself famous:

> There exist against me enmities on the part of people I have never seen – enmities which date from the obtrusive noise caused by my name at that time. I have friendships which also originated then. How many people envied me my triumph that evening, who little knew that I had passed the night on a mattress upon the ground at the bedside of a dying Mother!

On the next day (Sunday) the little room in Monsieur Deviolaine's house, which he and his mother had occupied ever since she had suffered her stroke, was filled with flowers which he laid on the poor lady's bed, the significance of which she could not understand. At two o'clock in the afternoon of the same day he received from a publisher six thousand francs in bank notes for the manuscript of his play. He was rich! Never had he had so much money in his life. He hurried up to M Deviolaine's apartment and showed him his roll of bank notes. M Deviolaine expressed astonishment. 'What's the meaning of this? Do you mean to say that there are imbeciles who have bought that manuscript from you?' But soon dropping his pose, he became positively affectionate and admitted that when Firmin brought Alexandre before the curtain at the end of the performance, he had 'cried like a calf' and throughout the play had been tormenting himself that it was his fault that had brought about Madame Dumas's illness. 'I could think of nothing else,' he said, and then added as an afterthought, 'but what will they say in the department?

Dumas showed him the Baron de Broval's letter. M Deviolaine read it through twice. 'Well, I'll be damned,' he said as he handed it back.

From Monsieur Deviolaine the young dramatist hastened to the banker Lafitte, proud to be able to discharge his debt so promptly. Dumas never forgot the service he had done him, which in the circumstances of his mother's illness had been of inestimable value; nor did he forget Béranger, who had effected his introduction; poor Béranger, who a fortnight later was to be fined ten thousand francs and given nine months' imprisonment for publishing *L'Ange gardien*, *La Gerontocratie* and *Le Sacre de Charles le Simple*, lampooning the monarchy. Dumas, too, nearly suffered from the oppressive censorship which existed under the reign of Charles X, for despite his intellectual and liberal-minded minister of fine arts, the Comte de Martignac, the ministry of interior (ie the police) was all-powerful. On his return to his temporary home, Dumas found a note summoning him to the Français with all urgency. Here he found the administration in a state of consternation: a letter had been received from the ministry of interior forbidding further performances of the play – an interdiction far more serious for Dumas than the stoppage of his salary.

Fortunately Baron Taylor was ready with a resource. Dumas was to write to M de Martignac immediately requesting an interview. An answer was received within two hours. M de Martignac would receive M Dumas at seven o'clock on the following morning. M de Martignac was all sympathy. The play, he said, would go on. In fact it was the Duc d'Orléans himself who intervened on Dumas's behalf: The Duke had sent word that he would be present at the second performance. During the interval he sent a note to the young playwright desiring to see him in his box.

'Well Monsieur Dumas,' he said, 'I hope you are satisfied? You have won your case against the world, against the public and against myself. There is no one more delighted, not even Broval, Deviolaine and Oudard. But do you know,' he continued with a smile, 'do you know that, with all that, you have nearly done me a very bad turn?'

'*You, monseigneur?*' replied the incredulous Dumas.

'Yes, me.'

'How can that be?'

'The King sent for me yesterday.'

'The King! About what, *monseigneur?*'

'About your drama.'

'About *Henri III?*'

' "Do you know, cousin," the King said to me (emphasising our title of relationship), "what they tell me? They tell me there is a young man in your bureau who has written a drama in which both you and I play a part – I that of Henri III and you that of the Duc de Guise?" '

'You might have replied, *monseigneur,*' said Dumas, 'that his Majesty was mistaken, and that the young man was no longer in your employ.'

'No', replied the Duke, 'I preferred to give a different answer, so as not to speak an untruth for I mean to keep you with me'. ' "Sire", I said "you are misinformed for three reasons; first, because I do not beat my wife; second, because the Duchesse d'Orléans is not unfaithful to me; and third, because your Majesty has no more loyal subject than me." '*

The interview ended as the curtain rose. 'Go and attend to your business,' said the Duke – mine is to listen to you,' and then, as though as an afterthought, he added: 'By the way, the Duchess desires to see you tomorrow morning to inquire after your mother.'

Dumas had 'arrived'. The Duke offered him various posts in his establishment but Dumas insisted on that of assistant librarian under Casimir Delavigne, a position which, as can be imagined, the 'classic playwright' resented, since the production of *Henri III* had interfered with the production of his own *Marino Faliero* (an adaptation from Byron), which was eventually relegated to the Porte Saint-Martin. This caused a great furore among the academic playwrights who now took the unexpected step of writing a petition to the King, supplicating him to forbid the performance of any plays at the Théâtre Royal except those in the given tradition of Corneille, Racine and Voltaire. It was signed A.V. Arnault, N. Lemercier, Viennet, Jovy, Andrieux, J. O. Leroy. Not that any of these gentlemen could possibly be said to rival, let alone compare with, Corneille or Racine. To this petition, which was as long as it was ridiculous, the King replied: 'Gentlemen – I can

---

* This verbatim conversation between Dumas and the Duke is taken directly from *Mes Mémoires*. In Dumas's *Souvenirs dramatiques* he tells us, however, that there was no interview between the King and his cousin, but that the exchange of views was carried on by correspondence.

do nothing to meet your wishes: Like every other Frenchman, I have only my place in the pit.'

Today, in the latter part of the twentieth century, the stir caused by the production of *Henri III* seems inconceivable. Now that in western society the greatest latitude in all branches of the arts is accepted, we are prepared to lose sight of the fact that all innovations in the theatre, music and graphic arts were met with the greatest hostility in the first half of this century. Innovations today are accepted as the norm. Dumas with *Henri III* had not only successfully blazed a trail, but had become a celebrity overnight.

Now that Dumas had money to spend, he spent it. He leased a small house at Passy for Catharine Labay and the little Alexandre; he acquired a ground-floor flat with a garden in the rue Madame for his mother, and an apartment for himself at number 25 rue de l'Université on the corner of the rue de Bac. Here not only could he enjoy the company of Mélanie Waldor in privacy, but also entertain the new school of poets, writers and artists who now recognised him as one of themselves, and whose acquaintance he had made at the Arsenal Library Salon,* reigned over by its curator, Charles Nodier, Dumas's first patron. Here after dinner Nodier, standing with his back to the fireplace, entertained the company 'with a fund of stories with infinite wit'. His stories, Dumas tells us, seemed like a mixture of the fairy tales of Perrault and the romances of Sir Walter Scott – stories of his youth, of love affairs, of battles during the war of the Vendée, tales of the Revolution, of the conspiracy of Cadoudal or Oudet – an apparently inexhaustible supply of fact and fantasy, all told in his inimitable Franc-Comtois accent. Suddenly he would break off – 'no one applauded, any more than one would applaud a running river'. Nodier would then turn to Hugo, de Vigny, Lamartine, de Musset or some other young poet to recite their verses. Ladies were not excluded from these delightful evenings. Sophie and Delphine Gay, the poets Mesdames Annabel Tastu and Desbordes-Valmore, Mesdames Hugo, Bixio, Ancelot and Mélanie Waldor were nearly always to be found

---

* The Arsenal Library derived its name from the fact that it was built on the site of the arsenal of François I, which had been destroyed in an explosion and several times rebuilt before it eventually became a library.

there, and of course Nodier's beautiful daughter Marie. After stories and poetry reading were concluded, Marie would sit down at the piano, to whose accompaniment the young people would dance while their elders played cards.

Presently Dumas had a permanent place laid for him at the Nodiers' table, between Marie and Madame Nodier. Dumas's inextinguishable cheerfulness, his wit and good-heartedness, his boyish enthusiasm, had quickly won the hearts of the Nodier family. 'He exempts me from talking,' Nodier used to say, for Dumas soon almost usurped his host's role as storyteller. He told tales of his childhood, of his father the General, of his hunting exploits and poaching in the forest of Villers-Cotterêts, of his brief glimpses of Napoleon and, more recently, of his differences with the tragedy queen, Mlle Mars. All were lively and amusing and listened to with appreciation. Dumas loved the sound of his own voice. Once, after dining out, when someone asked him, 'How did the evening go?' he replied. 'Well, if I hadn't been there I would have been terribly bored.'

This young man, whose lack of knowledge on so many subjects was staggering, had a profound respect for Nodier who, as he himself put it, 'knew everything and a great deal more'. Nodier in turn was fond of Dumas and did his best to refine his taste, for it must be admitted, however charming and witty the young man might have been, he was both boastful and an exhibitionist. As soon as he had money he indulged in sartorial extravagances: he bought tight-fitting coats, vividly coloured waistcoats, fobs, multiple watch-chains (like Thackeray's Jos Sedley), trinkets, and a gold-mounted cane; he even sported a quite unnecessary monocle.

He never resented Nodier's criticisms. Others might hurt his feelings, but he felt himself in too strong a position to waste his time in taking umbrage. All he needed was to feel self-confidence, to know at every moment that he was as good as, if not better than, his critics. This certainly produced an occasional note of conceit in his voice.* It would be difficult to blame this twenty-nine-year-old dramatist for some degree of conceit. Deveria the artist made a portrait drawing of him in lithograph, which was on sale in all the principal print-shops, and the sculptor David d'Angers made a medallion of him. Any other reaction would have been unnatural of this country boy who was now

* André Maurois, *The Three Musketeers*, trans., Jonathan Cape, 1957.

the talk of the town and invited to the homes of the great, including the Comte Sosthène de la Rochefoucauld and Barras, the same Barras, now an old man, who on 13 Vendémiaire 1795 had called upon the young Bonaparte to suppress the rioting mob with his famous 'whiff of grape-shot' and put the Corsican on his first steps to glory. Here too Dumas met the Princess de Chimay, formerly Madame Tallien. Such meetings remind us how close Dumas was to the Revolution. Is it surprising, in the circumstances, that he was somewhat arrogant of his achievement where other men of reputation had failed? But it is ridiculous to suggest that he went through life with a chip on his shoulder (as at least one biographer has asserted) or that he had 'an inferiority complex' because of his mulatto background. This was something he never sought to deny; in fact, all his life he boasted of his father, the Schwartze Teufel as the Austrians had called the hero of Brixen. He never resented being reminded of his coloured background so long as it was done in a friendly way, as by Nodier when he teased him for his love of gewgaws 'so typical of his African origin', but if personally insulted, he was always prepared to challenge his man to a duel. His duels, indeed mostly farcical, could make a chapter on their own.

Dumas's friendship with Nodier lasted until the older man's death in 1844. If Charles Nodier is remembered today it is not for his own literary works, which are light, fanciful trifles, but because he acted as an impetus to the young Romanticists. He was the first to perceive the greatness in Béranger, Lamartine, de Vigny and Hugo, Gérard de Nerval, Mérimée and Gautier; in 1834 he was to write a preface to the collected plays of Dumas anticipating his future greatness. Dumas wrote of this kindly man:

> Everything died at the Arsenal with Nodier, joy, life and light . . . each of us lost something of himself in losing Nodier. As for me – I scarcely know how to express it – something died in me when Nodier died. That is why I speak of him so much.

Dumas soon awoke to the fact that the miserable pittance he received as assistant librarian to M Casimir Delavigne was quite insufficient to support him in the style of living to which he had now become accustomed, and that the long run of *Henri III* could not continue for ever.

At this time his affair with Mélanie Waldor was still at its most ardent. Mélanie had not been an easy conquest; her highly respectable Walloon husband had taught her little about the arts of love and, like Juliette Recamier, she 'would have liked love's year to stop in the spring so that it might last the longer'. Dumas, with his hot-blooded nature, was not at all the man to accept this situation. Mélanie had withstood his passionate advances from 3 June 1827, the day on which she first met him, until 27 September, three and a half long months. She had first been shocked when the lusty young man had taken her by surprise, crushing her in his arms and smothering her with kisses. He inundated her with daily letters, letters which were passionate, sensual and promises of love more than human: 'I send your lips a thousand kisses and to every inch of your body yet other kisses to set you trembling and to fill you with assurance of all delights.'*

In September he hired a room, prior to his acquisition of an apartment in the rue de l'Université, where she finally agreed to visit him and consented to become his mistress.

All this cost money. Dumas now decided to rewrite *Christine*. He took a seat in an empty diligence bound for Le Havre and on the way there and back he revised the whole play. Unlike Trollope, who wrote many of his works while travelling in railway trains, he certainly did not rewrite the whole play while jolting through the countryside. He may have revised it in his head, but he certainly could not have written it without reference to Schiller, as we shall see later. No doubt, as he rumbled along in the great empty coach, he decided to add a prologue in Stockholm, an epilogue in Rome, and build up a secondary intrigue, introducing the character of Paula, Mondaleschi's mistress. The treachery, therefore, which prompted the queen's vengeance was no longer dictated by politics but by sentiment. In so doing, Dumas once again entirely broke away from the classical tradition, by disregarding the dramatic 'unities' – one scene, one action.

It was in his apartment in the rue de l'Université that he read his revised *Christine* to a group of friends (including Adolphe de Leuven). Though not a patch on *Henri III*, it was now immensely improved. Soulié's *Christine* had fallen flat at the Odéon. Félix Harel, director of that theatre, wrote to Dumas offering to produce his new version. Feeling some scruple in the matter, Dumas consulted Soulié, who

* Bibliothèque Nationale, Dep. des Manuscrits, NAF 24641, folio 280.

replied: 'Pick up the scraps of my *Christine* ... drop them in the basket of the first rag-and-bone-man you meet – and go ahead' (quoted by Charles Ginel). Dumas went ahead.

Harel had taken over the Odéon in 1829 when this theatre was on the point of being closed down. Félix Harel, who had been auditor to the *conseil d'état, inspecteur des ponts et chaussées* and, under the empire, prefect of *les Landes*, finding his career as an administrator cut short by the Restoration, had turned theatrical manager, for the very good reason that he was in love with Mlle Georges, whose favours Napoleon had once enjoyed. He had a genius for publicity and was to become the herald of the Romantic drama. Mlle Georges, although no longer in her first youth and far from sylphlike, was cast in the role of Christine.

Christine was by no means one of Dumas's best plays, but it enjoyed considerable success, although overshadowed by Hugo's *Hernani* (of which more later), a fact which made little difference to the friendship between the two young dramatists. Hugo had promised, as did most of Dumas's literary friends including Alfred de Vigny, to attend the first performance. After the première Dumas gave a celebratory party in his new-found apartment. Elated as he was, Dumas was not entirely satisfied with the production and wished to make various alterations. The epilogue required to be cut, while at the same time some additional dialogue was needed. How was this to be done in time for the following night?

> Hugo and Vigny took the manuscript and told me not to bother about anything. They shut themselves up in my study, and while the rest of us ate, drank and sang, they worked ... They laboured at the play for four hours with the ardour, conscientiousness and the intensity that they would have devoted to their own work. When they emerged at daybreak to find us supine on chairs and couches, they left the manuscript on the mantelpiece, and without waking anyone, these two rivals (they had recently had a violent quarrel) went out arm in arm like brothers ...
>
> We were awakened from our sleep in the morning by the arrival of Barbar, the publisher, who came to offer me 12,000 francs for the manuscript of *Christine* – double the amount I had received for *Henri III*.

CHAPTER TEN

The Play Factory

So much has been written of Dumas's plagiarism and his so-called 'factory' (*vide* the famous story of him when, on meeting his son, he is reputed to have said, 'Have you read my last novel?' To which the son replies: 'No, have you?') that the method he used in writing *Christine* and *Henri III et sa Cour*, a method which he continued to use, must be explained.

There were two stages in Dumas's system of 'plagiarism'. The first was when he was content to depend on his own industry and could borrow and adapt by himself from dead authors, which was the case when writing his early plays. As already mentioned, he possessed a phenomenally retentive memory and, thanks to his very extensive reading, he made notes and he pigeonholed situations and whole lines from authors he admired for possible future use.

Later, finding this system too laborious, he passed to the ordinary system of collaboration, joining with two or three others in the composition of a play. In the writing of *Christine*, which he wrote alone, he borrowed almost all the text from the works of Schiller. The queen falls into the waters of Stockholm, just as Fiescho fell into the waters of Genoa. A whole monologue is taken almost verbatim from *Egmont*. A scene in the same act, in which Sentenelle is making a bargain with the soldiers, is taken almost word for word from *Wallenstein*. When Christine is abdicating, she paraphrases a whole speech from Hugo's *Hernani*, though in *Hernani* the speech is put into the mouth of Charles V when *ascending* the throne. A scene in which Christine is speaking to Mondaleschi of a treason she suspected in others, is taken from Lope de Vega's *Love and Honour*. To use or paraphrase lines written by foreign authors long dead is all very well, but when Dumas puts into Mondaleschi's mouth a speech four pages in length taken almost directly from Hugo's *Le Dernier jour d'un Condamné*, it is not merely plagiarism but downright theft. On the other hand, it should not be forgotten that after the opening night of *Christine*, Hugo (with de Vigny) had himself volunteered to revise some of the text, and must have acquiesced to this inclusion.

But *Christine* in Dumas's hands was no mere patchwork. No one possessed dramatic instinct to a more perfect degree than he, nor can it be said that he lacked imagination – far from it. The ingenuity with which he blatantly introduced into his plays the words of other writers, often out of context with his own plot, was nothing less than masterly. The strangest phenomenon was that this method should have produced works which, as a whole, were spirited and glowing and had a perfect air of originality. *Henri III et sa Cour*, which was to make him famous, was almost an 'arrangement on a theme of Schiller'. Perhaps one could draw an anology between Stravinsky's *Le Baiser de la Fée* (Stravinsky–Tchaikovsky), but while Stravinsky made no attempt to disguise his inspiration, Dumas remained secretive. Dumas's supporters were apt to cite the example of artist painters, who constantly 'borrowed' from each other. No critics have ever found any fault in this practice. It is sometimes forgotten that Dumas was born just after the turn of the eighteenth century; no one had ever complained that during the last two or three hundred years musicians had constantly 'borrowed' from each other. Examples are too numerous to mention here – Handel and Bach being two of the greatest offenders. It was not until the nineteenth century that plagiarism was regarded as almost a crime. Was it not Brahms who when accused of plagiarising Beethoven – but to what effect! – remarked caustically, 'Any donkey can see that.' Not that the plot of *Christine* was other than Dumas's own invention; though, again, 'invention' is possibly not the right word, for it was an amalgamation of historical anecdotes, which when fused together made an admirable plot. It was Dumas's genius that enabled him to piece together disparate historical anecdotes and make them into a whole, and it was also genius to dig deep into his knowledge of Schiller to find whole passages from the German master which, with little adaptation, suited his purpose.

The strange thing is that although the classicists slated his Romantic plays, few at first seemed to have noticed how much he 'borrowed'. One of Dumas's most telling scenes, in which the jealous Duc de Guise seizes his wife's arm in his mailed fist as he forces her to write the letter which is to condemn her lover to death, a scene which brought the house down, is almost pure Scott, as was the bolting of the door of her chamber by thrusting her arm through the staple.*

It was the critic Granier de Cassagnac who was the first to expose Dumas's *supercherie*. Take for example the following (the translation is by Percy Fitzgerald, 1873):

Schiller, *Don Carlos*,
Act 2, Scene 4

DON CARLOS A letter for me! From whom is this key? and both sent with such mystery! Where was this given to you?

PAGE As far as I could make out, the lady seemed to prefer that her name should be guessed rather than told.

CARLOS A lady! What! How! Who are you then?

PAGE Page to her Majesty the Queen.

CARLOS (*putting his hand on the other's mouth*) Be silent as the grave. I know sufficient now. (*He reads the letter*) And she herself gave you this?

PAGE With her own hand.

CARLOS You must not trifle with me. I have never seen her handwriting. If this be a falsehood, confess it openly, and don't attempt to deceive me.

PAGE Deceive you!

CARLOS (*reads*) 'This key will open the room behind the Queen's pavilion.' Then it is not a dream. It is not delirium. Yes, there in my right hand, there is my sword, the written words of the letter. Yes all is real. I am loved! I am loved!

Dumas, *Henri III*,
Act 4, Scene 1

ST MEGRIM This letter and this key for me? You say yes. For the Count St Megrim? From whom had you it?

ARTHUR Although you did not expect it, could you not make a guess at the person?

ST MEGRIM The person! How? And who are you, then?

ARTHUR Don't you recognise the arms of two Royal Houses?

ST MEGRIM The Duchess! (*Putting his hand on the other's mouth*) Silence! I know all (*he reads the letter*) And she herself gave you this?

ARTHUR She herself.

ST MEGRIM Boy, do not attempt to trifle with me. I do not know her handwriting. If this be a falsehood, confess you have been trying to deceive me.

ARTHUR Deceive you!

ST MEGRIM (*Reads*) 'The rooms of the Duchess are on the second floor, and this key will open the door.' It is not a dream! My brain is not wandering! This key, these written lines; all is true. I am loved! ARTHUR Count, let me remind you –silence.

* From Scott's *The Abbot*.

113

PAGE Prince, this is hardly the place – you seem to forget . . .

CARLOS You are right, my friend. Thank you, I was not myself. What you have just seen must be buried within you as in the tomb. You are a child. Be so always and show the same gaiety. How wise and prudent she was, who chose you her messenger of love! It is not among such that the King chooses his vile spies.

PAGE And I, Prince, am proud to know by this secret I am superior to the King himself.

CARLOS Boyish, foolish vanity. Should we meet in public, approach me with timidity and submission. Let not your vanity ever seduce you into letting it be seen that the infanta is well inclined towards you.

ST MEGRIM You are right. Silence. Forget what you have done and seen. Never recall my name or that of my mistress. She has shown me prudence in entrusting you with this message. It is not among children one ought to fear spies.

ARTHUR And I, Count, am proud to have a secret that belongs to no other.

ST MEGRIM Yes, but a terrible secret. One of the secrets that kill! Should we meet in public, pass on without knowing, without perceiving me.

The years 1829–30 were years of revolution, both political and artistic. In the artistic field battle had already been joined between classicists and Romantics. The great Talma had infused life into the second-rate classical productions, such as *Sylla*, *Marius at Miturnac*, and *Caractacus*, feeble invitations of Corneille and Racine with 'Romanised' Frenchmen acting the roles of heroes of antiquity, clad in pseudo-classical costume, often wearing helmets more reminiscent of those worn by *pompiers* (firemen) than the genuine article; the latter gave rise to the expression, still used today, *l'art pompier*, applicable not only to the theatre but to the most conservative type of painting once so favoured by the Salon and the British Royal Academy. But this government-sponsored art was beginning to pall on the French public. Dumas himself felt the need for 'a national theatre of our own, original and French, not Greek, English or German . . . *Henri III* was at least an original drama drawn from our own history, and though you may find in it the influences of other theatres, it imitates none.'

'Romantic' was a strange name for a school which featured violence

114

and brutality in every way. The enthusiasm which it aroused among the people had a certain unreal basis largely encouraged by the efforts to suppress it. The wretched government of Charles X tried with a stupid vigour to put down all these novelties, whether on stage, on canvas or on paper. Prosecutions were instituted against newspapers; the publisher of Béranger's *chansons* was indicted, and Béranger, as we have noted, was himself fined and imprisoned. The censor, striking right and left, refused admission to paintings, suppressed books and forbade plays to be performed. Hugo's *Marion Delorme* was competed for by half a dozen managers, put into rehearsal, then banned forthwith. The court trembled before this series of portrayals of a decadent monarchy, however remote, and no doubt regretted that they had tolerated the example of Dumas. An attempt was made to buy over Hugo by trebling his pension, which he had the spirit to refuse. When in 1827, as a very young man, he wrote *Cromwell*, he prefixed the published text with a programme of his dramatic principles: 'All that we see in nature belongs to art; the drama itself results from the union of the sublime with the true and familiar and should, at the same time, be the expression of modern life and manners.' This would seem to justify the exhibition on the stage of crude passions and what the conservative critics regarded as 'coarse scenes', which had hitherto been excluded from the French theatre. Hugo, faithful to his principles, was a true poet and was never coarse. Shakespeare recreated 'crude passions' and was an immediate success with the Romantic school, but was frowned upon by the so-called classicists. Whatever would they have thought of Wycherley or Congreve?

The première of Hugo's *Hernani* was to be one famous in the annals of the stage: irritated at the malicious and persistent efforts of the old conservative party to crush the new school, the young brigade assembled in force, already preparing for the serious business of revolution, determined to carry through the piece of their distinguished leader, as Hugo was regarded. The night was 26 March 1830. Julius Janin, who was present, recalled how they waited in the darkened theatre for six hours before the doors were opened and talked and whispered like conspirators; how as each party appeared at the box office doors, a storm of hissing or applause burst forth according to which faction they were known to favour. Throughout the whole play the battle was continued; but its incontestable merits and the exertions of Hugo's friends carried it through.

It was not until a year later that Dumas's *Antony* was eventually completed and produced, its production having been delayed by the three day revolution of 1830. It was to cause an even greater sensation than *Hernani*.

The year 1830 was to be a crucial one both in the political arena and for the Romantic movement. As André Maurois writes:

> It was a red-hot period, with battle everywhere – in the theatres, on the barricades, even between husbands and wives. Great passions are necessary to the romantic ... The light-hearted Dumas was not of a nature to indulge in self-torment, but had all the same to follow the fashion. In order to be like everyone else, he had to be jealous of somebody, and for this purpose chose Captain Waldor, his mistress's peace-loving husband.*

When Dumas learnt that the Captain, after a long absence, was about to spend his leave in Paris, he rushed to the War Ministry, where he had an officer friend, to ask him to arrange for the Captain's leave to be cancelled. 'The thought of his presence will drive me mad!' he said. This madness was confined to words. The husband did not put in an appearance, but the comedy began again – more than once.

While still writing passionate love letters to Mélanie, he lost no opportunity to be unfaithful to her. Although Mélanie still remained his principal 'angel' he was surrounded by a host of lesser 'angels' – Virginie Bourbier of the Comédie-Française (or the Théâtre Royal as it still was); Louise Despreaux, (whose lovely legs in her role of page in *Henri III* had entranced him); Marie Dorval, who had accosted him in a cab and had almost thrown herself at him; and the lovely Belle Krelsamer (Mélanie Serre on the stage), who had played the role of the Duchesse de Guise on tour. Mélanie the second was not only beautiful but intelligent, and it was with her he spent most of his time while Mélanie Waldor was spending a long holiday with her mother on the family estate of La Jarrie in the Vendée.

---

* André Maurois, *Les Trois Dumas*, 1957. Maurois might also have mentioned that this was the year which saw the performance of Berlioz's *Symphonie Fantastique*, the most revolutionary piece of music performed up until Stravinsky's *Rite of Spring* in 1913.

Despite these love affairs he continued to write innumerable letters to Mélanie the first; he spoke to her of their 'burning, grievous kisses'; he threatened to mingle love with death and even to kill her unfortunate spouse. All these literary posturings were to result in the composition of a new play – *Antony*, which he started to write in 1829. He even incorporated whole passages from his own letters to his mistress. Of the conception of *Antony* he tells us that 'One day, when I was strolling along the Boulevards, I stopped short all at once, and said to myself, "Suppose a man, surprised by the husband of his mistress, was to kill her, saying that she had resisted him, and was thus to save her honour, etc." There was the idea of *Antony*.' No mention is made of his friend Emile Souvestre who, it was stated openly, had furnished him with the story. A more curious fact connected with this play was that when, sometime later, Victor Hugo brought out his *Marion Delorme*, it seemed as though the poet had stolen Didier, his principal protagonist, from Dumas's play. Hugo never attempted to clear himself. The truth was that after attending a reading of *Marion Delorme*, which it will be recollected had been indicted by the censor and not performed until 1831, Dumas borrowed a copy and appropriated his friend's principal character. The main characters – Antony and Didier – were almost the same. Both were illegitimate, both misanthropists and both were to die on the scaffold for a woman. However, twenty years later, just glancing at the truth, Dumas wrote in his characteristic way: 'The reading of *Marion Delorme* had not merely produced an immense effect upon my mind, but it had done me a great deal of good; it had really opened for me brilliant unseen horizons . . . and furnished me with the first idea of *Antony*.'

It was not Hugo who drew attention to this plagiarism, but Casimir Delavigne. Nevertheless, it is certainly Mélanie Waldor whom Dumas had in mind when he wrote the play. In one of his many letters to her he tells her: 'You will find many things in *Antony* which have been taken from our life together . . . The public will make nothing of them, though in us they will awake eternal memories. Antony himself will, I am almost sure, be recognised, for he is a madman with a remarkable resemblance to me.'

Briefly, the plot of the play is as follows: Antony, the social rebel and bastard, is unable to marry Adèle, the girl he loves, because he has no family, position or fortune. Adèle is given in marriage to a Colonel Baron d'Hervey (the simple Captain Waldor has been promoted for the purposes of the play). One day Antony reappears to stop the runaway horses of Adèle's carriage. He is injured and taken to her house. The two young people mutually confess their love, but Adèle, a slave to convention, tries to resist. She attempts to flee to her husband who is in garrison at Strasbourg. Antony, having led her into a trap, continues to spend a night of love with her at the inn of Ittenheim. Here the guilty lovers are surprised by the arrival of the colonel.

ADELE Someone is coming upstairs . . . it is my husband . . . Fly! . . . Fly!
ANTONY I will not . . . You told me a long while ago that you have no fear of death.
ADELE Nor have I! . . . Oh! kill me, kill me for pity's sake.
ANTONY A death that may save your reputation and your daughter's?
ADELE I ask it of you on my knees!
A VOICE (*without*) Open! open I say . . . Break down the door.
ANTONY Say with your last breath you do not hate your murderer.
ADELE Nay, I bless him! But hasten, hasten . . . the door . . .
ANTONY Have no fear, death will be here – before him. Think upon it . . . think on death.
ADELE I ask it of you – I want it – I beg for it (*throwing herself into his arms*) – I long to meet it.
ANTONY (*kissing her*) Then die! (*Stabs her*)
ADELE (*falling into an armchair*) Ah! . . .
At this moment the door (off) is broken in and Colonel d'Hervey rushes onto the stage.
D'HERVEY Villain! What do I see? Adèle dead!
ANTONY Yes, dead . . . She resisted me and so I killed her!
(*He throws his dagger at Colonel d'Hervey's feet*)

CURTAIN

What is remarkable about *Antony* is that, for the first time in many years, Dumas had transferred what might have been an historical play into contemporary times. Certainly it would never have been produced under the strict censorship existing during the reign of Charles X. Only after the days of July did it become possible to depict the morals of contemporary society frankly and without gloss. To quote André Maurois again:

This recovered freedom gave us Balzac. But when Dumas wrote *Antony* [that is to say, before 1830] the censorship was still severe. Dumas could not merely point to the fact of adultery; he had to condemn and punish it. Balzac could allow himself a high degree of cynicism. Diane de

118

Maufrigneuse and the Princesse de Cardigman, could pass with impunity through flames which burned Adèle d'Hervey alive. But [when Dumas wrote the play] he had not the right to say in a public theatre that a woman might be at once, guilty and happy, however much he might think it — perhaps wrongly, for his own code of facile morals made more than one mistress in real life truly miserable.

But perhaps *Antony* would not have enjoyed the success it ultimately achieved without the famous last lines. The Romantic school, we said, was preoccupied with assassinations and brutal scenes. Dumas himself was obsessed with death scenes, particularly in his novels, in which he reveals a morbid fascination with death by decapitation, often horrific — rolling heads that bite, speak or kiss — for example in the final scene of *Le Bâtard de Mauléon* (1846), in *Mille et un Fantômes* (1849), in *La Femme au collier de Velours* (1851). Of ten plays by Dumas and Victor Hugo, eight of the characters are adulteresses; five are common prostitutes; six are seduced; four mothers are in love with their sons or sons-in-law; eleven persons are murdered; and in no less than six of these plays the leading character is either a foundling or a bastard.

CHAPTER ELEVEN

Revolution and the Seizure of the Soissons Arsenal

The autocratic regime of Charles X, the violent strictures on personal liberties, the dissolution of the Chambre des Députés, not to mention the economic crises affecting the country and consequent unemployment, had led to an ever growing dissatisfaction among the people. The Polignac ministry saw revolution everywhere, even in the most harmless writings.

So often, when an unpopular government finds itself in such a position that it fears a popular rising, it will hope to dazzle a disaffected people with some military and diplomatic success. This is precisely the action taken by the ministers of the last of the Bourbons. On the slender excuse that the French consul had been insulted by the Bey of Algiers, and that despite punitive naval expeditions mounted by the British, Americans and Dutch to destroy the fleets of the Barbary corsairs, piracy had not been entirely eliminated, the French now in turn dispatched an amphibious force, not merely to destroy the Algerian fleet, but to capture Algiers itself and occupy the country. In fact it was a war of colonial expansion. France had already lost so many of her colonial possessions during and after the Napoleonic wars, that to acquire new territories on her very doorstep could not be other than popular and add lustre to the throne. The expedition, though costly in lives, was successful.

The capture of Algiers suggested to Dumas a dashing scheme – to visit the newly acquired colony and bring back some 'lively impressions of travel'. *Antony* was all but finished; he had money in his pocket; Mélanie Waldor was in the Vendée; he was free to travel.

He planned to leave on Monday 26 July. Mélanie the second was to accompany him as far as Marseille.

On the very morning of his planned departure, his friend Achille Comte burst into his rooms at eight o'clock in the morning with the news that the *Moniteur* had published the decrees of the Polignac ministry against the freedom of the press and the prorogation of the chamber. 'Will you still be leaving for Algiers?' asked Comte. 'I am not so stupid,' replied Dumas. 'What we will see here will be much more interesting than anything I might see over there.' Then, summoning his servant: 'Joseph,' he said, 'go to the gunsmith and bring me back my double-barrelled gun, with two hundred cartridges.'

Dumas was convinced, as were many others, that these decrees spelt the end of the monarchy and that Paris would soon be up in arms.

With the 'three glorious days' of the July revolution which drove Charles X from the throne and replaced him by Louis-Philippe, the 'citizen king', a new chapter opened in the life of Dumas. The theatre was temporarily forgotten; Algiers and *Antony* were put aside. Paris was now his stage and he cast himself in the role of one of the principal protagonists. One can smile today at his vanity and bombast, but it is impossible to deny that his account of certain scenes and of his own exploits during those exciting days is enthralling.

His friend Janin wrote happily of him that he saw everything about him with dramatic eyes; with his keen and picturesque sense, everything fell into the shape of a scene on the stage. His story was a good deal ridiculed at the time but, as will be seen, the facts are in the main correct.

After giving the order for the two hundred bullets, Dumas went out into the town with his friend. Everything was still tranquil. He looked in at the Café du Roi, and found the coterie of royalist newspaper editors quite confident, and loudly applauding the steps that had been taken. The day passed by in some excitement, but without any act of violence taking place. The editors of the leading liberal journals, including Thiers, had signed a protest against the unconstitutional action of ministers; and the following day, when Dumas went out with Carrel of the *National*, they witnessed a curious scene that was taking place at the offices of the newspaper *Le Temps*. A commissary of police, with a party of gendarmes, was preparing to break in, with the intention of destroying the presses; but though locksmith after locksmith was fetched, the crowd contrived to spirit them away and the doors remained firmly closed. Dumas wandered about all day, and it seemed probable that all would pass without any major disturbance, when suddenly towards seven o'clock, the sound of firing was heard in the direction of the Palais Royal. There had been some stone-throwing at the soldiers, who had fired and killed a woman. Dumas was well acquainted with a number of the militant liberals, among them his friend Stephen Arago, the first journalist to have given him a favourable review, who took a leading part in the street skirmishing. It was the morning of 26 July and the time was come for Dumas to act. He took his gun, with some of the 'two hundred bullets', and descended into the street. He tells us that he was at once constituted a leader. He forthwith ordered barricades to be constructed. He was asked for arms, and pointed, significantly, to three soldiers in the distance. D'Artagnan or Aramis would have made the same answer. He led on his men to the attack of the Hôtel de Ville, was allowed to pass by an officer who addressed him by his name and paid him compliments on *Christine*, and with whom, too, he exchanged compliments of the most chivalrous kind, promising tickets for his new play (*Antony*), and then went on to the attack, which was repulsed. He reached home safely after this *début*; and, indeed, according to his vivacious account, the taste for revolution in Paris is easily explained by the fascination and excitement, the 'turning out' of friends for 'sport', and the certain chances they afford for bringing obscure persons into importance with very little exertion.

Next day he was awakened to learn from his servant Joseph that the famous artillery museum was being attacked; he was struck with horror at the notion of this precious historic collection of arms and armour being pillaged. When it was captured he saw it was hopeless to think of saving it; all he could do was to plunder for the nation. So, seizing some arms that had belonged to Francis I and Charles IX, he carried off a helmet, shield and sword to his rooms. He called briefly on Belle Krelsamer to assure her that he was still safe and sound, then set off again to join in the attack on the Louvre. The scene was an exciting one. He and his band advanced along the *quai*, by the *Institut*, and from the other side of the river saw the long line of windows of the great picture-gallery thrown open, with two scarlet-clad Swiss guards, musket in hand, posted at each. The balcony was filled with more Swiss, who had protected themselves with a rampart of mattresses. All along the *quai* were lines of Cuirassiers, while on the right, the great colonnade facing St Germain l'Auxerrois was half-hidden in rolling clouds of smoke. The air was thick, seeming to vibrate with distant musketry and the sound of tolling bells, while a fiery sun blazed luridly in the heavens. Dumas witnessed the whole attack, and frankly confesses that he secured a safe 'ambuscade' behind a bronze lion. At times clouds of smoke enveloped the whole palace; these would break, and disclose glimpses of the Swiss guards. Then he saw a regular attack marshalled, and an attempt made, chiefly by youths, to cross the bridge connecting the *Institut* with the right bank. A cannon commanding it now opened fire and swept it from end to end with grape-shot, causing many casualties. Dumas found this altogether too dangerous, and got away as fast as he could. Later, he made his way round to the other side of the river, saw the Tuileries carried; and heard the shouts caused by the spectacle of what seemed an enormous flight of pigeons fluttering from the windows. These were letters to Napoleon, Louis and Charles, all torn up and thrown out by the mob. He rushed in with the rest, witnessed the odd scenes that followed, including a crowd of laughing men and women gathered round the royal bed on which a young couple were making love, and the naïve astonishment of the populace as they wandered through the state rooms.

He takes care to tell that he saw on a work-table in the library of the Duchesse de Berry a copy of *Christine* bound in violet morocco, adorned with her arms, which he carried off. Afterwards he reached the Hôtel de Ville, where he found La Fayette and many other important personages whom he knew. He chanced to look in a mirror, and hardly recognised himself – unwashed, unshaven for three days, his face blistered by the sun, his clothes torn, and his shoes daubed with the blood of a poor wretch whom he had helped out of the conflict. He listened to the excited discussions as to what was to be done. He describes with humour the proclamations signed by the provisional government, whose members no one could find, and by uniformed self-promoted generals who were only too easily found.

He had heard La Fayette say that if the King (who was at Rambouillet) were to advance on Paris there would not be sufficient powder to fight. On hearing this, Alexandre conceived a bold scheme. He proposed to La Fayette to set off for Soissons – a town he knew well – and seize the magazines there. La Fayette laughed at the idea, but consented to give him a letter to General Gérard, to which Dumas

123

coolly added the words, 'and we recommend his scheme to you'. From Gérard he obtained, though not without difficulty, a requisition addressed to the authorities of the town for the powder; and in this he ingeniously interpolated the words 'Minister of War' – a rank which no one but himself had conferred on the general. With this official document he returned to La Fayette, and persuaded the old patriot to give him a sort of letter of introduction to the citizens of Soissons, recommending to them 'M Alexandre Dumas, one of our combatants', as a fit and proper person to whom they should hand over their powder. Then our hero – for such he was on this occasion – prepared himself for as spirited and dramatic an adventure as any to be found in his Romantic novels.

It was now about three o'clock in the afternoon of 30 July. As he was hurrying away, he met a young painter named Bard, who was only nineteen, whom he asked to join in his adventure. The other agreed with alacrity, and Alexandre, sending him back for his double-barrelled pistols and horse, set off himself in a cabriolet for Le Bourget, then the first post on the road to Soissons. Arrived there, he exhibited his letters from La Fayette and Gérard to the postmaster, and demanded a chaise and horses for his mission. The postmaster was friendly, and even eager to help, and supplied him at once with what he asked. He then went out to buy some pieces of calico – red, white and blue – which were sewn into a tricolour flag and fixed to a broomstick, which was then tied to the chaise. With this ensign they set off, in hopes of getting to Soissons before the city gates were closed at eleven o'clock. The postmaster shook his head but, as he sagaciously remarked, 'so many miracles had been performed during the last three days that it might be possible'. As they hurried through the various villages the flag caused great excitement. His fellow-traveller, delighted, declared that all was going splendidly, 'but that they ought to have some sort of rallying cry'.

'Shout away,' said Dumas, 'and while you are shouting I'll take some sleep.'

The only difficulty was what to shout. With some hesitation the now well-worn and tattered *vive la république!* was decided on. Accordingly the young painter, his head out of the window and his flag waving, roared on. On the high road they met a chaise going to Paris, and a middle-aged traveller stopped to ask for news.

'The Louvre is taken; the Bourbons fled; provisional government established – *vive la république!* the excited painter poured out. The middle-aged gentleman scratched his ear, and continued his journey calmly. On the next stage of the journey they had an old postilion, who persisted in driving at a steady trot and who, to every remonstrance, answered doggedly, 'Leave it to me. A man ought to know his own business.' At last, from the chaise window, Dumas laid on the backs of the horses with a stick, and made them gallop. In a rage the postilion pulled up, swore he would unyoke his horses, and actually proceeded to do so. Dumas fired at him with a blank cartridge, and so scared him that he rolled on the ground. Alexandre then put on the huge posting-boots and, mounting, galloped on to the next post. They had soon reached the old familiar Villers-Cotterêts. The whole town was thrown into intense excitement when it was known that the chaise with the tricolour contained their Alexandre Dumas. Late as it was, every house poured out its inhabitants, who rushed to the post-house. A thousand eager questions were put to him – what did it mean, the flag, the guns? It was insisted that he should stay a short time and have something to eat, and he was carried off to the house of his old friend Cartier where a hasty supper was got ready. A number of young men who had been boys with him in the little town gathered round, listening eagerly as Alexandre declaimed and recounted his adventures between every mouthful. As he dashed in for them, which he could do so admirably, vivid sketches of these thrilling scenes, he was listened to with delight and wonder, but when he came to explain that the object of his present expedition was to capture, single-handed, all the powder that was in a military town containing eight thousand inhabitants and a garrison of eight hundred men, they looked at him doubtfully. This was, of course, welcome to Alexandre, who always delighted to be the centre of a dramatic situation. He turned to his companion, Bard:

'What were my words when proposing this expedition to you?'

'You asked,' was the reply, 'was I inclined to get myself shot with you.'

'But what do you say now?'

'I am still ready.'

All were confounded at such gallantry. One of his old friends, Hutin, now stepped forward and offered to get him into Soissons without difficulty, as he had a friend at the gates. Then Alexandre, always anticipating d'Artagnan, raised his glass and drank to his own return to them on the next evening. 'Have dinner ready,' he called to his host, 'for twenty people, and it is to be eaten just the same whether we be alive or dead. Here are two hundred francs.' The other answered that he might pay on the morrow. 'But if I should be shot?' 'Then I shall pay.' A shout arose, 'Hurrah for Cartier!' Dumas drank off his wine and, with that curtain line, rose to leave. It was now eleven o'clock. The horses were put to, the chaise was waiting, and the bold trio, Dumas, Bard and Hutin, drove away on their daring expedition. By one o'clock they had reached the gates of Soissons, through which they were allowed to pass, 'the door-keeper little dreaming', says the great *farceur* 'that he was admitting the revolution!'

They went straight to the house of Hutin's mother, where their first business was the manufacture of a large tricolour flag. She contributed her blue and red curtains and a white tablecloth, and all the women of the household were set to work to sew the pieces together. By daybreak the work was completed. The pole, of course, gave no trouble, as the one from which the Bourbon white flag was floating would answer. 'For a flagstaff,' as Dumas says, 'has no political opinions.'

The plan they had arranged was quixotic in its extravagance. Making all allowance for Dumas's bombast, it will be seen that at the most his account has been guilty only of a novelist's exaggeration; and though at the time the story of the adventure was ridiculed, it could not be disproved in its facts, which are given with the most minute details of dates, names, and places. It was settled that Bard and Hutin were to take the flag and contrive to get into the cathedral under pretence of watching the sunrise from the tower. If the sacristan made any resistance he was to be flung over the parapet. Then having dragged down the white flag of the Bourbons, and set the tricolour floating from the tower, Bard was to hurry on to lend his aid to Dumas, who would be engaged at the powder magazine. Such was the plan of the three men.

They started at daybreak; Dumas made his way to Fort St Jean, where a small pavilion, close to the gateway, was used as the magazine. He dared not attempt the gate, but stealing round, climbed up the wall cautiously, and took a peep into the fort. He saw two soldiers busy hoeing in a little garden at the corner. He let himself down again, and looked over at the distant cathedral. He saw distinctly against the sky a dark outline of some figures; then the white

126

flag tossed about 'in an extraordinary fashion that could not have been owing to the wind', and finally disappeared, while the tricolour took its place. Now was the moment; his companions had done their part. He slung his double-barrelled gun over his shoulder and began to climb the wall. When he reached the top he saw the two soldiers staring with wonder at the strange flag on the cathedral – cocking both barrels of his gun, he leaped down and stood before them. One was named Captain Mollard; the other, Sergeant Ragon. He advanced on them and presenting his gun, made them a courteous but hurried speech, explaining who he was and what was his errand. He was Monsieur Alexandre Dumas, son of General Dumas, etc. He came in the name of General Gérard to demand the surrender of the powder – there was his order, signed by the general, which he presented with one hand, while he held his cocked gun in the other. The pair, taken aback, were at a loss what to do, when they were spared from their dilemma, by the appearance of Colonel Dorcour, commandant of the fort. The matter was explained to him, and after many courteous phrases a treaty was arranged, by which the two officers and sergeant promised their neutrality, and engaged to keep within doors. Thus the powder magazine would seem to have been captured by Dumas single-handed. He omits to mention that three of his friends were waiting for him at the gate. It has the air of a very brilliant achievement, and the picture of the hero alone in the fort, his fingers on the triggers of his gun, courteously but firmly controlling his three opponents, is a most dramatic scene.

Thus successful, Dumas opened the gate and found his friends Bard and Hutin awaiting him. To them he handed over the charge of the magazine, while he went away to deal with the commandant of the town, Colonel Liniers. He found this officer just risen, discussing the news of the sudden appearance of the flag on the cathedral. Dumas laid down his gun at the door and, introducing himself, demanded an order from Liniers to hand over the powder. Liniers declined to acknowledge General Gérard's requisition, and claimed moreover that there was scarcely any powder in the magazine. The commandant seemed, in fact, rather amused, and smiled scornfully when Dumas answered that the party at the magazine were his prisoners and that he would go back at once and bring proof that the powder was there. He then made his bow, and retired. He flew back, found that he was right, and returned presently with satisfactory proof that a large quantity of powder was indeed in the magazine. But when he reached the commandant's office he found that the party had been increased during his absence by Lenferna, an officer of gendarmes, and Bonvilliers, colonel of the engineers, who were in full uniform and armed. The commandant addressed him in a sort of bantering tone, telling him that he had sent for those officers who, with him, were in command of the town, in order that they might have the pleasure of hearing M Dumas explain his mission. The young man saw that boldness was his only recourse, and coolly told them that he had been engaged by La Fayette to bring the powder to Paris, or to lose his life, and again insisted on the commandant's handing over the powder. The officers passed on Gérard's order from one to the other with a sort of smiling contempt.

'And so,' said the commandant, in the same tone – 'so, single-handed, Monsieur Dumas – I think you said that was your name – you propose to force me to do this. You see we are four.'

The young man saw that matters were coming to a crisis, and took prompt action. He stepped back, pulled his double-barrelled pistols from his pockets, and presented them at the startled party. 'You are four,' he said, 'gentlemen; but I am five! If that order is not signed in five seconds, I give you my word of honour I will blow all your brains out, beginning with the commandant there!'

He confesses that he felt a little nervous, but he was determined.

'Take care,' he went on; 'I mean what I say. I am going to count; one – two – three –'

At this critical moment a side door was flung open, and a lady flung herself among them in a paroxysm of alarm.

'Agree! agree!' she cried. 'Oh, this is another revolt of the Negroes! Think of my poor father and mother, whom they murdered in Saint Domingo!'

Alexandre admits that the lady's mistake was excusable, considering his own natural tint (deepened by recent exposure to the sun), and the peculiar character of his hair and voice. The commandant could not resist the entreaties of his wife. Alexandre declared that he had infinite respect for the lady, but entreated her husband to send her away, and let men finish the business. The poor commandant protested that his honour must be respected. He could not decently yield to a single man. Alexandre then offered to sign a paper to the effect that the order had been extorted at 'the mouth of

128

the pistol-barrel'. 'Or would you prefer,' he added, 'that I should fetch two or three of my companions, so that you should seem to have yielded to a more respectable force?' The commandant accepted this proposal, and Alexandre left him, bluntly declaring that no advantage must be taken of the delay, or he would return and 'blow all their brains out', and that the whole party must give their word of honour that they would remain as they were.

'Yes, yes,' cried the lady. Alexandre made her a low bow, but declared that it was not her word that he wanted. The commandant gave what was required of him, and Alexandre, hurrying away, speedily returned with two or three of his men, (Hutin had by now enlisted the help of a number of his friends in Soissons), whom he placed in the courtyard. Opening the window, he called to them, and bade them inform the gentlemen inside that they were ready to fire on them at the first signal; an appeal answered by the significant sound of the cocking of guns. The commandant understood, and going to his desk, wrote out a formal order.

After this the rest was comparatively easy. The magazine was broken open, carts procured and loaded, and at about five o'clock they were outside the town. Dumas was so exhausted that he sank down on the grass, under a hedge, and fell fast asleep. Roused presently, he started on the journey, and by eight o'clock reached Villers-Cotterêts, where they found the supper ready which had been ordered the evening before. After a jovial meal they set out once more, and by three o'clock in the morning were close to Paris, at the post-house whence they had started. At nine he presented himself, with his powder, at the Hôtel de Ville having triumphantly accomplished his mission.

When Alexandre told this adventure, there was many a shrug of the shoulders and much laughter. Such a romance as this was not thought worth serious refutation coming from this amusing and notorious gasconader, an uncomplimentary appreciation which he owed to his incurable vanity which always made him set his own person in the most effective and dramatic positions. But the story is perfectly true, apart from some harmless exaggeration. It is to be found in an official report, published at La Fayette's direction in the *Moniteur* of 9 August 1830, and signed by Dumas and the friends who assisted him in the expedition. The names of the various officers whom he forced to submit to him are given at length. When the *Mémoires* were published in 1853, the son of the commandant, Liniers, came forward with an indignant 'reclamation' to clear the memory of his father, who was then dead; but his testimony (for he was present at the scene in the commandant's office) only confirms Dumas's account. The purport of the son's letter is merely this: the town was already ripe for revolt before Dumas's arrival, and that when the latter returned with his friends, these were taken to be the chiefs of the National Guard, already known to be disaffected. In short, that the officer yielded, not to Dumas, but to the overpowering force behind him. His son describes Dumas parading his pistols, and menacing the commandant, but declares that the presence of the four officers both armed and intimidated was a fiction of the novelist. He admits, however, that he himself and the secretary — with Madame de Liniers — were present. On the whole, the adventure, so splendidly told, may be accepted in all faith.

CHAPTER TWELVE

The Republican who Loved Royalty

The three day revolution of July 1830 was over. For Dumas the change in the dynasty, the accession to the throne of the Duc d'Orléans, his friend and patron, soon to be Louis-Philippe – king, not of France but of the French – the royal duke who had secured the admission of his play to the Français, who had made him his assistant librarian – a sinecure post which he had continued to hold despite the antipathy he felt for Casimir Delavigne – augured the brightest prospects. He might well imagine that his future was made.

Dumas, it must be said, does not appear now to the best advantage. He was convinced that he would be rewarded for his actions during *les trois glorieuse*, as the three days of the revolution were to be called. He even thought he might be made a minister by a grateful sovereign. He lost no time, therefore, in presenting himself at the Palais Royal. Here he found the Duke in conversation with Casimir Delavigne and others. The Duke, all smiles, on seeing him held out his hand, saying, 'M Dumas, you have just produced your best play.' This compliment might have been a sign of great favour, but if we are to believe Dumas (*vide* his memoirs), he had already had his suspicions of the Duke awakened. He was amazed at certain signs of duplicity in his behaviour. His portrait of Louis-Philippe during those days is drawn with singular effect and a vigour which is more than malicious. But one cannot help feeling that this portrait is prompted more by what he regarded as a personal slight than by his political faith. True, he had cried *vive la république* as he made his dash to seize the ammunition at Soissons and had hoisted the tricolour flag on the cathedral tower, but

131

unlike Thiers – who had belonged to that enthusiastic group of clever young men who had written fiery articles in the papers attacking the unconstitutional government of Charles X but who, when the revolution came, were acute enough to glide cleverly into Orléanism – Dumas would have us believe that he found the new regime thoroughly distasteful and that pure republicanism was still his only creed.

Dumas ascribes his antipathy and mistrust of the Duke to the moment he witnessed the mob come to the Palais, shouting for his Royal Highness. Here, he tells us, the crowd was regaled with wine by servants in handsome livery of the House of Orléans, but it was remarked that the wine was of the cheapest. 'The crowd found the liveries splendid, but the liquor bad. When replete, fresh mobs would arrive under the balcony waving for the Duke.' Dumas describes him as rushing to the balcony again and again, joining in the 'Marseillaise', his wig all awry, his face covered with perspiration. He would wash his hands and face, while heartily execrating the whole business.

It was after witnessing scenes like this, or so Dumas would have us believe, that he became so utterly shocked and disgusted, that casting the dust off his shoes and sorrowfully renouncing his royal patron, he quitted the Palais Royal for ever. 'The spectacle of a prince begging for a crown like a street beggar' wounded him to the very soul. He had merely to go to the Palais, he says, to ask for some mission to Prussia, Russia or Spain – but no, 'I would have nothing to do with them. I had sworn never to put my foot in the Palais Royal again.' In vain did Oudard (who had sat on the fence, waiting to see how things would turn out) try to sooth him, dangling the cross of the Légion d'Honneur before his eyes and 'offering to send [him] to St Petersburg with M Athalin, who was just starting out as ambassador extraordinary to the Emperor Nicholas'. In vain did his mother congratulate him on his fortune being made; his sister arrived post-haste from the country to solicit his interest and good offices in favour of her husband. But no, he was inflexible. 'Poor dear mother! I took care not to let her know that far from being able to advance others, I considered that my own career was ended for ever.' He told Oudard that he must consider him as no longer attached to the establishment.

This picture of self-abnegation and the story of such noble political integrity must have made those who knew Alexandre smile. The truth was that the Duke was displeased that one of his household should have taken part with the more violent of the revolutionary party. Dumas's vanity, leading him to suppose that he had been one of the principal personages to have placed his former patron on the throne, had thoroughly displeased the Duke, who had coldly refused to acknowledge his pretensions and demands. Despite his claims it seems unlikely Oudard had ever offered him the cross of the Légion d'Honneur or the post of secretary to the ambassador to St Petersburg. One can be sure that it was he who solicited these honours. It was disappointment at being refused recognition for what he regarded as his invaluable services that led him to portray the Duke as dishonest and contemptible. Twenty years later, after Louis-Philippe's fall in 1848, when he might have thought of past favours and kindnesses, Dumas shows in his memoirs he was still brooding over what he regarded as an injustice.

In fact, Dumas, although associated with the *ultras*, was not a true revolutionary; he was a republican by reason, a royalist by instinct:

> In politics there was within him a perpetual conflict between impulse and reflection, idealism and realism ... it was with Dumas as with Scott. Pageantry, remnants of past splendour, the heritage of past tradition, these he revered ... He tried to separate men from their ideas, and in this the writer defeated the politician. His failure was not to realise that in politics men cannot be separate from their ideologies.'*

Dumas now took another truly quixotic step. He tells us that he went to see La Fayette, to whom he proposed another expedition, not quite so daring perhaps as his expedition to Soissons, but one which was in character with his Romantic spirit. This was a mission into the Vendée – not a very intelligible sort; indeed, it is most confusing. 'General,' said Dumas, 'I come to ask you for something.' 'Bah,' replied the old man, 'I suppose you want a *préfecture*.' No, replied Dumas, all he asked was to be authorized to travel through the Vendée and organize a national guard. His contention was that the Vendée was as royalist as ever and that Charles X's friends would be active in trying to excite a reaction against Louis-Philippe. His theory was that a powerful middle class had grown up who held republican views and who only wanted rallying and proper organisation. In the ghastly civil

* A. C. Bell, *Alexandre Dumas*, Cassell & Co Ltd, 1950.

war of 1793 (described in my book *Banners of the King**) the peasants and *gentilhommes* of the west had fought heroically to overthrow the republican convention. In 1830 the chance of another rising, either by the peasants and *petite noblesse* to restore a Bourbon to the throne or by the middle classes to restore a republic, was remote. Admittedly there were a number of Carlistes (supporters of Charles X) who regarded Louis-Philippe as a usurper, but the attempted *coup* by the Duchesse de Berry (the widow of Charles X's second son) to stir the Vendée to revolt in 1832 in favour of her son, Henri, Duc de Bordeaux, ended in ignominious failure. Nevertheless, La Fayette, according to Dumas, willingly agreed to his suggestion and provided him with a letter of authorisation. This obtained, Dumas requested permission *'to wear some description of uniform'*. 'By all means,' replied the General, *'get them to make you something like an aide-de-camp's dress.* How much time do you want?' 'Only sufficient to get my uniform made.' Was his real purpose perhaps merely to visit Mélanie Waldor at La Jarrie, where her family possessed a country estate, and boast to her of his exploits? A uniform would of course be essential if he were to impress her sufficiently. On leaving La Fayette he met a friend riding by in the Place de Carrousel, dressed in the most flamboyant uniform, worthy of Murat, with a plume of tricolour ostrich feathers, a tunic of royal blue, with silver braid and silver sash. Dumas was enchanted by the effect and rushed after him to inquire the name of the corps. It turned out to be an invention of the wearer, who had thought of establishing what he called the 'mounted national guard', but which was not yet in being. Dumas, having obtained the name of his friend's tailor, immediately dashed off to have a similar costume made for himself. Having procured his uniform and obtained a horse, he set forth. It is difficult to believe that La Fayette ever took Dumas's self-appointed mission with any seriousness. Dumas, for his part, made little attempt to recruit a mounted national guard. He was faced with increasing hostility the further he proceeded west and was obliged to discard his all too conspicuous uniform. He would have us believe that he was often in danger of his life, but one may be certain that this was just his habitual 'gasconading'. Needless to say, his mission was pointless; nevertheless it has provided us with some

---

* Michael Ross, *Banners of the King: The War of the Vendée 1793–94*, Leo Cooper and Seeley Service, London, 1975.

delightful chapters both in his *Mémoires* and in his *La Vendée après le 29 juillet*, published by the *Revue des Deux Mondes* and which later gave him the material for his romance, *Les Louves de Machecoul* (1858).

On his return to Paris, he was sent for by the King (or so he claims), who wished to hear all about his mission.

Dumas now really surpasses himself in fantasy. He tells us that he spoke out boldly and fearlessly that the west was prepared to rise again, as in 1793. When the King said that he had no fears from the Vendée, Dumas replied, laughing (so he maintains), 'The King will perhaps excuse my attempting to refute his opinion, but will allow me to retain my own. May I say what I think?' 'You mean on the state of La Vendée?' 'Yes; and also on *your present policy*.' Dumas, seizing the opportunity, then tells us he spoke out and said: 'This critical state of the Vendée is a capital pretext for putting aside the notion of a war on the Rhine or in Italy. I know that this [war] would be popular; but the King is not inclined for it, and is glad to have such an excuse for avoiding it.' 'Ah,' said the King, wincing under the thrust and biting his lips(!). 'Politics is a hard profession, you had better leave it to kings and ministers – you are a poet; better stick to your poetry.' 'Sire,' replied Dumas, 'the ancients called the poets *prophets*.' Unable to endure any more of these 'bitter thrusts' the King waved him off impatiently and terminated the interview.

Alexandre came out triumphant and meeting Oudard, who was waiting on the staircase, said, 'Yesterday the King and I had only half quarrelled, but today I have broken with him for ever!' Dumas says that he then sat down and wrote the following letter of resignation:

SIRE:
My political opinions not being in harmony with those Your Majesty is entitled to require in the persons who hold office in Your Majesty's household, I must ask Your Majesty to accept my resignation.
I have the honour to remain, etc,
Alex Dumas

Dumas seems to overlook the fact that he has already told his readers that he had given in his resignation to Oudard sometime earlier. The whole story is absurd. That he had an interview with the King is probable enough, but it seems almost too certain that it was not for the object of cocking a snook at his patron, but of obsequiously pressing his claims. Now, as though to show his contempt for the monarch, he enrolled in the newly formed artillery of the national guard, a body of hot-headed republicans who did not hesitate to conceal their political leanings. Dumas, however, as already mentioned, was 'a republican by reason but a royalist by instinct', for though thus flaunting his republicanism, he nevertheless went to the Palais Royal on New Year's Day to pay his compliments to the King, making a complete fool of himself by appearing in uniform, not realising that the corps had been disbanded on the previous day by royal decree. This visit to the King surely shows that he was still eager to win back the royal favour, but he was once again snubbed. The King not unnaturally thought that Dumas was wearing the uniform out of bravado. He looked our hero up and down with a smile and remarked: 'Ah, there you are Dumas. That's you all over,' and passed on.

'On the same table on which I wrote my resignation was a letter in handwriting which I recognised as that of Harel. I opened it trembling in case he was talking once again about that unfortunate drama on Napoleon.' Harel, he tells us, had previously approached him during the July revolution to write a play on the Empire. Dumas claims that he haughtily answered him: 'Ask that of a man who has not fought, of a man who has seen nothing, of a poet who has a country estate and who by chance stayed there during the three glorious days – he would do it marvellously well. But I who have seen, I who have participated, I who have taken part in the action, I could do nothing good, and never match up to what I have seen.'

But the revolution was now behind him and he once more turned his attention to the theatre. The letter was indeed from Harel, but he was not attracted by the subject, complaining that his knowledge of history was *nil* – strange to say, this was true, and as we shall see he was to be entirely dependent on collaborators; for although a tireless worker, he could never be bothered with research. Harel refused to take no for an answer. He invited him to dinner and prepared a study for him, installed a bed, armchair and desk, stacked it with pens, ink, paper and a library of Napoleonic literature. After dinner he decoyed his guest into the study, informing him that the room was at his disposal until *Napoléon* was written, and locked the door on him. Without too much protest, Alexandre accepted his enforced captivity and in eight days turned out a drama of twenty-four tableaux and nine thousand lines. From a literary point of view the play was without merit, and the success it enjoyed was entirely due to Frédérick Lemaître's superb performance in the title role.

Free of Harel and *Napoléon*, Dumas could now devote his attention once again to *Antony*.

CHAPTER THIRTEEN

Antony

In 1831 *Antony* was accepted at the Français with Mlle Mars cast as Adèle, the heroine, and Firmin as the Byronic misanthropic hero. Neither of these two artists approved of the role assigned to them. Dumas describes them as gradually pruning away 'this and that extravagance' out of mere whim. The result, says Dumas, was that 'after three months of rehearsal, Adèle and Antony were just two charming lovers, such as might be seen at the Gymnase. They might just as well have been called Monsieur Arthur and Mlle Céleste.'* No doubt Mlle Mars and Firmin were not altogether wrong in their assessment of the play, because later, on de Vigny's advice, Dumas was to delete some of his more outrageous dialogue in reference to Antony's atheism. Nevertheless, it was quite obvious that neither Mlle Mars nor Firmin were in sympathy with their roles and both were miscast.

From the start, the play had been received with no great enthusiasm by the Français, but the committee, after the phenomenal success of *Henri III*, had found it almost impossible to turn down a play by the now famous Alexandre Dumas. When Dumas abruptly withdrew the play, it was to the consternation of all concerned, except perhaps to Mlle Mars. It was Firmin who told Dumas that she would never play the role of Adèle and that it was ideally suited for Marie Dorval, while Pierre Bocage should play the part of the Byronic hero. This was precisely what the young author himself had been thinking for some time. He at once offered the play to the director of the Porte Saint-Martin, who received it cordially. He read it to Dorval. Dorval was

* *Souvenirs dramatiques.*

small, dark and fragile, with a curly fringe, quivering lips and a poetic face. According to Théophile Gautier (*Histoire de l'art dramatique*) she was more than an actress. 'She was spirit incarnate . . . Her figure was like a flexible reed, responsive to every mysterious breeze.' Marie Dorval was the natural child of two poor strolling players and had been brought up 'among sordid and violent passions'. When in a temper she could swear like a fishwife. Though twice married, she had numerous lovers, including, as already mentioned, Dumas himself. To quote de Banville and George Sand: 'There is nothing she could not turn her hand to, the ravaged face, the wildly passionate lips, the eyes burned dry with tears, the body quivering from head to toe, the thin, pale arms emaciated with fever.'* 'With her everything, every single thing, was resolved in terms of passion, motherhood, art, friendship, devotion, indignation, yearning. And since she could not moderate or suppress anything, her whole existence was lived out in such violent superlatives, that one was terrified.'†

There was no doubt that Marie Dorval was ideal for the part of Adèle, infinitely better than Mlle Mars. Indeed far from pruning down, Dorval was entranced by her part. As Dumas read it to her, she wept hysterically – or so Dumas recounts – and almost choked him in a passionate embrace. 'It was no longer her bosom that rose and sank; it was her heart that beat against my shoulders.' The last act, however, she thought still lacking in power. Dumas agreed; it must be rewritten that very night. Fortunately there was a vacant room in her apartment, usually occupied by another gentleman (presumably de Vigny, with whom she was now having an affair) who was fortunately absent. 'During the night I will come and visit you,' said Dorval, 'to see how you are getting on, and in the morning you will read it to me.' At eleven o'clock he set to work on his fifth act. It was finished by three in the morning. Dorval was delighted and read her lines to perfection.

On 3 May 1831 the curtain of the Théâtre Porte Saint-Martin rose for the first time on what was to be one of the most sensational plays of the century. 'All the young men were there: writers, painters, craftsmen. Strange fierce faces were to be seen by the score, pointed beards, long curling hair, extravagant doublets, dress coats with velvet lapels . . . The ladies a bit nervous . . . with their hair done *à la*

* Théodore de Banville, *Caméos parisiennes*, 2nd series.

† George Sand, *Histoire de ma vie*, vol IX.

giraffe, their great tortoiseshell combs, their leg-of-mutton sleeves, their short skirts revealing feet shod in high-heeled boots.'* The success was immense. Frédérick Lemaître maintained that the fourth act of *Antony*, as played by Bocage and Dorval, was the finest thing he had ever seen. The fifth act was Dorval's own. As *Le Figaro* announced the next day: 'She cried as people do cry, with genuine tears; she shrieked as people do shriek, cursed as women do curse, tearing her hair . . .'

Dumas was so nervous that he was unable to remain in the theatre, and with his friend Bixio, hurried out to pace the boulevards.

When he returned, the audience and actors were all in a tumult of excitement. The applause was still continuing after the fourth act. 'A hundred francs if you can get the curtain up before they have done applauding,' Dumas shouted to the scene-shifters – a stimulant which needed no further prompting. If the audience had been enthralled by the previous acts, it can be imagined what was the effect of the dénouement of the final scene, when Antony flings the dagger at the colonel's feet and cries, *'Elle me resistait; je l'ai assassiné.'* As the curtain fell for the last time, 'shouts of terror and grief burst from the audience'. The whole house was stupified and confounded. An ovation awaited the author behind the scenes. His young friends, 'pale, agitated and panting', flung themselves upon him. 'I was dragged to the right and left,' he recalls; 'I had on a green suit, buttoned from top to bottom, which was torn to pieces.' No wonder he looked back fondly to this night of bewildering triumph.

But there was a sad side to the triumph, of which Dumas seems to have been quite oblivious. The remains of his tattered coat were among the souvenirs kept to the last by Catharine Labay, but Mélanie Waldor did not even have this much – only bitter memories. She sat alone in the *loge* Dumas had reserved for her. 'I shall try to visit you in your box,' he had written, but he never came. Was he ashamed to face her? Like everyone else in Paris, that is to say in the world of the arts, she had immediately recognised the resemblance between herself and Adèle Hervey – the officer husband, the only daughter, as well as certain details of dress and peculiarities of speech, all made recognition easy; but she alone could recognise in the impassioned words put into Antony's mouth the very same impassionate words

---

* Théophile Gautier, *Histoire du Romantisme*.

Dumas had so recently addressed to herself. There were further aggravating circumstances. She was aware that Mlle Dorval had been her lover's mistress and that he was now living with Belle Krelsamer who, under her stage name of Mélanie Serre, was playing a minor role. No doubt she also recognised Catharine Labay among the audience. Dumas, as Maurois writes, belonged to that category of Don Juans who is neither satanic nor vicious: 'He has no wish to cause pain to any of his mistresses, but tries to keep all of them, which . . . is apt to be exhausting, and since they are jealous, compels him to lie to all of them, with the result that he finds himself in the special district of Hell reserved for liars – the Circle of Insecurity.'

Mélanie Waldor, who had longed to have a child by Dumas, was also aware that Mélanie the second had already borne him a daughter (Marie-Alexandrine, born 5 March 1831), a fact which caused her further anguish. But Mélanie Waldor was an exceptional woman and although still deeply in love with the faithless Alexandre, she presented a brave face to the world and continued to invite him to her *salons*. He was to see her often at the houses of literary friends, but his love for her was dead. He was now living openly with Belle Krelsamer, who had persuaded him to acknowledge her child legally. It was Belle who now persuaded Dumas to apply for custody of his son Alexandre, on the grounds that Catharine was vulgar and altogether unfitted to bring up his child. Of course it was Catharine Labay, 'a simple, upright and honest woman, a hard worker, a devout churchgoer, and orderly by temperament in all things'* who was far more suitable as a parent than his inconsiderate, happy-go-lucky, volatile father. The official custody of Alexandre was, however, granted to Dumas on 17 March 1831. Catharine, who loved her son, a love reciprocated by the young Alexandre, contested the judgement and instituted proceedings against the father. A long-drawn-out wrangle followed, in which Catharine, due to a technicality in French law, was the loser. The tribunal ordered that the seven-year-old boy should be taken in charge by the police commissioners and placed in a boarding school. It was a traumatic experience for the child, who never altogether forgave his father.

When later Dumas *père* withdrew his son from school to live under

---

* Maurice Spronck, '*Alexandre Dumas fils, ses origines et ses débuts*', *Revue de Deux Mondes*, 15 March 1898.

the same roof as himself and Belle Krelsamer, Dumas *fils* proved so intractable that his father sent him back to boarding school. It was his mother who fitted him out with school clothes out of her meagre earnings, something that the boy never forgot and for which he was forever grateful.

Despite the success of *Antony* and the more liberal censorship, there was still powerful opposition to a play that departed so radically from the norm of classical productions and so blatantly portrayed adultery. As Dumas himself points out, this was sheer hypocrisy. Had he placed the setting a few hundred years previously no one would have objected.

One of his sternest critics was a M Jay, a member of the Chamber of Deputies as well as being editor of the *Constitutionnel*, who was openly living with a married woman. Nevertheless the play was performed 130 times and frequently played in the provinces. It was not until 1834, when it was transferred to the Théâtre Royal, that its performance was officially proscribed, with the usual excuse that it was degrading to put on such an 'immoral' play in a state-subsidised theatre. Two or three years after its première, *Antony* was still a favourite and was the play chosen for benefit performances. At one such, in which Dorval and Bocage were playing, the stage manager inadvertently ordered the curtain to drop as Antony plunged his dagger into Adèle's heart, thus depriving the audience of the now famous last lines. A furious public shouted repeatedly, '*Le dénouement! Le dénouement!*' So vociferous were the cries that the unfortunate stage manager begged the artists to be allowed to raise the curtain and finish the scene. Dorval, always a good trouper, resumed her post as the murdered Adèle; but Bocage, who had already retired to his dressing room, obstinately refused to return to the stage. The audience continued to shout 'Bocage! Dorval!' and threatened even to break up the seats.

The stage manager raised the curtain, hoping that by so doing Bocage would feel obliged to return. But no; Bocage refused. The public waited. A full minute elapsed. Meanwhile Dorval lay as though lifeless in the armchair into which she had fallen, her arms hanging loose, her head thrown back. But when Bocage failed to appear the public once more began to shout and stamp even more wildly. Dorval, sensing that at any moment the audience would get out of hand, lifted her head and, rising as it were from the dead, advanced to the footlights; in the sudden hush which followed her first movement, she addressed the audience: '*Messieurs,*' she said, '*je lui resistais, il m'a assassiné.*' She then made a graceful curtsy and left the stage to a thunder of applause.

'The curtain fell and the spectators left enchanted. They had had their dénouement, a variant it is true, but a variant which was so *spirituel* that one would be a poor fellow not to have preferred it to the original.'

But to return to the year 1831. Paris had not been satisfied by the three day revolution of July. All the political factions were at loggerheads – Orléanists and ardent republicans, Bonapartists and Carlists. There were frequent anti-royalist demonstrations. At a dinner party organised by the republican faction, attended by Dumas, the anti-royalist speeches inveighing against Louis-Philippe became so heated that Dumas thought it wiser to leave the gathering by jumping out of the window rather than compromise himself.

'I went home,' he writes, 'much troubled in mind, for it was plain that the business would have awkward consequences.' Relieved that no notice was taken of his part in the banquet, he indulged in a little agitation, regarding the question of the 'Cross of July'. The distribution of this decoration was in the hands of 'a sort of republican committee' and the history of this trifling affair gives a graphic picture of the imbecile government which despite the revolution still oppressed France. Dumas applied for this decoration – which he certainly deserved – but was refused on the grounds that he had taken no part in the 'glorious days'. This refusal came from the King himself. The committee thereupon proceeded to elect a subcommittee of fourteen. Alexandre found himself fourteenth on the committee and last on the list of nominees. A report was adopted, repudiating all interference on the part of the King or of anyone else. A long discussion took place on the important question of the colour of the ribbon. As we might have guessed, Dumas took a prominent part in a matter so directly connected with clothes. The colour mentioned in the royal decree was adopted with much opposition. Dumas would have none of it. He must have forseen that this quite idiotic wrangle would take place, for he had brought with him yards of ribbon of his own choice with which he proceeded to decorate the buttonholes of those nearest. The immediate possession of a *boutonnière* of gay ribbon was a bait too tempting to be resisted, even at the expense of principle. 'As soon as twenty or so were seen to be thus decorated,' Dumas records, 'an eager desire seized on every one to be thus adorned.' Messengers were sent to procure further lengths of ribbon, and within a short while, not only the fourteen members of the subcommittee, but a whole crowd of people, on learning that Dumas was distributing honours, surged into the room to receive the ribbon 'awarded by the people' but which was to be denied to the royal house.

Politics naturally extended to writers and artists. The founders of the Romantic movement were split. Lamartine had entered the political arena, Saint-Beuve and Hugo were not on speaking terms, despite the fact that he considered Hugo an infinitely better dramatist than Dumas.

All this political excitement was unfavourable for literature. Riots and literary rivalry, Dumas admits, took up too much of his time and money. He therefore decided to leave Paris and make an excursion to the country in search of peace of mind and for reasons of economy. With Belle Krelsamer and little Alexandre, he travelled north to Normandy with no clear idea of where to stay. At Le Havre he was recommended Trouville as a quiet spot in which to spend a month or six weeks. Trouville at that time was nothing more than a fishing village, not even marked on the map. He remembered that a painter friend of his had once extolled its virtues, telling him that to stay there was almost like visiting a foreign country and that the fisher-folk did not even speak French but a speech peculiar to Normandy. There was only one inn, kept by *la mère* Oseraie, a magnificent cook who made special terms for artists and, in Dumas's case, for a poet – to whom she charged the present day equivalent of eightpence for two rooms and board.

Dumas has left us a delightful account of his visit. He went for walks and bathed (he was an excellent swimmer) and was once pursued by an enormous porpoise. Unfortunately, in those days, it was not appreciated that this 'enormous fish', as he describes it, was a playful, friendly creature. Supposing it to be some sort of shark, he tells us how he managed to regain the beach, and how he ran to the inn, dripping wet in his bathing costume, much to the shock of a charming lady visitor, to retrieve his carbine and return to shoot 'the beast!' Between bathing, walking and shooting, he still found time to write a five-act poetical drama, *Charles VII chez ses grands vassaux** containing some of the best verse he ever wrote. In the meanwhile he had met an acquaintance, a young man named Beudin who had come expressly to Trouville to consult him on an idea for a drama which he was writing together with another would-be dramatist named Gobeaux. So far Beudin and Gobeaux had got no further than writing the prologue (with which neither aspiring author was satisfied), and had merely sketched out the ensuing plot. Dumas was interested and promised, on his return to Paris, to collaborate, but insisted modestly that his name should not appear as co-author.

Three months later, on 20 October, *Charles VII chez ses grands vassaux* was given its première at the Odéon. On the opening night it received a cold reception. 'The audience taking ill the sacrifice of movement to poetry, did not "believe" it.' The seven-year-old Dumas *fils* was present at the dismal première. Father and son walked home together hand in hand; the father, for once silent and depressed. That sad walk home stayed for ever in the memory of the boy, and is vividly recollected in *Le Fils naturel*. Although the first night was received coldly, the play, despite adverse press reviews, had a successful run. Dumas, however, was far from satisfied. He now turned his attention to *Richard Darlington*, the play outlined to him by Beudin. He had already revised or entirely rewritten (it is difficult to know which) the prologue, or first act.

The plot, which could not fail to fascinate Dumas, was as follows: A man, masked and duly mysterious, attended by a lady, arrives at a roadside inn on his way to Dover, and then calls for a doctor to attend the lady, who has suddenly been taken ill. Without removing his mask he confides to the doctor that he is flying with the lady from an angry father. This doctor, who is one of those grave, sagacious and benevolent practitioners found chiefly on the stage, discovers that the lady is about to be delivered of a child, and presently has to announce the birth of a boy. At this critical moment the angry parent arrives. The *accouchée* rushes [*sic*] from the adjoining room, and flinging herself at his feet protests she will not be separated from her lover. The father then snatches the mask from the latter's face and bids her stay with him if she will – for he is the common executioner! So much for the prologue. The next act takes place twenty-five years later. The

* Based on Racine's *Andromaque*.

offspring of this union has grown up and is married to the doctor's daughter. Beyond this, Beudin admitted that he was 'stuck'. It is difficult to assess how much of the subsequent acts are entirely the work of Dumas, or how much Beudin and Gobeaux contributed. Dumas, later, was to claim that *Richard Darlington* was *his* best play. The final acts certainly have the Dumas touch, but like so much of his work are a patchwork of other writers. The plot of the prologue is borrowed from the English *Chronicles of the Canongate* (with which presumably Beudin and Gobeaux were familiar), while the subsequent plot is derived from Scott's *The Surgeon's Daughter*, and whole passages, as Dumas frankly admits (but only after his *modus operandi* had been exposed by the critics) are borrowed from Schiller. At the point where Beudin admitted that he was stuck, Dumas conceived the idea, borrowed from Scott, that the young man, now grown up and married to the doctor's daughter, becomes ambitious and, seduced by the prospect of an aristocratic alliance, plots how to get rid of his lawful wife. Divorce? That was altogether a too simple and undramatic solution. No, she must be murdered. The problem of how to get rid of his lawful wife was one which was to involve Dumas in many lengthy discussions with his co-authors. Dumas had the genius to realise that to depict actual murder on the stage was much less dramatic than to have the murder committed offstage. Dumas's solution to the murder scene – which he tells us occurred to him during the night, when he leapt from his bed, crying 'Eureka', was to have Darlington open the french windows of the room in which he was confronting his wife and force her out into the open, closing the windows behind him. Then follows a pause. Darlington re-enters the room alone. A ghastly green light shines on the villain's face. All is left to the imagination. It was a brilliant dénouement.

Richard Darlington was performed on 10 December 1832 to a house crowded to the roof. 'The last act,' writes Dumas modestly, 'was one of the most terrible things I have ever seen on the stage. When Jenny [Darlington's wife] asked him what he was about to do, and he answered, "I know not – but say your prayers at once," a great shudder passed over the audience, and a murmur of fear issuing from every bosom worked up into a regular cry of terror.' Dumas, however, affected to repudiate all responsibility for the authorship, taking his seat among the audience as 'a mere stranger'. The manager, as the excitement increased, implored him to let his name be announced. Dumas refused. Once again the manager returned with Beudin and Gobeaux, who gallantly insisted that he, Dumas, had written it all. But our young hero – it must not be forgotten that he was still only twenty-nine years of age – remained inflexible. 'I embraced them, but refused. I had tears in my eyes.'

When the curtain fell to frenzied applause, he rushed behind the scenes to greet the actors, meeting on the way the young Alfred de Musset, 'very pale and agitated'. 'What ails you, *mon cher poète?*' asked Dumas. 'Nothing. *I am only choking,*' was the reply. 'This was,' adds Dumas, 'the very highest praise he could give to a play.' If this anecdote is true, and we have no reason to doubt it, it certainly was praise from the young, spoilt poet-dandy, who now at the age of twenty had already been accepted into the cenacle of Victor Hugo and was no admirer of Dumas as a dramatist. This almost paranoid young man, who affected to like no one's work but his own, with perhaps the exception of Victor Hugo and later of George Sand (with whom he had a tumultous and disastrous love affair two years later), was highly emotional and was quite probably strongly moved by this realistic melodrama.

Although Dumas did not entertain the same feelings towards the cast as he did in the case of Dorval and Bocage, he had every reason to congratulate them. As a light on Dumas's attitude towards women, it is interesting to note what he has to say of Mlle Noblet, who played the part of Jenny, Darlington's murdered wife: 'Between me and Mlle Noblet, pretty, attractive, as she was at this time, there existed merely relations based on art; she only interested me as a young and pretty person, with a hopeful career before her.' With what delightful candour Dumas announces this fact, as though relations other than platonic friendship, 'based on art', were something out of the ordinary.

Now, with renewed confidence after the success of *Richard Darlington*, he tells us how he dashed off a play – *Térésa* – while on a flying visit to Villers-Cotterêts, where he was fêted and lionised and enjoyed hunting-parties. 'Dashed off a play' is a hyperbole if ever there was one. In fact *Térésa*, like so much of Dumas's work, was not original. Bocage, who had the happiest memories of *Antony*, had submitted to him the draft of the play, by Anicet Bourgeois, who already had a number of melodramas to his credit. Dumas did not really care for *Térésa* apart from the fact that it contained a part for a young girl of whom he said, with characteristic immodesty, 'She is a flower from the same garden as Miranda in *The Tempest* and Klärchen in *Egmont*.'

It was Bocage who suggested for this part a beginner who, he assured Dumas, had considerable talent. 'She is called Ida,' he said, 'acts at Montmartre and Belleville: but she is highly gifted, quite ravishing and the part should fit her like a glove.'

To quote André Maurois:* 'Ravishing would seem to be an optimistic epithet when applied to Ida Ferrier. Small, with an indifferent figure, she had little in her favour beyond fine eyes, a good complexion, and thick fair hair. She tried to imitate Dorval, "to speak with her shoulders and make undulating motions, like a turtle dove".' On the other hand, Théophile Gautier writes that at the time, she had considerable talent and possessed a graceful figure. Ida Ferrier's real name was Marguerite Ferrand. She dragged a widowed mother at her heels wherever she went. Small though her part was, she made a considerable success in *Térésa*, and flung herself in a highly emotional state into the author's arms, saying that he had assured her future.

She did not then know how true those words were. Dumas gave her supper, took her home and made her his mistress. (Belle Krelsamer was on tour at the time.) He was never tired of wondering at the youth, beauty and poetry of his new conquest. He even praised her chastity.

It was said Ida managed to create an illusion. But once she had become Dumas's mistress, and knew that in future there would be a part for her in any new play written by her lover, she neglected her craft and sank to a level 'well below that of mediocrity'. The critic Maurice Descotes wrote of her that she was 'a minor Dorval . . . She waved her arms like a scythe and opened her mouth to chew over a lot of words she did not understand.'

She was a serious danger to Dumas. So long as the Romantics wrote for performers of genius they could get away with anything. A commonplace phrase spoken by Dorval could sweep an audience off its feet, but when spoken by Ida Ferrier it 'showed up for the sad stuff it was'.†

---

* André Maurois, *The Three Musketeers*, Jonathan Cape, 1957. Unfortunately, Maurois does not provide the source of this description. Probably Fontenay, but I have been unable to confirm this.

† André Maurois, *The Three Musketeers*.

By now it is clear from reading Fonteney's diary that Dumas's increasingly numerous collaborations were beginning to damage his reputation in literary circles. Fonteney wrote: *'Monday 6 February 1831:* Went to see *Térésa* at the Opéra Comique – it is a great success – still about adultery, but this time in double harness . . . the play is announced as by Dumas. There is another author as well, but he had to agree that his name shall not appear. *Thursday 16 February:* Lunched with Dumas and his lady friend and Gobeaux . . . Later to Madame Gay. Dumas was there, solemnly talking Republic and Revolution. They want to make him pay for the powder he brought back from Soissons: a good joke! He had with him M Anicet Bourgeois, who collaborated with him over *Térésa*. They are busy with four other plays, all written in the same way. *For shame!'*

CHAPTER FOURTEEN

Birth of a Historian

The year 1832 marked a turning point in the life of Alexandre Dumas. He now seriously considered turning his talents to historical fiction covering the whole history of France. Dumas was not the first among contemporary French writers to interpret history in terms of fiction. As early as 1826, Vigny had published *Cinq Mars*, a novel set in the time of Richelieu; in 1829 there had appeared Mérimée's *Chronique du Regne de Charles IX* and Balzac's *Les Chouans*. Two years later Victor Hugo had taken the literary world by storm with his *Notre-Dame de Paris*. It was therefore hardly surprising that Dumas, already an admirer of Scott, should consider applying his talents to the Romantic historical novel.

Never one to do anything by halves, Dumas plunged into history. True, he was more or less familiar with French history from the fifteenth century up to the Napoleonic epoch, but only very superficially. Dumas never had the patience for serious research. The first history book he obtained was a schoolboy manual by the Abbé Gauthier, which consisted of no more than a set of doggerel verses of the type learnt by English schoolboys at the beginning of this century. 'In fourteen hundred and ninety-two/Columbus sailed over the seas so blue.' Gauthier's doggerel was no better: '*En l'an quatre cent trois Pharamond premier roi, / Est connu seulement par la salique loi.*' Fortunately for Dumas his friend Delanoue entered his work room at the very moment that he was reading this trivia. Dumas hastily attempted to hide the book, but Delanoue was quick to notice his movement.

'What are you reading?' he asked.

'Oh nothing.'

'What do you mean "nothing"? You are holding a book.'

Rather than have his friend believe that he was reading a pornographic work, an extremely embarrassed Dumas confessed that the book in question was none other than Gauthier's elementary schoolboy primer. When he explained that he wished 'to learn something about the first centuries of our history,' Delanoue, who was an extremely well-read young man and fond of Dumas, gave him the benefit of his knowledge. Instead of teasing him he advised him to read Châteaubriand and Thierry, Barante and Michelet. From now onwards, putting everything else aside – politics, society, love affairs, even meals – Dumas plunged into history. Barente and Thierry were his favourites. It was fortunate, too, that at this time a moribund fortnightly magazine – *Le Journal des Voyages* – was acquired from M Ribbing de Leuven by an enterprising printer named Buloz, a rough diamond, but with a genuine flair for spotting literary talent, just as Ambrose Vollard a few decades later was to recognise the talent of Renoir, Monet and other Impressionist painters. According to Dumas, it was he and Adolphe who persuaded the latter's father to sell the journal. Buloz, Bocage, and two others of Dumas's friends raised the money to make the purchase.

All this happened in 1830 or 1831. 'Each of us did our best for this journal, which was given the title of the *Revue des Deux Mondes*, which we looked upon as a child hatched in common, and which we loved with paternal affection.' 'The first milk I gave it to suckle' (writes Dumas, somewhat mixing his metaphors) 'was my *Voyage en Vendée.*' This led him on to write *Isabel de Bavière*, based on his reading of Barente's *Histoire des ducs de Bourgogne*. With his knowledge of the theatre, this was not a dry historical work but, as he admitted, a hybrid between romance and history, dialogue alternating with narrative. The figure of the haughty and adulterous Isabel of Bavaria, the blasé face of Louis of Orléans, and other protagonists in this melodrama passed before his eyes like actors on a stage. 'From this time,' Dumas writes, 'I became aware of my two principal qualities . . . dialogue, the backbone of the drama; narrative, the backbone of the novel. These qualities – everyone knows with what candour I speak of myself – I possess to the highest degree. I had not yet discovered my two others, no less important, which are derived from each other: *la gaieté* and *la verre amusante* [gaiety and wit].'

From this time too dated his unbounded enthusiasm for Thierry:

I perceived a living world buried twelve centuries in the past . . . I realised that in the last nine years I had learnt next to nothing. I recalled my conversation with Lassagne ('but history is so dull'), I understood that the past held more than the future. It is terrible not to know at the age of thirty what most schoolboys know at twelve. The study of play writing had taken me five or six years. How long then would the study of history take me?

From now on Dumas became more and more immersed in Barante, Thierry and Michelet. Now with the vista of the past unfolded before his eyes, he began to realise that he had discovered his true *métier* – not merely to be a playwright, but a writer of history as well. He admits that he did not feel competent as yet to undertake the task of writing a full-blooded romance in the manner of Walter Scott.

Dumas, by the age of thirty, had a very wide circle of friends and acquaintances, but he had also earned himself a number of enemies. He wrote of himself in middle life, 'I have many friendships, I have not one hatred.' His friendship extended not only to actors and actresses and everyone connected with the theatrical world, but also embraced musicians, including Liszt and Rossini (Berlioz mentions him twice in his *Mémoires* with gratitude), artists, painters, journalists and politicians of all ages, and of course former colleagues from the royal household.

It was his friend, the actor Bocage who first suggested to Dumas that he should give a fancy-dress ball in the New Year, to which *tout Paris* was to be invited. It was customary for the King to give a ball at carnival time, and it no doubt amused Dumas to think that he too should give a ball which, though not to be compared with the splendour and elegance of the royal function at the Tuileries, would certainly outshine it in wit and talent. He decided to invite three or four hundred guests, including some of the most distinguished society in Paris. His self-assurance convinced him that his invitations would not be refused; nor was he disappointed. The only inconvenience was that his apartment in the Place d'Orléans was not large enough to accommodate all whom he had invited. However, this difficulty was soon overcome. The apartment adjacent to his own was empty; this his landlord obligingly put at his disposal. All that was necessary was to decorate the rooms. The decorators were none other than Eugène

Delacroix, Louis and Clément Boulanger, and other well-known artists of the time. Some were to take a subject from a novel or play by one of the authors who would be present, others were to paint decorative panels and portraits of their literary friends. Four or five days prior to the party the walls were to be hung with canvas; pots of distemper and brushes were to be provided. The artists, only too delighted to oblige, undertook not to quit their tasks, not even to sleep, until all was finished. Dumas agreed to provide them with food and drink.

One thing of the greatest importance remained – what to provide for the supper. This presented no great difficulty to our hero. By permission of M Deviolaine, he set off with some young companions to hunt in the forests of Ferté-Vidame. Dumas has left us a delightful account of this hunting party in the snow-clad woods, 'like those surrounding the castle of the Sleeping Beauty'. How admirably he conveys the gaiety of youth, the wintry landscape, a picnic in the snow around a blazing bonfire . . . Needless to say Dumas is the hero of the party. He brings down three roebuck with two shots, to the astonishment of his companions. The happy band returns to Paris with nine deer and three hares. Two of the deer were to be roasted whole, three others were exchanged for a gigantic salmon and a fifty-pound sturgeon, another for an immense galantine; the hares were made into a delicious pâté to Dumas's own recipe.

Three days before the ball, all the artists were at their posts. Only Delacroix was absent.

It was a strange sight to watch this 'steeplechase' between ten painters of equal merit . . . None, especially the Johannot brothers, who were engravers and the designers of vignettes and easel painters, was accustomed to the use of distemper. But the painters of large canvasses soon became accustomed to its use. Louis and Clément Boulanger, like some others, seemed never to have used any other medium. Jadin and Decamps discovered in this new method of execution the most marvellous tones . . . We waited with impatience the arrival of Delacroix, whose facility of execution has become proverbial.

By the evening, only the two Johannot brothers were behind-hand . . . In consequence, while the rest of us played cards, smoked and chatted, the two of them, as night fell, continued their daytime work, congratulating themselves on the superiority of lamplight to achieve beautiful colour effects, which were eventually to be observed by the light of candles.

On the following day, when daylight came, Alfred and Tony uttered cries of despair. By lamplight they had taken yellow for white and white for yellow, green for blue and blue for green. The two pictures looked like immense *omelettes aux fines herbes*.

At this moment old Père Ciceri entered. [Ciceri was a scene painter who had been responsible for painting the ceilings, hanging the canvasses and providing paints and brushes.]

'Good,' said he, 'so we have a green sky and yellow clouds? Not to worry.'

He took up his brushes and, in the space of a minute, he had broadly and vigorously repainted the skies of the two pictures. One calm, serene, all azure, allowing one to glimpse Dante's paradise through the blue of the firmament; the other, lowering and cloudy, charged with electricity and ready to be torn apart by a flash of lightning.

All these young men learnt in a moment the science of decorative art, which on the previous evening they had been stumblingly seeking for hours on end. No one now thought of working at night. Thanks to the lesson given by Ciceri, work proceeded with giant strides ... On the evening of the second day, I sent [to Delacroix] to ask him if he had forgotten that the ball was fixed for the following day. He told me not to worry and that he would arrive on the morrow *à l'heure du déjeuner*.

Delacroix duly arrived, glanced round the four rooms and made appropriate complimentary comments. Then, after lunching, without even removing his short black frock-coat or rolling up his sleeves, he picked up his charcoal and in three or four strokes sketched in a horse; in five or six more, a mounted knight; in seven or eight, a landscape, dead and dying men, figures in flight; and then having made this sketch, only intelligible to himself, he took up his brushes and began to paint.

Then in an instant one saw appear a mortally wounded knight, all covered in blood, mounted on a horse ... All around, before and behind him, lie heaps of dead ... As far as the eye can see lies a terrible bloody battlefield. Above all this, a glowing sun, like a red-hot metal buckler straight from the forge, sinks behind a blood-stained horizon. Then finally, a blue sky melts into green in the receding distance.

It was wonderful to watch. A circle formed around the master, and every man, without jealousy, without envy, had quit their tasks to applaud this second Rubens, who could improvise composition and execution at the same time.

In two or three hours everything was finished. At five o'clock in the afternoon, thanks to a huge fire, all was dry and it was possible to place seats against the walls.

The news of the ball had made a tremendous stir. Artists and writers whom Dumas had forgotten to include in his list of invitations begged to be allowed to come; many *femmes du monde* solicited invitations, but demanded to come masked. This Dumas refused. The ball was to be a costume ball, but not masked: Belle Krelsamer was very strict on this point and had laid in two dozen dominos for those guests, no matter what their position, who attempted to contravene the rules.

At seven o'clock the fifty-pound salmon and a roebuck, roasted whole, set on a silver platter 'which might have been taken from the dresser of Gargantua', were brought in, together with a gigantic pâté.' Three hundred bottles of Bordeaux and three hundred of Burgundy had already been subjected to the right temperature, while a further five hundred bottles of champagne were on ice. Dumas himself wore 'a charming costume of 1525, copied from an engraving'. The hostess, Belle Krelsamer, was dressed as Helena Fourment, Rubens's second wife. The elderly, courtly La Fayette came dressed in Venetian costume.

> La Fayette, the man who has shaken the hand of Washington, the man who had obliged Marat to hide in his cellars; this man who had lost his popularity by trying to save the life of the Queen, who had fought against Mirabeau; this man, who on 6 October, had said to ten centuries of royalty, 'Bow before the royalty of today – the People!' This man who in 1814 had cast down Napoleon from his throne, who had helped Louis-Philippe to mount his, this man who, instead of falling like the others, had grown in stature with each revolution; here was this man *simple comme la grandeur, bon comme la force, naïf comme le génie.*

Rossini was there too, dressed as Figaro, and rivalled La Fayette in popularity. All the world of the theatre was represented wearing their theatrical costumes. A Monsieur Beauchêne, well known for his monarchist views, arrived dressed to perfection as a Vendéan peasant of 1793.* Catching sight of him, La Fayette addressed him with a charming smile: 'Monsieur de Beauchêne, pray tell me, by virtue of what privilege are you the only person here not in fancy dress?' A

---

* The Vendéan peasants of 1793, it will be remembered, were royalist almost to a man.

155

quarter of an hour later Beauchêne was playing cards with the republican of 1789 and 1830, with gold pieces bearing the effigy of Henri V. The party broke up at nine o'clock on the following morning, with a final joyous *galop* which extended all the way from the Place d'Orléans through the rue de Trois-Frères to the boulevard.

CHAPTER FIFTEEN

The End of the Party

It is hardly surprising that this prodigal party and his other extravagances left Dumas in financial difficulties. He was obliged not only to plunge once more into his work for the *Revue des Deux Mondes* with his *Scènes Historiques*, but dashed off one of his worst plays – *Edith aux longs Cheveux* for, as yet still unknown as a novelist, he continued to write for the theatre. Scarcely had he finished these two works than cholera broke out in Paris. The epidemic had already been making terrible progress across Europe, but it was not until it was learnt that London was stricken that Paris became seriously alarmed. Dumas was to remember in detail that Saturday morning of 29 March, when the news went round that the epidemic had arrived. It was a lovely day, he tells us; the sun was shining in a sapphire sky, never did the gardens of the Tuileries look more beautiful; and what seemed to Dumas a higher charm than the attraction of nature was, as he puts it, that 'the gardens were literally enamelled with beautiful women'. 'Suddenly,' he writes, 'a terrible cry arose . . . the cholera! A man had just been found dead in the rue Chauchat!'

At once everything changed. Happy strollers in the streets were seen hurrying home to shut themselves up crying, 'The cholera!' just as they had cried, 'The Cossacks!' 'Who could ever forget this time,' continues Dumas, 'with its steady blue sky, with its mocking sun, its deserted boulevards, the theatres like vaults.'

No wonder few people wished to go to the theatre. Once indeed the audience at the Odéon consisted of only one person, who refused to take back his money and insisted that the play should be performed in its entirety. Legally, he was within his rights. He had paid his money and by law the actors were obliged to perform. In the circumstances, it can be well imagined that they 'did their worst'. The audience (of one) hissed. Harel, the manager, always a man of initiative, summoned the police and charged him with disturbance of the peace. He was ejected and the relieved actors returned to their homes.

The play in question was a melodrama entitled *Ten Years in the Life of a Woman,* a mediocre piece by any standards, but one in which Harel had invested a considerable sum of money. He therefore inserted the following advertisement in the newspapers:

> It had been noted with much astonishment that the theatres are literally the only places – no matter how crowded – *where not a single case of cholera has appeared.* We have this fact – and we defy contradiction – from invesitgation by the most eminent scientists.

There was little response.

It was, as it so happened, on 28 March, the very eve of the day when cholera first made its appearance in Paris, that Dumas was visited by a charming young actress, Martine Dupont, an excellent soubrette from the Théâtre Français, to tell him that her benefit night was fixed and that she had come with a request for a little original scene for the occasion. This was Friday evening and the benefit was to be on the Tuesday or Wednesday following. Dumas promised, if she should give him an entire week, to furnish her with not only one scene, but a whole short play. The circumstances proved hardly propitious. From the windows of his room in the rue Saint-Lazare, Place d'Orléans, Dumas was to watch fifty or sixty funerals passing every day on their way to the cemetery of Montmartre. Nevertheless, with death all around him, he dashed off one of his gayest and most delightful plays – *Le Mari de la Veuve* – in twenty-four hours.*

Dashed off in twenty-four hours! At least this is what Dumas claims. In *Le Mari de la Veuve* he was assisted by one Durieu and his old ally, Anicet Bourgeois. He might have fairly given these two their share of credit, though no doubt the arrangement was in the form of a fair bargain. They were very content to have the cash and the substantial aid of his undoubted powers. But when due acknowledgement had to be made, Dumas tells us loftily that he had a friend Durieu 'who was always provided with some story or plot for a

---

* With Mlle Mars in the principal role and Mlle Dupont in support, the play proved an instant success and was revived many times.

piece in one, or two, or three acts', but nothing had been seriously agreed upon. He sent for him, he tells us, and told him to run over the list of his subjects. 'I want a one-act piece for Dupont's benefit,' he said. Durieu asked was he mad, as the benefit was to be in a few days' time. 'That is my business,' replied Dumas. '*There is one day in which to write the piece*, another to have it copied, a third for the reading. There is plenty of margin, you see, for study and rehearsal.'

Durieu suggested a number of plots. *Le Mari de la Veuve* was chosen: in fact what Dumas had done was to send Durieu off to Anicet Bourgeois who wished for an entrée to the Théâtre Français. 'Go and find him,' he said, 'settle the arrangement of the scenes with him, then come and dine with me, and we will map the whole out together.' Now here was a play for which Dumas claimed the whole credit, but of which in fact not only the plot, but the very arrangement of the scenes, were found by two others, while he contributed the dialogue. Anyone who reads the play will see that it is not of such a trifling sort that it could be knocked off in twenty-four hours. It is long, carefully and deliberately written. It may fairly be suspected, from what he was later to do with *La Tour de Nesle*, that his friends brought him the scenes ready-written and that he set himself to rewrite and recast it with that light and airy touch which was particularly his own.

Dumas had now dropped his mask as the misanthropic Manfred or Childe Harold – a mask he had worn exceedingly badly – and had reverted to his normal gaiety and good humour. Despite the cholera, which before it left France accounted for more than 20,000 victims, our irrepressible hero refused to be downhearted. Every evening he invited friends to his apartment – celebrated, agreeable, witty friends, who 'passed the time with anecdotes, discussions, laughter aided by warmth and comfort, good food and good wine'. To these evenings came Hugo, again on friendly terms, Boulanger, Delanoue, Châtillon and Liszt, who 'without any pressing, pounded away on a wretched piano, cursing at it all the time he played'. Here, Harel, no longer on amicable terms with Hugo, turned up every other night to inveigle Dumas into rewriting a play by an unknown dramatist, a certain Frédéric Gaillardet, an ambitious young provincial from Tonnerre. The play was called *La Tour de Nesle*. The plot, according to Harel, was admirably suited to Dumas's genius, but as it stood quite unactable; in Dumas's hands it would take Paris by storm. Dumas kept on putting off Harel, telling him that the plot had already been offered to him twice, once by Roger de Beauvoir and a second time by Fourcade, the brother of Dumas's old friend of Villers-Cotterêts days, the same who had saved him from embarrassment by supplying him with a pair of gloves at the country ball.

On the evening of 15 April, just as Dumas had bade *au revoir* to his guests, he felt a slight trembling in his hands and turned as cold as ice. 'It's strange,' he said to his servant Catherine, as he began to shiver; 'I feel cold.' Catherine immediately recognised the symptoms. 'Oh, *mon dieu*,' she cried. '*Monsieur qui a le choléra!*' Dumas undressed himself as best he could and leapt into bed. He felt his strength ebbing. He told the distraught Catherine to bring him a lump of sugar soaked in ether, and call the doctor. The poor girl, half out of her mind with worry, brought him instead a wine glass filled with neat spirit which the now half-delirious Dumas swallowed in a single draught. For two hours he remained unconscious. When he eventually reopened his eyes, he found himself in a form of vapour bath, effected by the introduction of a tube emitting steam beneath his sheets, in addition to which had been added a warming pan. 'I don't know what will happen to me in Hell,' he writes in his memoirs, 'but I have never been so nearly roasted as I was on that night.' For five or six days, he was confined to bed, which did not prevent Harel calling every day with is *Tour de Nesle*. Finding Dumas too exhausted to read, he narrated the story of the play, or rather it was Verteuil, an actor friend, who was called in to give the readings. Harel, taking no chances, had already approached Janin with a request that he should revise Gaillardet's text. Janin, however, after making some minor improvements on the original, cast it aside. Thus, if one includes Janin, three authors were responsible for the final version, but there is no doubt that at least a large part (Harel claimed four-fifths) of the definitive dialogue was the work of Dumas. It was Dumas who supplied the truly dramatic passages with which the play abounds and provided it with a certain magic quality which held the stage well into the Second Empire.

This collaboration – Gaillardet, Janin and Dumas – created a stir at the time, and it becomes important to consider it in some detail, as it throws a light on 'the great Dumas system'. The attempt to rob a young writer of the reputation and profit from his work cannot be justified, but more discreditable was the garbled, confusing account given by Dumas of how rights and attributes of royalties were finally settled. It must be admitted that the play would never have been the success it proved to be without Dumas, but both Gaillardet and Janin deserved more consideration than he was prepared to give them. That he had twice been offered the plot, as he claims, once by Beauvoir and a second time by Fourcade, and that he had turned it down seems highly improbable, since it was just the sort of plot that would have had an immense appeal to him. Today the plot would seem outrageously outdated – just as *Murder in the Red Barn* is. Briefly, it turns on the nymphomaniac Queen Marguerite of Burgundy, wife of Louis X, and her sisters-in-law, Blanche de la Marche and Jeanne de Poitiers, luring young men into her secret apartments in the gloomy tower – La Tour de Nesle – where, once having satisfied their lust, they had the unfortunate lovers thrown into the Seine. Finally the queen is outsmarted by one Buridan, a man of determined character, who threatens to reveal her identity. However absurd the plot may seem today, Dumas's inimitable gift of dialogue assured it an immediate success. It did not matter that the details of the play were quite imaginary. What is historically correct, however, is that Marguerite and her sisters-in-law were accused of adultery. Louis X (1289–1316) had the queen, after a long imprisonment, smothered between two mattresses and her sisters-in-law banished.

When the play was completed, it was agreed that it should appear under the name of Gaillardet, who by law would enjoy the whole of the author's rights, namely the equivalent today of two pounds per night and sixty tickets which he could sell. These perquisites were not to be divided; the young man was to have the whole. This, at least, was the contract which Gaillardet signed with Harel. What at the time the young man did not know was that, by a private arrangement, Harel had agreed to give Dumas the equivalent of fourteen pounds a night, in addition to the usual free tickets.

Omitting to mention the private transaction he had concluded with Harel, Dumas wrote to Gaillardet. He told him that Harel had consulted him in reference to his play; that he had given his views with pleasure, that he was 'delighted to introduce to the stage a young confrère whom I have not the pleasure of knowing, but whose success I warmly desire . . . It is hardly necessary for me to say you will be the sole author and that my name is not to be mentioned. This little service you must allow me to offer you and not sell you.'

Gaillardet could not accept the sincerity of this letter. He wrote to Harel that he had wanted no help and needed none. He had never asked for his play to be 'revised'. Harel apologised, but explained that it was too late – the play was already in rehearsal. Gaillardet, he added, could of course go to law if he chose, but surely Monsieur Dumas had done him a good turn, etc. Gaillardet seems to have been no fool. There had already been talk of Dumas's methods. Some drudge of a young tyro furnished a good plot for which he would be paid; Dumas would then touch it up or even rewrite it altogether. He would then have the chief credit and the major profits. No doubt there were many young writers who would be delighted to work on such terms, but such an arrangement in the present instance was not acceptable to the impetuous young Gaillardet.

Was Gaillardet really the victim of a grave injustice? The impetuous young man from Tonnerre certainly thought so, but the critic and writer Jules Janin had already expressed his view that the original version was worthless, and Janin was a critic on whom one can rely – was he not the first to champion Hector Berlioz? We may be sure that without Dumas's inimitable touch, *La Tour du Nesle* would never have seen the light of day.

On its opening night the play caused a furore. That evening Dumas dined with Odilon Barrot, and brought 'the great tribune', as our hero calls him, to the theatre. Throughout dinner he had been on thorns to get away from the table. But all was well; the trio arrived in time to see the curtain rise. Scene succeeded scene; 'it was all terrible, men and women trembling with excitement', as Dumas loves to describe it. 'Success was in the very air.' Harel, the manager, saw here a great success for his theatre, and flew to Dumas to impore him to allow his name to appear on the play bills. But Dumas was firm. The piece was destined to be played eight hundred times. This prestige and glory he determined to sacrifice. He held firm, and amid tumultous applause and shouts for 'Author!' M Frédéric Gaillardet was proclaimed sole author.

This might seem to Dumas's credit, but on the other hand he had to all intents stolen Gaillardet's plot (it is beside the point that Gaillardet had himself 'borrowed' the story) and Dumas was financially the gainer. Secondly, one can be sure that he kept it no secret that he, not Gaillardet, was the real author. No one really would believe that he just touched it up here and there. He insisted that he had come to an agreement with the 'young man', as he persisted in styling him (to the young man's annoyance), which was quite untrue. Dumas's secret arrangement with Harel had been made without Gaillardet's knowledge. Dumas seems to have been surprised that the young man should be anxious for more prestige. Did he not have his name as author on the play bills, did he not obtain his two tickets and his two pounds a night?

But despite Dumas's insistence that his own name should not appear on the play bills, Harel was far less scrupulous. Seeing, on the reception of the first night, what a run he might expect for the piece, he coolly announced in the newspapers of the next morning that the play was 'by MM *** et Gaillardet'. Everyone would of course know for whom the three stars stood. Dumas tells us that he immediately went to Harel to protest. He found him chuckling over the business. 'My dear sir, we shall have a tremendous success. All we needed was a little scandal. Gaillardet will make a fuss – there we will have it. At all events he will have *done something for the piece*.'

The play had been running for two years – not night after night, but at judicious intervals. The dispute between the parties had become more and more embittered. The indefatigable Gaillardet could fight his own battle with spirit, and actually summoned Dumas before the 'committee of authors'. No less than six decisions were given by the courts, all adverse to Dumas. After two years the public began to forget the dispute, until it was revived again by an allusion of Gaillardet's in a periodical. This called out angry and recriminating letters on both sides; correspondence thus wound up by Gaillardet: 'Do you know, M Dumas – you, who affect to treat me as if I was some poor devil – the sort of answer I ought to make you? But I have too much politeness to tell you.' He then speaks of 'disgrace', 'apostasy', 'shame'.

This indignant exposé of Dumas's behaviour and methods of work was so cutting and so damaging that only one sort of reply could be sent. This was a challenge; and a duel was fixed for 17 October 1834.

A duel was fought, or at least pistol shots were exchanged, but neither party was hurt. For a while Dumas's reputation was damaged, but soon other extravagances of the writer caused the matter to be forgotten. Twenty-five years later, when he wrote his memoirs, one might have thought he would allow this episode to be forgotten; a shrewd and sensible man would wisely have done so. Dumas, however, revives the whole with all the offensive letters, and protests 'that God knew he would not for the world say anything that would rouse slumbering susceptibilities of M Gaillardet'. He had heard, indeed, that the latter had made a fortune in America, 'to my sincere joy', to his still greater joy he had learned that his (Dumas's) books had something to do with that good fortune. Such is his retrospect of the affair. Dumas's publishers, however, took care to produce a letter written by Gaillardet at a still later period, when the play was being revived. 'As you are reviving the piece,' he wrote to the manager, 'I give you full permission, and would ask you at the same time to join with my name that of M Alexandre Dumas, my partner, to whom I am anxious to show that I have forgotten our old disputes, and recollect only our friendly relations of later years, and the important share which his incomparable talent had in the success of *La Tour de Nesle*.'

CHAPTER SIXTEEN

Temporary Exile

Before his dispute with Gaillardet was composed, Dumas was again to be involved in his usual impetuous way in further political troubles. The noisy and turbulent republicans with whom he associated, and whom nothing could satisfy, were eagerly seeking every pretext for another demonstration. This was soon found on the occasion of the funeral of Lamarque, an old Bonapartist general. General Lamarque had known Dumas's father and had been initmate with the son. The general's family had therefore requested Alexandre to act as director of the solemnities, which gave him a welcome opportunity of again figuring in uniform on a public occasion.

The artillery National Guard had been reorganised on a new footing. All the revolutionary elements were present in a vast procession, and it seems to have been arranged that an attempt should be made to renew the scenes of July, which had been so successful. As the funeral procession passed along, it was interrupted by various incidents, which had nearly led to riots; but the 'commissary' of the cortège, as Alexandre dubbed himself, was always at hand. 'I ran forward to find out the cause of the stoppage. Thanks to my uniform, and to a certain popularity which always attended me, and, above all, to a tricoloured scarf, fringed with gold, which I wore on my left arm, the crowd opened before me.' Every moment, he recounts, a murderous riot was on the point of breaking out. A gendarme, in a scuffle with a man, cut his assailant's throat with a sword. The crowd might well have torn him to pieces; but when the gendarme saw Dumas and his uniform, he rushed to him, shouting, 'Oh, save me!' and the 'commissary', pushing him into the ranks of the artillery, rescued him from the mob.

When the bridge was reached where the speech-making was to

165

commence, Alexandre began to feel exhausted and ready to faint. He had not yet recovered from his attack of cholera, and with some friends left his duties to go and dine at a café. While there, sounds of musketry were heard; fighting had begun. He was now anxious to get home to exchange his uniform for plain clothes. Once more in civilian dress, he attended a meeting at which La Fayette and the financier Laffitte were present, but where, he says, he found nothing but talk: 'I left unobtrusively, and this was easy enough, as I was a very unimportant personage and not likely to be missed by any one. My intention was to go to the office of the *National*, but, when I got to the boulevard, I found that fighting was going on in that direction. I could hardly stand from weakness, and was burning with fever. I took a cabriolet and was brought home, fainted away on mounting the stair, and was found insensible on the landing.'

He was undressed and put to bed. After a feverish night, and still very weak, he visited his friend Arago in search of news. Arago, not unnaturally, asked him behind what barricade he had passed the night. 'In my bed, unfortunately,' Dumas replied. Arago told him that he was on his way to visit the King with a deputation to demand that the King should repudiate the excesses of the night before, or grant indulgence now that the riot had collapsed. Alexandre and other young men waited anxiously to hear the result of the delibration. He is proud to be able to quote from the republican historian Louis Blanc who mentions his share in the revolt. 'When Arago came out from the meeting [writes Blanc], he was met by Savary and Alexandre Dumas, by a savant and a poet. Both were greatly excited; and, as soon as they learned what had passed inside, broke out into bitter expostulations, declaring that Paris had only waited for open encouragement to rise, and that the deputies who could thus repudiate the exertions of the people were very guilty in the eyes of their country.'

Later, as he was sitting at the door of the Café de Paris, 'too weak to stand up', he saw the King go by, shaking the outstretched hands of national guards, when the following strange reflection occurred to him. 'Seeing him pass so calm, smiling, and indifferent to danger, I felt a sort of bewilderment, and asked myself, if this man, thus greeted so enthusiastically, were not indeed a chosen man, and whether any one had the right to make attempts against a power which God, by ranging Himself on its side, seemed to sanction?'

Whatever his reflections might have been at that moment, his behaviour during the revolt had certainly been sufficient to compromise him. One newspaper announced that he had been taken fighting in the streets, tried summarily by court martial, and shot at three o'clock in the morning! He had even given away arms to the mob and, though these were only stage muskets, the authorities would hardly entertain such nice distinctions. He indeed received a warning from an aide-de-camp of the King that the question of his arrest was under discussion, and with a friendly hint suggested that he had better travel for a few months until the matter had blown over.

To leave Paris at this moment was far from convenient, as he was busy on a new play for the Porte St-Martin – *Le Fils de l'Emigré* – which the manager was eager he should finish, promising him 250 louis for his expenses if he set seriously to work. Dumas, therefore, sent for his friend and assistant, Anicet Bourgeois, 'that conscientious labourer and indefatigable researcher . . . No one could do his part more handsomely in à joint composition. It was he who had brought me the plan of *Térésa*, ready made. I supplied him with the idea of *Angèle*. The idea of the *Fils de l'Emigré* was his; the execution, especially of the first three acts, was mine. We wrote the last two acts together.' Dumas is profuse in these acknowledgements of assistance in his *Mémoires*; but this was after the *exposé* of his practices. This task accomplished, his eyes turned towards Switzerland, a country he longed to visit. He proposed to Gosselin, his publisher, to write a book of travels, and frankly owns that the latter 'could not see it'. The subject was stale and used up. His doctor, too, declared that his health would be benefited, so that both his political and medical advisers recommend a change of scene. He determined to look on the expédition as a sacrifice paid to health, and also as time fatally lost so far as pecuniary profit was concerned. Having completed *Le Fils de l'Emigré*, one of the worst melodramas he ever wrote, he left Paris on the first of his many exhilarating wanderings.

His infatuation for Belle Krelsamer had run its usual course, but although no longer in love, he could not altogether discard her since she had borne him a daughter, Marie-Alexandrine, on whom he doted. He acquired an apartment for mother and daughter, and left alone.

Disappointment at Gosselin's refusal to consider a travel book on Switzerland was soon forgotten. Our indefatigable hero was determined not only to enjoy his holiday, but to turn it to profitable account. From Montereau, at the start of his journey, to Brig, where his tour ended, he was never without pencil and notebook. Every evening he jotted down the day's events. A ruined castle, a man chasing a runaway donkey, the strange name of an inn or of a town or village, anything extraordinary or intriguing – it was not enough for him to know they were there, he must know *why* they were there. The guide books will give us the descriptions, even the legends, but they cannot give us Dumas, with the events and characters that come in his train. 'Everything in him was emotion and therefore enjoyment. He loved the society of others, but never tired of his own.' So he wrote of d'Artagnan.* Dumas is obviously thinking of himself there, and it is because of this that he was equally master of monologue and dialogue. Of the two he preferred the latter. 'Solitary travel, to have no one with whom to share one's emotions of joy or fear, is a sorry business . . . To hope or fear for another is the one emotion which gives man the supreme proof of his own being,' he writes in *Voyage en Suisse*.

In consequence of his preference for company, Dumas took care never to be long without a companion, and if there is none to be found, he will invent one. He will even take a friend with him in his imagination.

He travelled by way of Montereau, Auxerre, Châlons, Mâcon and Lyon. At Saint-Genis, learning that he was no longer on French soil, he descended from his coach and visited the birthplace of Jean-Jacques Rousseau. 'I breath again,' he wrote to a friend; 'I am in a republican land.' At Ferney he made a pilgrimage to the house of Voltaire, 'the god of those who do not believe in God'. And at Coppet, he paid homage to the memory of Madame de Staël.

From Ferney he travelled via Lausanne to Vevey and Clarence, saw the castle of Chillon and fished in the lake by night with the aid of a lantern. His next halt was at the Hôtel de la Poste at Martigny, where he tells us he enjoyed a delicious bear steak, a story which gained such credence after the publication of *Voyage en Suisse* that the unfortunate landlord of the hotel was driven frantic by the number of tourists demanding bear steaks. (There were of course no bears in Switzerland). The highlights of this tour were his meeting with Balmar, the first man to scale Mont Blanc; his visit to the Saint

* *Le Vicomte de Bragelonne.*

168

Bernard Hospice and the macabre spectacle of its morgue filled with corpses and its floor thick with human dust; his ascent of the Dent du Chat at midnight by the light of torches, and his meeting with the boy Francesco, one of the most charming characters in his book, who was to act as his guide. At Obergestelen he astonished the company at the inn with a masterpiece of an omelette, remarking that 'an omelette is to cookery what the sonnet is to poetry'. It was between Brunnen and Scwyz that Dumas and Francesco fell in with the obstinate donkey which inspired his delightful series of vignettes *Histoire d'un ane, d'un homme, d'un chien et d'une femme*. At Lucerne a very shy Dumas called on his hero, Châteaubriand. The old exile, ex-politician and 'father of Romanticism', invited Dumas to breakfast, and soon put the younger man at his ease. They talked of France and politics. Dumas could not help observing that Châteaubriand's theories were *'royalistes comme la forme [mais] étaient républicaines par le fond'*. To which the old man replied with a smile: *'Cela vous étonne? Mais ça m'étonne bien davantage* [it astonishes me even more]. *J'ai marché sans le vouloir comme un rocher que le torrent roule; et maintenant, voilà que je me trouve plus près de vous que vous de moi.'* (Without meaning to, I have been carried along like a rock in a torrent; and so now here am I, closer to you than you are to me.')

The old man then took Dumas outside while he fed his chickens and then escorted him to see the famous Lion of Lucerne, carved in the rock, which had been commissioned by a republican canton to honour the memory of the 792 gallant Swiss officers and men who died on 10 August 1792 in defence of the Tuileries and royalty. At Staffel he acted as second for a Frenchman who had a duel with an Englishman; next, gun on shoulder, he accompanied a chamois hunter on a hunting expedition. He visited the school of Reichenau where, as a young man and an exile, the future king of France, Louis-Philippe d'Orléans, then Duc de Chartres, had taught geography and history for five francs a day. It was from here that he wrote a pompous letter to the present young Duc d'Orléans, now heir to the throne: 'I tear a page from my notebook, not addressed to the son of the King of France, but to the son of the humble schoolmaster who, etc.'

Dumas, the ardent republican, was always anxious to keep on good terms with the court. In all fairness to Dumas, the young duke seems to have had a genuine liking for his father's former employee which was reciprocated. In fact the young duke was a good friend and however much he might have smiled at Dumas's somewhat absurd letter, he was probably astute enough to realise that Dumas sincerely believed that he was writing something becoming and heroic, however ridiculous. Sycophantic perhaps, but as already mentioned, Dumas humbugged himself just as much as he humbugged others. The young prince even went so far as to solicit Guizot, Minister of the Interior, and later of Public Instruction, to found a theatre especially for the Romantic school. Guizot, in turn, addressed himself to the King, who, though congratulating his son on his artistic tastes, pointed out that neither the privy purse nor the government were prepared to forward a plan which would make both himself and the country bankrupt.

From Reichenau, Dumas proceeded to Arenenberg where Hortense, ex-queen of Holland, stepdaughter and sister-in-law of Napoleon, was living out her exile. Together they walked arm in arm round the garden of her château. The conversation turned to politics; she asked him his opinion on the state of affairs in Paris and finally asked him 'what counsel he would give to a Bonaparte who dreamed of restoring the power and glory of Napoleon'. In reply Dumas made this astonishing statement: 'I would tell him to get his exile revoked, to buy a plot of land in France, and thanks to the immense popularity of his name to get himself elected as deputy, to use his talent to win over the chamber, and to make sure of it to depose Louis-Philippe and become king in his place.' The statement (if he really made it) is astounding, since nineteen years later his advice was realised in the *coup d'état* of 1851.

Dumas spent three days at Arenenberg, and it was here that he saw French newspapers for the first time since his departure from Aix. He was horrified to read headlines in the *Constitutionnel*: '*THEATRE DE LA PORTE SAINT-MARTIN. Le Fils de l'Emigré. Drame par MM Anicet Bourgeois et Alexandre Dumas.*' Before leaving for Switzerland, he had specifically requested that his name should not appear as co-author. Dumas's reason for insisting that his name should not appear on the play bills, just as he had originally refused to acknowledge his share of the authorship of *La Tour de Nesle*, was probably because of the severe notices he had received from the critics for his *Charles VII chez ses grands vassaux*; and he hoped that they would be more lenient towards a new and comparatively unknown author. By the omission of his name, however, just as with the *Tour de Nesle*, he stood to lose no money should the play prove to be a success.

Unfortunately the manager of the Porte Saint-Martin had paid no heed to Dumas's wishes. The reviews could hardly have been more damning. The strange thing is that Dumas gives us in his memoirs a complete synopsis of this play, something he would have been wiser to have forgotten. It is difficult to believe that he could have ever collaborated in such a farrago of adultery, vengeance, murder and incest. In the final act, the audience actually hissed and left the theatre in disgust. It is hardly surprising therefore that on his return to Paris, Dumas temporarily forsook the theatre and plunged into his history, *Gaule et la France*. Throughout the winter of 1832–3 he shut himself up in his rooms and refused for once to be distracted by any social life whatsoever. By the spring, *Gaule et la France* was ready for publication, as were his delightful series of vignettes of his Swiss travels.

Many critics wrote derisively of Dumas's pretensions to historical learning, but Thierry found 'in M Dumas's work boldness, colour, poetry and depth'. But this was not the real Dumas. He himself, in his *Une Vie d'Artiste*, wrote of it that 'it belongs to that class of works that might be made interesting with only half the talent employed by their authors in making them tedious'. It is, of course, a compilation rather than an original creation, but how many histories or biographies are other than compilations? Certainly not the sparkling witty Dumas of *En Suisse*, the first of his *Impressions de Voyage*. The really extraordinary thing about his history is his clairvoyance. He writes:

> We have concluded our work with the death of Charles IV because with the accession of Philippe de Valois a new era commenced for France. The monarchial power had reached its culmination, and was to descend step by step from the feudal domination of Hugues Capet to *the 'Citizen King' Louis-Philippe, the last king, in all probability, of our race.*

He also foretold the re-establishment of a French republic with a five-year government, and a president springing from the people, possessing only a moderate personal fortune with a restricted civil list.

CHAPTER SEVENTEEN

The Return of the Hero

With *Gaule et la France* in the press and *Voyage en Suisse* already appearing in the *Revue des Deux Mondes* in serial form, Dumas threw himself into society life. Now with money in his pocket, earned from the above – especially the infinitely entertaining *En Suisse* – this tall, lanky young man, with his brilliantly coloured waistcoats, elegant frock-coats and multiple trinkets, was once more a familiar figure in all his old haunts. He attended every soirée and himself gave dinner parties every Wednesday, with dishes prepared by himself.

His interest in cooking remained with him all his life and his last great work (unfinished), *Le grand dictionnaire de la Cuisine* (1863), written in the year of his death, is a fascinating combination of recipes (many fantastic), historical anecdotes and autobiographical reminiscences, truly gargantuan in scale. Dumas liked eating – eating well and plentifully, but a gourmet rather than a gourmand. He by no means confined himself only to *la cuisine française*. He did not have to wait for the siege of Paris, when the population were reduced to eating rats and animals from the zoo, before recommending the trunk of a young elephant as excellent as any boiled beef. Dumas never considers the quantity or cost of his recipes; for his *dindon à la Sainte Menehould*, he recommends eighteen right legs of turkeys; left legs, he claims, are tougher, because it is with the left leg that the turkey scratches itself; while for another recipe he recommends 'fifteen stomachs of young sharks'. However, all is not fantasy; Dumas, who never drank spirits or coffee (it was Balzac who was the coffee addict), devotes a whole chapter to this stimulating beverage, which he regarded as a vice. He also disapproved of smoking, since the habit precluded ladies from joining the gentlemen after dinner, thus denying them the benefit of their witty conversation. Presumably he forgave his friend George Sand, to whom he referred as his *bon ami et bonne amie*.

Despite his love of food, the popular image of Dumas as an obese elderly gentleman is misleading. It was not until his later years that he put on weight. We have already mentioned that as a young boy he was exceptionally good-looking. In his thirties, as we can see from the excellent lithograph portrait by his friend Deveria, he was still slim and elegant. Roger de Beauvoir, one of Dumas's close friends, a well-known journalist and wit, describes him at this time as 'a man of fantastic clothes, dazzling waistcoats, dinners of Sardanapalus. He kills horses and loves women.'

Although his *Fils de l'Emigré* was admitted by almost everyone to be a thoroughly bad work which must have done his literary reputation no good, such was Dumas's personal magic, his charisma, that he still drew around him a whole galaxy of wits, writers, painters and musicians. Although not musical (the reader will remember his failure even to tune his violin as a child), he was on the friendliest terms with Rossini and Liszt, and, although he scarcely mentions the great Hector Berlioz in his *Mémoires*, he must have known him well, for Berlioz in his memoirs mentions Dumas three times and on one occasion writes: 'All his life, Dumas was kind to me,'* and in a letter to Liszt, dated March 1834, Berlioz writes '*Je ne puis aller avec vous ce soir chez Dumas*,' which suggests that he was one of those more or less regular guests at Dumas's Wednesday evening dinner parties. We know that Berlioz attended a performance of *Antony* (certainly not the première, as some biographers have suggested, for in 1831 Berlioz was still in Rome); furthermore Dumas's familiarity with Berlioz can be assumed from the fact that at a performance of a very indifferent opera, *Esmeralda* (by Louise Bertin, based on a book by Victor Hugo), one aria alone showed any merit, which in contrast to the rest of the work was loudly applauded. It was rumoured that it had been written by Berlioz and that Dumas 'in his stentorian mulatto voice,† shouted, above the general hubbub, 'It *is* by Berlioz.'

* Like Paganini, who helped him financially.
† Hector Berlioz, *Mémoires*, trans. David Cairns, Victor Gollancz, 1969.

If Dumas quarrelled with anyone it was nearly always forgotten the next day. Of course he fought duels, but most of these were farcical encounters. Of course, too, he had many detractors, but as Eugène Delacroix wrote of him: 'Here is an artist in all the meaning of the word, full of faults impossible to defend, full of excellent qualities impossible to contest, over whom friends and enemies, admirers and detractors alike can rage as they will.'

In these comparatively unproductive years of 1832–5 he had to divide his life between Belle Krelsamer and Ida Ferrier. During the first of these two years he kept house with Bel (as he called her) in his apartment in the Place d'Orléans (where he gave his famous party) or visited Trouville and other Normandy fishing villages. In 1833, he was sharing Ida's apartment in the rue Bleu, a luxurious home very much suited to Dumas's sybaritic tastes. There seem to have been no jealous quarrels between the ladies, probably because both as actresses were more or less dependent on Alexandre's influence to keep them in work. It was Ida, the lesser artist of the two, who was the more ambitious, and also the more extravagant. Of the two, despite her plump figure and lack of talent, it was she who was to become the reigning sultana. But even the two charmers and his enjoyment of artistic society were not sufficient to quench Dumas's thirst for travel. Perhaps he would have left Paris earlier but for the fact that with two mistresses to maintain and his habitual extravagance, not to mention an allowance to his mother (though regrettably meagre – she was obliged to supplement her income by taking in needlework) and school fees for young Alexandre,* he was obliged to write another drama with the aid of Anicet Bourgeois. This was *Angèle*, which was quickly followed by *Catherine Howard*. Although, from a literary point of view, both plays were of mediocre quality, they were financially successful.

Dumas was now in a position to indulge in his zest for travel. The success of Lamartine's *Souvenirs d'Orient*, published in 1832, had 'given him a gigantic idea'. His intention was 'to travel round the Mediterranean, exploring, investigating, visiting places known and unknown and then complete from my researches a vast history, such as had never yet been written'. He says he was heartily sick of writing for the theatre.

---

* Alexandre *fils* was sent to an exclusive school run by Goubeaux, the same who had collaborated with Dumas on *Richard Darlington*, where the boy was made thoroughly miserable by the snobbish pupils who never let him forget he was a bastard and 'half a nigger'.

He may have been heartily sick of writing plays, but it is also true to say that despite the success of *Angèle* and *Catherine Howard*, the more discerning public was beginning to tire of the cloak and dagger, adultery and incest of the so-called realistic plays, although in the provinces these were continuing to enjoy success, especially *Antony* and *La Tour de Nesle*, which were still bringing him in handsome royalties. Heartily sick of the theatre he may have been, but while there was money to be made his career as a dramatist was by no means finished.

Now, with money in his pocket, he visited Lamartine to ask him to work out an itinerary, with which the poet-politician willingly obliged him. Dumas was happy to put Paris behind him. Although he had enjoyed the companionship of café society, life had not been altogether smooth. He had quarrelled with Hugo, the Gaillardet duel had brought ridicule on him (though he preferred to make light of this) and more and more critics were beginning to accuse him of plagiarism and unoriginality, particularly Cassagnac, the champion of Hugo.

On 15 October 1835, provided with letters of credit and accompanied by his friend Jadin the painter, who was to supply him with illustrations for his book, and with the latter's inseparable companion Milord, an English bulldog, Dumas set out for the south.

The trio travelled in a leisurely fashion from Fontainebleau to Marseille. Here Dumas, Jadin and Milord spent a week with Alexandre's friend Méry, a witty author and political satirist. It was while staying with Méry that Dumas learnt the local story of the *chasse au chastre* (*chastre* is a species of wild pigeon), which he was to turn into the successful novel of that name six years later. Here too he met the Catalans (it will be recollected that Edmond Dantès, the hero of *Monte-Cristo*, fell in love with a Catalan girl from Marseille) and saw for the first time the famous Château d'If. At that time tourists went there to see the prison of Mirabeau and the coffin of Kléber, as did Dumas. After 1844, the year *Monte-Cristo* was first published, Mirabeau and Kléber were forgotten, and visitors flocked to visit Dante's supposed cell and the dungeon of the Abbé Faria.

From Marseille the trio continued on their journey by way of Toulon to Florence.* Here they stayed a week while Dumas wrote

---

* His journey was interrupted by a short visit to Paris to superintend the production of *Angèle*.

the first draft of his fantastic drama *Don Juan de Marana*, partly based on *Faust*, while the effective portion can be traced to Mérimée's *Ames en Purgatoire*.

He was now determined to spend some years in Italy. He says he received 'a mission' from M de Remusat, the Minister of the Interior, to visit that country. To these journeys we owe those delightful *Impressions de voyage dans le midi*.

As an avowed republican, Dumas was unable to obtain a passport to visit Naples. He therefore borrowed one from a friend, a M Guichard, and successfully passed the frontier only to be arrested a few days later. With the greatest aplomb, when threatened with prison, Dumas admitted his real identity and produced three letters of introduction, one from the Minister of Foreign Affairs, one from the Minister of the Interior. As for a third letter, he forbade the police commissary to touch it. 'Allow me to show it to you from a distance,' he said. 'It is signed *MARIE-AMELIE,* that is one of the noblest and most holy names to be found on this earth.'* Marie-Amélie, whom Dumas often quotes with an almost holy reverence, was Marie-Amélie de Bourbon, Queen of the French by her marraige to Louis-Philippe. She was daughter of Ferdinand I, King of the Two Sicilies (and thus of Naples). When Dumas had been a member of the Duc d'Orléans' household, the Duke it will be remembered had offered him the post of reader to the Duchess. Naturally the signature of the daughter of the King of the Two Sicilies left no doubt in the mind of the commissary of police that Dumas was a man to be treated with respect. Apologies followed and our hero was treated with all the respect that he considered as his desert.

From Naples, Dumas and Jadin returned to Rome, where he was granted an audience by the Pope. He had brought no court dress, which caused him, he says, considerable embarrassment, for his dress suit was badly worn. The difficulty was represented to his Holiness (Gregory XVI), who good-naturedly waived ceremony. This was once more thanks to the letter of Queen Marie-Amélie.

Dumas felt exceedingly nervous as he ascended the steps of the Vatican. His limbs tottered beneath him; he was obliged to stop. The account of his interview, which took place in November 1835, is a delicious specimen of Dumas's best manner. As he kissed the Pope's

* *Impressions de voyage.*

foot he exclaimed, '*Tibi et Petro,*' an allusion which made the Pope smile. After talking of the missions in India (of which we can be assured Dumas knew nothing) and other subjects, his Holiness then came to the subject of our hero himself. 'Has it ever occurred to you, my son, that in these days of ours the stage ought to be a pulpit, whence the word of God should flow. You seem to speak like a child who, wandering away for a time has not yet forgotten the universal mother of the Church.'

What plays of Dumas had his Holiness ever read? Murder, adultery, incest, horror piled on horror . . . '*wandering away for a time*' indeed!

Dumas claims that he answered: 'One would think that your Holiness had read to the very bottom of my soul.' He said he wished to act as a missionary, but that he did not dare. The real authors of the corruption were, he said, Voltaire and Beaumarchais. This from the author of *Térésa* and *Antony*. But if encouraged by his Holiness he might attempt the task. Had he chosen a subject? asked the Pope. Dumas replied that he had long had the idea of writing a play on Caligula. His Holiness suggested that the early Christians might be introduced. Dumas hinted at dramatic difficulties, but would consider the matter; he tactfully made no mention of Messalina.

It is quite possible that he did really entertain the Pope with conversation of this kind. He probably believed that all he recorded was true. As a near-contemporary of his wrote: 'He was so far genuine that he lived in delusions and distortions of every kind, his vanity and impulsiveness blending his mental and corporal vision to the most extravagant degree.'*

Notwithstanding the cordial reception from his Holiness, he was nevertheless again arrested, this time by the papal police, and sent to the frontier under the escort of two *carabinieri* who never left his side. It would seem that throughout his whole journey the news had preceded him that he was a dangerous revolutionary. Considering that he had been obliged to leave Paris only three years previously for his republican opinions, this was perhaps not surprising. He tells us that he complained to the French ambassador and in consequence received handsome apologies from the Pope.

From the Papal States he visited Florence and there passed some time. In the same year he made a tour round Sicily in a small vessel,

* Percy Fitzgerald, 1873.

the account of which journey he published under the title of *Le Capitaine Aréna* in 1842. All his Italian adventures were written up either by himself or under his direction. Included in *Impressions de voyage*, were *Corricolo* (published 1843), an account of Naples, and *Le Speronare** (1842) and an account of Florence, which, according to his detractors, was written by a friend, one Fiorentino, but it has nevertheless the genuine Dumas touch. All his 'impressions' are full of wit and originality with little of the pilferings from other writers.

Dumas wrote that the three months spent on the *Speronare* in the company of his Sicilian sailors were the happiest in his life. Certainly these three months were packed with adventure from beginning to end. From the first minute to the last, their journey was filled with memorable happenings – dangers from volcanoes, water-spouts, whirlwinds, and the ever present fear of *banditti*. They explored Capri, Messina, Catánia, climbed Etna, visited Syracuse, made the ascent of Stromboli and put in for a few days at Palermo (where twenty-five years later Dumas was to meet Garibaldi); they also visited Maida, where, on 1 July 1806, a British force under General Stuart had confronted for the first time the so far invincible Napoleonic troops, commanded by General Reynier, and despite the difficulty of an amphibious landing, had achieved an overwhelming victory, a victory which would have been even more decisive had Stuart possessed cavalry to follow up the routed enemy. How many Englishmen realise today that a district of London, Maida Vale, is named after General Stuart's victory?

In February 1836 Dumas was back in Paris. A great deal had happened in France during his absence. There had occurred the abortive 'legitimist' rising of the Duchesse de Berry in favour of her son 'Henri V', and her ignominious capture in Nantes where she was found hiding in a chimney-piece – an occasion which caused considerable stir. There had been other Carlist and republican plots against the reigning monarchy. Once again there had been barricades in the streets. In 1835 an attempt on the King's life by Fieschi had failed, but eighteen members of the royal entourage had been killed, including Marshal Marmont.

---

* A light sailing vessel. Giuseppe Aréna was the captain of this little craft.

The press was henceforth severely indicted, and to call oneself a republican was tantamount to treason. Even the partisans of Louis-Philippe were divided. The popular newspaper *Le Siècle* had been founded by Odilon Barrot and La Fayette, and had as its slogan '*la gauche dynastique*'; and *Le Constitutionnel*, directed by Thiers, advocated a parliamentary regime on the English model; there was also the *Tiers Parti* which attempted to take a middle course (among whose members was Dupin, president of the Chambre des Députés), and finally the *Centre droit*, with Guizot and Molé, who edited the *Journal des Débats* (which was secretly subsidised by the court), and which advocated fuller political powers to the King. In fact the various shades of Orléanist opinion, all basically conservative, were influenced not so much by any particular political or social programme, as by political ambition on the part of their editors. There was also the republican or radical side, represented by Armand Carrel, Auguste Blanqui, Ledru-Rollin and Armand Barbé's *Le Figaro*, and the literary *Revue des Deux Mondes*; newspapers were proliferating and thriving.

Such was the Paris to which Dumas returned. But his whole life had been passed in such turbulent times that little seemed to have changed. On the domestic side he found that Ida had grown even more plump; his mother was now an ageing, bed-ridden old woman; his son, the twelve-year-old Alexandre, was a tall, unhappy, gangly schoolboy, living under the same roof as Ida. Their dislike of each other was mutual.

On his return Dumas was immediately badgered by Harel to write another play. He made all haste to secure a performance of *Don Juan de Marana*, which was to mark his comeback to the stage after nearly two years' silence.* *Don Juan* proved a miserable failure. Played at the Porte Saint-Martin on 30 April 1836, it met with a cold reception from public and critics as well. It is hardly a play at all and is perhaps best described as a hurriedly concocted 'mystery' partly in prose, partly in verse, partly, as already mentioned, based on Goethe, partly on Merimée, with music, spirits, devils, scenes in heaven, earth and hell and all the Don Juan legends jumbled pellmell. *Caligula*, too, was an ignominious failure. However, if *Don Juan* and *Caligula* were failures, *Kean* was a tremendous success. With Frédérick Lemaître in

---

* A list of his other writings at this period will be found in the Appendix.

the leading role, who in character was so like the great English actor himself, it could scarcely fail. But apart from Lemaître, it was a good play and even today, in a revised version by Jean-Paul Sartre, it has proved its merits.

CHAPTER EIGHTEEN

New Experiments

In 1837 there occurred the marriage of Dumas's young friend and patron the Duc d'Orléans. Louis-Philippe had tried to get one of the Austrian archduchesses as a bride for his son, but 'the family of kings' cold-shouldered the 'usurper'. Instead he was obliged to fall back on a German princess, Helena von Mecklenburg-Schwerin. The young duke was probably lucky, since Helena was a cultivated, charming young woman, very different from the stiff, protocol-ridden Habsburg archduchesses.

Louis-Philippe announced that the occasion was to be celebrated by a banquet at Versailles followed by a splendid ball and a performance of Molière's *Le Misanthrope* (presumably only one act, as the play is so long) in which Mlle Mars was to perform. At the same time a special honours list was proclaimed, which included Victor Hugo. In the first draft of those to be honoured Dumas's name had appeared, but had been struck out by the King. He was prepared to invite him to the festivities, but was averse to honouring a well-known republican, an artillery man of the National Guard and an insubordinate junior clerk at the Palais Royal. Dumas was deeply hurt and returned the invitation sent to him for the festivities. Victor Hugo, who by now was quite reconciled with Dumas, was completely on the side of his colleague. He generously wrote to the Duc d'Orléans, explaining that he too would not be present and gave the reasons for his abstention. The royal duke who was a great admirer of both writers was extremely disappointed, as was the young duchess, who had been looking forward to meeting her two favourite authors. Both petitioned the King who, thanks to their joint solicitation, granted Dumas the coveted honour of *chevalier* of the Légion d'Honneur.

Another version of the story, that is to say Dumas's version, is that on the occasion of the Duke's marriage, the King allowed his son the disposal of four crosses. The grand cross was for Arago; the rosette of an officer's cross for Thierry and Hugo, while that of a simple cross of a *chevalier* was given to Dumas and at the same time, as if to mortify him, a similar cross was given 'to an obscure person'. 'Thereupon,' Dumas tells us, 'instead of hanging it from my buttonhole, I put it in my pocket.' I cannot believe this for a moment. There is plenty of evidence to show that Dumas was as pleased as punch with his decoration and would walk the whole length of the boulevard wearing an enormous cross, together with the Order of Isabella the Catholic, a Belgian decoration, the Swedish Cross of Gustavus Vasa and the Order of St John of Jerusalem. In every country he visited he always solicited a decoration and bought any that were for sale. According to Théophile Gautier, 'His coat on high days and holidays was a regular show piece of medals and ribbons.'

Following Dumas's comparative failures with *Don Juan de Marana* and *Caligula,* and despite the success of *Kean,* two years passed without a return to the stage. He had written a dozen successful plays and it certainly was not the failure of *Don Juan* and *Caligula* that now made him turn his hand to other literary fields. He was a born experimenter and he was not content to rest upon his laurels. In the following two years he was forever studying; learning and trying out new fields. The short story, the *chronique* history, the novel, historical romance (he had discovered Froissart and Scott's *Quentin Durward* and had realised the possibilities of an historical *French* novel, as opposed to a play), travel impressions, autobiography, *causeries* and poetry. With the exception of the first and last he was to be successful in all, but it was the historical novel that was to earn him immortal fame.

In all this whirl of work he was to receive a heavy shock in the loss of his mother.

It was on 1 August 1836, while writing one of his first historical novels, *Acté**, that a messenger came running to his door to tell him

---

* A bad novel. Acté was the Christian mistress of the Emperor Nero.

that Madame Dumas had been seized with a stroke at her humble lodgings in the Faubourg du Roule. Dumas immediately hurried to her side to find her unconscious. This was the second attack of its kind from which she had suffered. Dumas, although, it must be admitted, a neglectful son, truly loved his mother, but even at her death bed the dramatist in him, rather than genuine filial love, was foremost, or so it would appear from his writing. 'I required a miracle – that she should live,' he wrote. 'If passionate prayers were uttered over the face of dying mothers, they were then . . . I wanted someone to whom to open my heart. I took a pen, sat down, and wrote to the Prince Royal.'

This very odd proceeding had its effect. Our republican hero wrote: 'Beside the bed of a dying mother I prayed that God would preserve to the Duke his mother and father.' In about an hour's time, a servant in royal livery presented himself at his door who explained he had come on behalf of the Prince to inquire after the health of Madame Dumas. 'Very bad – no hope,' replied her son; 'thank his Highness most heartily for me.' 'I ought to tell you, *monsieur*,' said the servant, 'that his Royal Highness is below.'

Dumas ran downstairs to find the Prince seated in his carriage. Dumas, in his account of the incident cannot help but be extravagant. The door of the carriage, he says, was open, he laid his head upon the Prince's knees, and wept there, in the open street, for a considerable time. He could not say for how long: 'All I know is that the night was calm, and I could see, through the window of the opposite door, the stars of heaven glittering.'

It seems very strange that of all people, in his moment of grief, he should have written to the heir to the throne. How intimate was their friendship?

The republican continued to seek the friendship and patronage of the court. Being on such good terms with the heir to the throne, it occurred to him that he might put his friendship to commercial purpose. The young duke was an enthusiastic soldier, who had distinguished himself in the field. Alexandre therefore proposed to him to write a 'History of the French Army' by regiments. The proposal was accepted, and the Prince agreed to give him the handsome sum of 320 *livres* a volume. This was in the year 1838, and Dumas must have known that he had too much work on hand to undertake the task. But unable to resist such a princely fee he farmed out the work to an assistant who was to receive eighty *livres* a volume for his share. Only three volumes were finished, containing the history of three regiments. The history was not only full of inaccuracies but badly written; nevertheless, Dumas, on the grounds that he had had to do so much research(!) pressed for another eighty *livres*. This was conceded by the Duke, who only deferred payment until completion of the work. The Duke's death in 1842 (to which I shall have occasion to refer later) stopped the project, although one volume was in fact published. Alexandre with all his sympathy for the Duchess Helena, the 'sainted widow' as he called her, pressed her for the 'few *sous*' (as he called it) that were owing to him. The secretary of the household refused the demand, whereupon Dumas, whose behaviour was often unpredictable, replied to the secretary: 'As for the eighty *livres*, the Duchess can keep them. I am only too well accustomed to publishers becoming bankrupt!'

It is often difficult to follow chronologically incidents in the life of Dumas. It may well have been prior to the Duc d'Orléans' wedding that he had proposed the writing of the military history, and it was thanks to the young prince that he had ingratiated himself with the King. One version of the story is that before undertaking this history, the Duke had observed that Dumas had become gloomy and had lost all his wit. Pressed for a reason, Dumas confessed that he was troubled in mind; in fact he wanted to be reconciled with the court. The Prince promised to do his best and often introduced his name, but the King only shrugged his shoulders when the name was mentioned. The good-natured Duke then thought of a little ruse. One day when the King was to pass through his galleries of Versailles, Dumas was posted in ambush, and as the King walked by, he rushed out and prostrated himself before his sovereign. Half displeased, half amused, Louis-Philippe bent forward, pinched his ear (a touch of Napoleon here) and raising him up, said in a loud voice, which everyone could hear: 'Grown-up schoolboy!' He then passed on, leaving Dumas in ecstasies at the reconciliation. Three days later the Cross of the Legion was sent to him.*

* This is the version from *Fabrique de Romans* (a work I have been unable to trace). Cited by P. Fitzgerald, 1873.

CHAPTER NINETEEN

Marriage and the Death of a Prince

Despite the pleasure Dumas received from his reconciliation with the throne and the decoration conferred on him, the loss of his mother made life in Paris for the time being intolerable. He decided to try to forget his grief in travel. He hastily finished *Acté*, which bore the dedication: *To the memory of my mother, who died while I was completing this work,* and set out for Germany, taking Ida with him.

He went by way of Brussels, Antwerp, Ghent, Bruges, Liège, Aix-la-Chapelle, Cologne. At Cologne he saw the Rhine for the first time. As he travelled up the river to Frankfurt, he caught something of its magic with its cliffs crowned with castles, its ruins and legends, which had inspired his favourite German authors. It had been arranged that at Frankfurt he was to meet Gérard de Nerval. The trio visited Mannheim, Heidelberg, and Baden-Baden. The holiday was a short one, but it restored Dumas's old exuberant spirits and resulted in a small travel book: *Excursions sur les Bords du Rhin*, which however was not published until three years later.

On his return to Paris in November, Dumas removed to 22 rue de Rivoli with Ida. Although he had only a short while ago made it clear that he had lost interest in the theatre, his short holiday had obviously been beneficial. He now set to work on two plays in collaboration with Nerval, *L'Alchimiste* and *Léo Burckhart*. The first had an Italian setting, the second, German. They were both inferior works, which proved unpopular, but a third, *Mademoiselle de Belle-Isle*, a comedy of manners set in the eighteenth century, which after five years of mental gestation he now put on paper, proved an unqualified success.

For the first time since *En Suisse*, everyone, with few exceptions, critics, rivals and friends, applauded his work.

By 1838 the Romantic drama was entering its last phase. Violence and brutality, blood and lust, had begun to sicken the most besotted of its supporters. The Romantics had trampled on Corneille, Racine and Molière in favour of what they called realism. Of course it was no more realistic than modern horror films, and, for all that, Hugo, Dumas and others might claim, plays such as *Antony, Richard Darlington, La Tour de Nesle, Le Fils de l'Emigré, Angèle* and *Le Roi s'amuse* owed little or nothing to Byron or Shakespeare.

Not only were the public tired of blood and lust, but suddenly with the appearance of the brilliant young Jewish actress Rachel on the boards of the Comédie-Française (her début was as Camille in Corneille's *Horace* on 12 June 1838), the French public suddenly awoke to the fact that the old classical tragedies of Racine and Corneille and the comedies of Molière were not the dull fustian that the younger generation of playwrights and their supporters had represented them to be, but were masterpieces.

The Théâtre Français, which for so long had been playing to empty houses, was now attracting a new public. Paris had discovered that it possessed a great literary heritage and the Français was packed.

With the Français now playing classical repertoire, the public flocking to see Rachel in the leading roles, and critics such as Janin, Veron, de Girardin, Saint-Beuve and de Musset rejoicing at the coming of an interpreter who could 'reinstate the true gods and chase the false ones from the sacred shrine', the Porte Saint-Martin had lost its popularity; Harel was desperately trying to transform it into a circus; the management of the Odéon had no further use for the Romantics. A year or two earlier, L'Alchimiste and *Léo Burckhart* might have proved successful, but with *Mademoiselle de Belle-Isle*, it would seem that Dumas had seen how the wind was blowing.

This delightful comedy was first produced at the Comédie-Française in 1839. It has a touch of Marivaux, Beaumarchais and even of Claude Crébillon. The story, set in the eighteenth century, is slight and tart. The greatest libertine of the time, the Duc Armand de Richelieu, wagers a group of roués that he will make the conquest of the first lady who passes through the gallery in which they are gathered, and will be received that very same evening at midnight in her chamber. At this point the arrival is announced of the Marquise de

Prie, the Duc de Bourbon's mistress, a lady whose reputation for her numerous love affairs quite equalled Richelieu's.

'Gentlemen,' says Richelieu, 'she does not count. I'd be stealing your money.'

Now, at the end of the gallery, appears Mlle de Belle-Isle, a young lady who has come to petition Bourbon's mistress to save her father, imprisoned in the Bastille. A certain young d'Aubigny says, 'I am to marry the lady! Monsieur de Richelieu means to dishonour her tonight? I answer for her.'

The bet stands.

In Act 2, the Marquise de Prie, who has taken the young girl under her wing, puts her into a carriage and sends her secretly to the Bastille to see her father. She then herself goes into Mlle de Belle-Isle's bedroom and waits in the darkness for the enterprising Duke.

'In point of fact,' wrote Saint-Beuve, who was never very favourable to Dumas, 'it is quite inconceivable that the Duke should not almost at once have realized from forensic medical reasons, the trick that was being played on him.' But as he points out a theatre audience will accept anything, especially the improbable, and in this case the public accepted the situation at its face value and was only too willing to believe that Richelieu really does think that when he creeps into bed with Madame de Prie that he is violating a virgin. Consequently, the Duke, in perfect good faith, sends a note to d'Aubigny announcing that he has won his wager.

To quote Maurois: 'Up to this point we have been moving in the world of Marivaux or rather of Crébillon. But it must not be forgotten that we are dealing with Dumas, "that churner up of passions" (as Théophile Gautier called him), who loved drama above all things and had a solid basis of popular morality. He had dishonoured many young girls in his time, but as a playwright he frowned on such villainy, and from the third act onwards, Dumas mixes feeling with comedy.' In the third act there is a scene in which d'Aubigny confronts his betrothed, who is unable to admit that she had secretly spent the evening visiting her father in the Bastille. 'What was begun as a wager had become an emotional torment.' All ends well, however, on a note of comedy, and the gaiety of the dénouement seems the sweeter for being unexpected. The Duc de Richelieu, to whom Mme de Prie has revealed the truth, appears in the nick of time to reassure everybody. The solemn d'Aubigny has the last word. He continues an introduction: 'Mademoiselle de Belle-Isle, my wife . . . Monsieur de Richelieu, my best friend.'

Although the success of *Mademoiselle de Belle-Isle* must have pleased him, Dumas was still unsure of himself. Between 1839 and 1842 he continued to write, but of all his works none stand out of any importance, with the exception of *La Chasse au Chastre* and *Le Capitaine Pamphile*, both short novels. These are the first two works of fiction from Dumas's pen to hold a permanent place in his vast output. It is true that with *Un Mariage sous Louis XV*, written in 1841 – another comedy for the theatre commissioned by Remusat, the Minister of the Interior, for the Théâtre Français – he nearly rose to the same heights as he had achieved with *Mademoiselle de Belle-Isle*. But it was not until 1843, with *Les Demoiselles de Saint Cyr*, the last of the trio of great comedies, that Dumas reached the peak of his career as a dramatist. This comedy of 1700, featuring Mesdames de Maintenon and Ursins as the two chief *intrigantes*, has been played the most frequently of all Dumas's plays, *Mademoiselle de Belle-Isle* excepted. Two hundred and twenty-six performances were given at the Comédie-Française alone up to 1892; and it was the play that Queen Victoria and Prince Albert chose to have performed on the occasion of their visit to Paris in 1855.*

After *Les Demoiselles de Saint-Cyr*, Dumas can be said to have turned his back on the theatre and now started on his career as novelist. This, as A. C. Bell points out,† does not mean to say that he lost interest in the theatre. After 1843 there followed almost as many plays as had preceded it, among them *Le Comte Hermann*, *Romulus*, *La Conscience* and *Catalina*, but at infrequent intervals. None of them is remembered today.‡

As already mentioned, Dumas had for some time been living with Ida Ferrier. Now in 1840, two years previous to writing *Les Demoiselles de St-Cyr*, he married her, much to the disgust of his son.

---

* A. C. Bell, *Alexandre Dumas.*

† ibid.

‡ For a detailed analysis of these plays, the reader is referred to Hippolyte Parigot, *Alexandre Dumas père*, Hachette, Paris, 1902.

Dumas had no illusions about her. Why then should he have married her? It was said that he had committed a social solecism by taking her to a reception given by Duc d'Orléans, hoping that she would pass unnoticed in the crowd of guests. The Prince, however, had noticed her and had said to him in a low voice, 'I am delighted to make the acquaintance of Madame Dumas, and hope that you will present your wife to us on a less formal occasion.' This, if the story be true, would have not only been a lesson in manners, but tantamount to a royal order. It is a good story but highly improbable. The duke was killed in a carriage accident, two years after his marriage. Viel-Castel maintains that the habitually extravagant Ida had brought back some bills which Dumas had backed and had then offered him the choice between marrying her or going to prison for debt. An actor, René Luguet, said that Dumas, when the question was put to him, had replied, 'I did it to get rid of her!'

Whether this story is true or not, the fact remains that after six years, Dumas was already tired of Ida. It would seem that he only married her to find an excuse to divorce her and get her off his shoulders for good!

There are so many conflicting stories about the marriage, that it is very difficult to unravel the truth. Even the date of the marriage was at one time a matter of dispute. It has however now been definitely established that the contract of marriage was signed in the presence of Maître Desmonèches at La Villette, on 1 February 1840. Witnesses for the husband were the Vicomte de Châteaubriand and François Villemain, minister of public instruction in the Guizot cabinet. Those for the bride were the Vicomte de Narbonne-Lara and the Vicomte de la Bonadière, councillor of state. A Monsieur Jacques Domange, appears for the first time in our story, the wealthy manager of a sewage disposal company; Dumas was at the time in hiding at his house (presumably from his creditors, or from the two Mélanies, Belle Krelsamer and Waldor, who were both furious with him). Domange was on the friendliest terms with Ida and had promised her a dowry of 120,000 francs in French gold and silver currency.

Gustave Claudin attributes to Châteaubriand a saying which is quoted by Maurois in his *Three Musketeers*, which may not be wholly apocryphal. Gazing at the corsage of the bride-to-be, 'the illustrious peer of France' is said to have remarked with some bitterness, referring to both the French monarchy and to Ida's sagging bosom, 'I would have you note that my destiny is always the same, no matter what I bless, it is sure to fall!'

Claudin's evidence, however, is not altogether to be trusted, for he mentions among the witnesses, Roger de Beauvoir, who in fact was not present, and also mentions that the ceremony took place in the chapel of the Chamber of Peers, whereas actually it was in the church of Saint Roch, the parish church of the bridal couple, who at that time were both living in the rue de Rivoli; Claudin also gets the date wrong. Châteaubriand, who was far from well on the appointed day, sent a substitute.

Apparently neither Villemain nor Nodier attended the nuptial mass, and were also represented by friends.

The *curé* of Saint Roch, not realising the substitution of witnesses, made a ridiculous address to the witnesses – none of whom, with the exception of the painter Boulanger, had any pretensions to fame – in the most flattering terms. It seemed, he said, assured that with such illustratious signatories to the marriage not only would Dumas write works (just as the Pope had suggested) which would be lessons in Christian morality, but they would earn him a seat among the immortals of the Académie Française. 'I trust that you, Monsieur de Châteaubriand, and you Monsieur Villemain,' turning to a somewhat obscure architect and to M Domange the sewage disposal contractor, 'will be responsible before God and before men for the literary conversion of this fiery and romantic heretic.'

It might well be supposed that Dumas's marriage to Ida was prompted by the fact he longed to be elected to the Académie (Hugo had recently been elected, a fact of which he was extremely jealous) and was aware that it was his notoriously libertine form of life that had earned him the disapproval of the straitlaced committee. Marriage might make all the difference.

Although Dumas and Ida had lived together for six years, there had never been any real love between them. She was happy to bask in the reflected fame of her lover, to have many roles assigned to her in his plays and to spend his money. As his mistress, Dumas was quite happy to enjoy the company of Ida, who was an admirable hostess and who was prepared to overlook his many infidelities, indeed as he was prepared to overlook hers. Almost immediately after their marriage she was conducting a liaison with Roger de Beauvoir. On one occasion Ida, expecting Dumas to be away from home for the evening, was entertaining de Beauvoir. Dumas, however, bored with his party, returned home early. At the sound of Dumas's footsteps, de Beauvoir leapt from Ida's bed and hid himself in a closet, hastily hiding his clothes. The evening was excessively cold and Dumas was happy to jump in between Ida's warm sheets. De Beauvoir in the closet, on the other hand, was soon too cold to bear this situation any longer and burst into the bedroom. Dumas, apparently not at all put out at the sight of one of his best friends shivering almost naked entering his nuptial chamber, threw him a blanket and told him to warm himself before the fire. But the fire soon died down and Roger's teeth were chattering with cold again. Dumas, unable to sleep, told him not to be a fool and to come to bed before he caught pneumonia. Roger obeyed, and soon the three were comfortably tucked up. Dumas's only comment was: 'What's the use of quarrelling between friends over a little matter like this!' The three were soon happily asleep.

But almost from the start of the marriage, as was obvious to all, particularly Dumas *fils*, it was bound to be a failure. Some years previously, when in Florence, Ida had made the conquest of a noble Italian, Eduardo Alliata, twelfth Prince of Villafranca, Duke of Saponara, Marquis of Santa-Lucia, Baron of Mastra, lord of Miru, Mangiavacca, Viagrande, Prince of the Holy Roman Empire, Count Palatine and Grandee of Spain.

She had, during the past few years – since 1840 – spent several months in Florence, where she was frequently joined by Dumas, who had no objections to her liaison with this immensely wealthy nobleman.

When in 1844 Dumas and Ida agreed on an amicable separation, it was to Florence that he sent her, no doubt in the hopes that his Serene Highness the Prince of Villafranca would relieve him of the financial burden of supporting her. However, for form's sake, by legal settlement dated 15 October 1844, he undertook to pay her an annual allowance of twelve thousand gold francs, with in addition three thousand francs for the upkeep of her carriage. He even offered to buy the lemon-wood furnishings of what had been their bed-chamber for an outright sum of nine thousand francs. On paper this munificence makes an impressive show. It cost him so little to distribute a non-existent allowance, and to undertake in writing to pay out sums of money in draft on a bank account without funds. Her future lay with Villafranca.

Dumas set great store by adopting what he imagined to be a chivalrous attitude towards women. A total breach without legal proceedings would have been out of the question. When Ida finally left for Italy he gave her a letter to the French ambassador:

Dear Ambassador – I send you Madame Dumas, who is as constant to you as is the eternal spring that you enjoy, and returns to claim the hospitality you so elegantly offered her. Be as good to her as you have always shown yourself to others, and some fine morning I shall set off myself to thank you and press your hand.

Yours, with all best wishes of my heart.

A. Dumas

Before the final break-up came, Dumas had already spent some time in Florence. He had taken up residence in the Villa Palmieri. 'It was at the Villa Palmieri,' he says with that wonderful complacency with which he places himself on the level of the great departed, 'that Boccacio had written the *Decameron*. I found that this name would bring me fortune, so I established my bureau in the very room where four hundred and ninety-three years ago the author of the hundred tales had had his.'

Dumas remained in Florence for almost a year. We are now in the year 1842. He became on very intimate terms with the former King of Westphalia, Jerome Napoleon, Prince de Montfort, and his family, whose two sons Jerome and Napoleon (all permanently banished from setting foot on French soil) were glad to cultivate the acquaintance of the now famous Alexandre Dumas.

One evening in July, Dumas was hurrying off to meet these two young men. When they came to meet him they wore gloomy faces. A rumour was abroad of a piece of news which they had hesitated to bring him. 'It concerns one,' they said, 'whom you love more than anyone in the world: the Duke of Orléans is said to have been killed falling out of a coach.' 'I became terribly pale. I felt myself totter and caught hold of Prince Napoleon, covering up my eyes with my hands.' Dumas then writes how he retired to a corner of the garden to weep at his leisure. 'Many loved him dearly no doubt, but few knew him as I did; few loved him as I did.'

This effusion is really too ridiculous for words. To understand the absurdity of this antic (which is here considerably condensed) it should be understood that it was addressed to a daily newspaper! Naturally, the famous Dumas, who loved his poor prince as no one else did, must be seen at the obsequies. He posted night and day and arrived in Paris by three o'clock on the morning of the funeral (2 August). He had a ticket for the *Tribune*, and with some college friends followed the corpse down to Dreux, where it was laid in a vault. He touched it in passing. 'One would have said that it wished to say one last good-bye to me.' Then follows much more in the same vein.

These accounts, published in the newspapers, were of course meant for the royal eye, but it was hopeless to make him see that his effusions were only presenting him in a more and more absurd light and actually frustrating the aim he had in view.

CHAPTER TWENTY

The Novelist is Born

Although Dumas had earlier expressed himself heartily sick of the theatre and was determined to devote himself to writing historical novels it was not until 1844 that he launched out on that enterprise which was to ensure his undying fame – the retelling of the history of France in fiction.

The reason why he was to devote himself almost entirely to the novel was partly circumstantial. The so-called realistic school of blood and thunder had by now almost lost its appeal – even to Dumas himself; with this, and with his three comedies, *Mademoiselle de Belle-Isle*, *Un Mariage sous Louis XV*, and *Les Demoiselles de Saint-Cyr* (the last of which had not quite achieved the success for which he hoped), he may have felt that he had reached the apogee of his career as a dramatist. Walter Scott, as we know, had always attracted him, as he had attracted other contemporary French writers, whose books had enjoyed great success with a minority élite. Hugo alone had reached a wider public. Dumas was not going to be left behind. Although an omniverous reader, he was neither a scholar nor had he the patience for research. It was now that he had the good fortune to renew his acquaintance with Auguste Maquet, a friend of Gérard de Nerval. Maquet was to play an extremely important part in Dumas's life. Maquet was at this time just turned twenty-five years of age. He was a handsome young man, the son of a rich industrialist, and had always entertained a passion for letters. Ever since 1833, at the age of twenty, he had been one of a small group of venturesome, anti-clerical writers and artists: Nerval, Théophile Gautier, Petrus Borel, Arsène Houssaye, and the painter Célestin Nanteuil. He was a teacher at the Lycée Charlemange, but had no enthusiasm for schoolmastering. In 1836 he joined the staff of the *Figaro* and tried his hand at writing plays. He submitted a drama entitled *Soir de Carnaval* to Joly, manager of the Renaissance Théâtre, which was rejected.

It was Gérard de Nerval who suggested that he should submit this 'unwanted child to Dumas, who was an orthopaedist renowned for his skill in straightening the limbs of plays born crooked'. In short, Dumas agreed to help Nerval's young friend. On 29 November 1838, Nerval wrote to the twenty-five-year-old Maquet: 'My dear friend: Dumas has completely rewritten the play in accordance with your original idea. Your name will appear. It has been accepted, has delighted everybody and will be put on ...'

The play was given a new title, *Bathilde*, and was produced on 4 January 1839. Young Maquet was delighted. During the course of the following year he submitted the draft of a novel, *Le Bonhomme Buvat*, to Dumas. The story deals with the conspiracy of Cellamare, the Spanish ambassador who had plotted against the regent. The story is told through the eyes of an obscure copyist, Buvat, who becomes involved in the conspiratorial activities without really understanding what is happening. Dumas found the story much to his liking. The period was one which he had recently used in one of his comedies, and he had 'the manners and atmosphere at his fingertips'. He therefore willingly agreed to refurbish and lengthen Maquet's text.

Thus began a collaboration which was to last many years. It should be noted that *Le Bonhomme Buvat* was a novel, and not a play. Here was Dumas's opportunity to pit his genius against that of Hugo, Balzac and the rest. The time could not have been more propitious. The 'serial story,' or the *feuilleton*, had already begun to make its appearance. For some two years, both Emile Girardin's *La Presse* and Ledru-Rollin's *Le Siècle* had been exerting every effort to extend their readership. The best way to keep up circulation was by publishing instalments of 'thrilling fiction'. 'To be continued in our next' was the formula invented in 1829 by Dr Vernon for use in the *Revue de Paris*. But it was not always the best authors who could write in serial form. Balzac is a good example – genius that he is, his books could never be divided into *feuilletons*. The long, topographical descriptions which occupy the first pages of his novels would inevitably fail to hold the readers' attention. On the other hand, Eugène Sue, Frédéric Soulié and Alexandre Dumas became masters of the *feuilleton*.

Dumas had given a great deal of thought to the serial form. Although he admired Walter Scott immensely, he realised that the Scottish writer would be incapable of writing a serial. Scott established his characters from the first page, by indulging in long descriptions of their peculiarities; but in a serial, which must hold its readers' attention from the very first lines, the author cannot permit himself a long-drawn-out beginning, and Dumas, capitalising on this, jumps immediately into dialogue and action. In practically every one of his many novels he supplies his readers in his opening paragraph with time, date and place. In a serial, Dumas realised, an author has no right ever to be boring. In 1838, one of his serial novels, *Le Capitaine Paul*, earned the *Siècle* five thousand new subscribers in three weeks. No wonder he was popular. He rarely leaves the reader in any doubt, from the very start, of the period and setting of his novel. For example, he writes, 'On Monday, the eighteenth day of the month of August 1572' (*La Reine Margot*). Often he omits the day of the week, merely a date, or vice versa, but gives exact times; for example, 'At the beginning of May in the year 1738, as ten o'clock sounded. . .' (*Amaury*); or again, 'In the early days of April 1784, at about a quarter past three in the afternoon . . .' (*Le Collier de la Reine*); or 'In the middle of the month of May in the year 1666, at nine o'clock in the morning, when the warmth of the sun was already drying the dew on the wall flowers of the Château of Blois . . .' He thus gives an impression of verisimilitude to his tale.

Another favourite gambit was to introduce his characters as though they appear to be crossing a 'threshold' into the story. Take for example the opening lines of the *Vicomte de Bragelonne:* 'Towards the middle of the month of May in the year 1666 . . . a small cavalcade of three horsemen and two pages *entered* by the *bridge* of the city . . . Or, 'It was on 10 July in the year of grace 1540, there *entered the precincts* of the University by the *gateway* of the church . . .'* (*Ascanio, ou l'orfèvre du roi*).

Again and again, with open (or sometimes closed) doors or frontiers, or over bridges, the reader is introduced into another world. This applies particularly to his earlier novels. In the later ones he assumes that the reader is already familiar with his 'inner world', taking for granted that his public has read his previous romances. Here is the beginning of *Le Collier de la Reine:* 'In the first days of

* My italics throughout.

Charles Nodier. 1824. Dumas's first patron.

Below (right) Auguste Maquet. Dumas's most faithful collaborator. *(left)* Adah Isaacs Menken. The last of Dumas's many loves.

(left) Contemporary caricature of Dumas striding across the Alps, published after the appearance of his travel book *En Suisse*.

(right) Contemporary title page for collected works by Dumas showing his 'folly' of Monte Cristo.

April 1784 . . . the old Maréchal de Richelieu, *our old acquaintance
. . .*' or again in *Vingt ans après*: 'In a chamber in the Palais-Cardinal,
which we already know . . .' He sometimes even goes as far as to write,
as in the opening lines of *La Comtesse de Charny*: 'If the reader would
be so good as to refer for a moment to our romance *Ange Pitou* and
open it at the second volume and glance for a moment at the chapter
entitled La Nuit du 5–6 Octobre, he will find there . . .'

So much for his method of immediately attracting the attention of
his readers, but it was the exciting and never-flagging turns of the
tales and the dramatically brisk and often witty dialogue that never
failed to hold the readers' attention.

When Dumas had finished remodelling Auguste Maquet's novel
under the title of *Le Chevalier d'Harmental*, he would gladly have
allowed the young man to share the credit with him, but the editors
would simply not agree. Dumas has often been accused of exploiting
other young authors, but it was scarcely his fault. Emile de Girardin
wrote: 'A serial bearing the name of Dumas is worth three francs a
line. Bearing the names of Dumas and Maquet it is worth thirty *sous*.'
The result was that Dumas alone was credited, but Maquet, unlike
Gaillardet, was quite happy with the arrangement. Dumas gave him
eight thousand francs – a not inconsiderable sum for those days, a sum
which Maquet could never have earned writing alone under his own
name. The success of *Le Chevalier d'Harmental* made Dumas
realise what a fortune there lay in romanticising history. When
Maquet furnished him with an idea for a novel about Louis XIII,
Cardinal Richelieu, Anne of Austria, and Buckingham, his
enthusiasm was aroused. The idea grew into *The Three Musketeers*.

In Cologne in 1700 and in Amsterdam in 1704, John Elzevir, the
publisher of whose existence Dumas had first heard from the lips of
Nodier many years before, had printed the *Mémoires of M
d'Artagnan, Captain-Lieutenant in the First Company of the King's
Musketeers*, a rare book written by one Gatien de Cortilz (sometimes
called Cortilz de Sandras or Sandras de Cortilz).

Whether it was Maquet or Dumas who discovered the book first is
immaterial. Maquet claimed that it was he, but a record in the
national library of Marseille shows that Dumas borrowed the book in
1842 and never returned it, which proves nothing more than that he
presumably read it, if not once, several times.

Certainly, along with the slightly changed names of Athos, Porthos, and Aramis, Dumas and Maquet borrowed many episodes from the *Mémoires d'Artagnan*; but Gatien de Cortilz was a scurrilous satirist of microscopic talent, and Maquet and Dumas had to transform even his best sequences – for example the story of Mme Bonacieux and that of Lady de Winter. To quote Maurois:

> If Maquet's role was that of mason, Dumas's was that of architect. With all his collaborators, Dumas had a nearly uniform method of working. The collaborator constructed a scenario. Dumas ... added a thousand details, which invested it with colour, wrote dialogues ... and lengthened the whole to satisfy the demands of publishers whose serials had to last a month and rivet the readers' interest without let-up.

He introduced new characters, like the wonderful taciturn valet Grimaud, who never replied with anything more than a monosyllable. This was an ingenious trick on the part of Dumas, for newspapers paid by the line. This was all ruined when *La Presse* and *Le Siècle* decided no longer to consider a line group which failed to extend more than halfway across a column as a complete line. Grimaud was immediately eliminated from the story. He had fulfilled his function.

A minor writer of the times, a certain Versmersch, later parodied these dialogues by Dumas:

'Have you seen him?'

'Who?'

'Him.'

'Who?'

'Dumas?'

'Père?'

'Yes.'

'What a man!'

'No doubt'

'How mad!'

'Surely.'

'How prolific!'

'Rather!'

In fact, Versmersch's parody is not far removed from a genuine dialogue by the great author himself.

'Ah, so it's you?'

'Yes, 'tis I.'

'I expected you.'

'Here I am.'
'And you have succeeded.'
'I have.'
'Quite certain.'
'What then?'
'The thing is done.'
'Then let us talk.'
'With all my heart,' etc.

Is it surprising that editors soon saw that they were being cheated? What is stranger is that the French reading public could have become enthralled with such daily snippets of a story. However, by the time he came to write *Monte-Cristo*, Dumas had been obliged to drop this lucrative method. According to Théophile Gautier, public interest in his *feuilletons* was quite extraordinary. He wrote: 'People found the characters so regularly and for so long every morning by their bedside, that they came at last to consider them as ordinary persons from daily life. Even the most busy could find a few minutes before leaving for their offices for half an hour's talk with d'Artagnan or Balsamo . . . I have often heard the remark, "Monte-Cristo has done so and so; *I think he was right,*" or wrong, as the case may be, exactly as one would praise or blame the proceedings of a living person.'

Human nature has not changed much. Today (1979–80) there is a large English-speaking public for whom characters in television and radio series such as *Coronation Street* and *The Archers* are more 'real' than their next-door neighbour.

Dumas tells us himself in his *Causeries* how he came to think of the subject for *Monte-Cristo*. On 14 March 1841, Jerome Bonaparte, ex-King of Westphalia, now an old man, as he describes him (in fact he was only fifty-seven), invited Dumas to the Villa Quarto, where he was now living, to suggest that he should take a sea voyage with his son, Prince Napoleon. 'I wish you to teach him France,' said the ex-King. There was to be no loss of dignity – each party was to contribute to the cost of the journey. This was an offer Dumas could not resist. A small vessel was hired and sailed first for Elba. On leaving here the travellers sighted a small, almost conical, deserted rock. Dumas inquired its name. 'Monte-Cristo,' he was told. 'Let's sail round it,' said the author; 'I would like to know its geographical position to note for a future story.'

Dumas admitted that he drew a great deal of his inspiration from places themselves. To write *Christine*, he tells us, he visited Fontainbleau; for *Henri III* he went to Blois; for *The Three Musketeers* to Boulogne and Bethune, and so on.

Local colour, however, is not everything, although wonderfully suggestive. Hence the germ of *Monte-Cristo*. The plot of the novel was based on a true story, a story which this time Dumas found for himself in a work by a certain Jacques Peuchet, entitled *Mémoires tirées des Archives de la Police de Paris.*

Peuchet had been keeper of the archives of the prefecture of police. From his files he had compiled six volumes which even today would be a rich mine for novelists.

Here in brief is the strange but true story which appealed to Dumas. In 1807 there lived in Paris a handsome young shoemaker named François Picaud, a native of Nîmes. He became engaged to a beautiful orphan girl named Marguerite Vigoroux, the possessor of a fortune of 100,000 gold francs. One Sunday, dressed in his best suit, he visited a café, the proprietor of which, a certain Mathieu Loupian, was his close acquaintance. Loupian, who was also from Nîmes, was a widower with two children, a boy – a feckless youth – and an angelically beautifully daughter. Although Loupian had a flourishing business he was madly jealous of other people's success.

In the café, Picaud met three other acquaintances, all originally from Nîmes. They teased him on his fine clothes and were dumbfounded when he explained that he was on his way to meet his rich fiancée; and was to be married on the following Tuesday.

No sooner had Picaud left, then the jealous Loupian exclaimed: 'I'll soon put a spoke in that wheel!' 'How?' asked the others. 'A police inspector is looking in later,' replied Loupian. 'I shall tell him that I suspect Picaud of being a secret agent in the pay of the English. He'll be questioned; he'll be very frightened and the marriage will be postponed.'

Of the three men from Nîmes, only one, a certain Antoine Allut, protested that he thought this a dirty trick. He knew that Napoleon's police did not take political crimes lightly, and it was not unusual to arrest and hold a man on mere suspicion, often without trial. But he was overruled; the others all regarded it as a good joke.

In due course the police inspector arrived, and anxious to

distinguish himself, took Loupian at his word, without more ado sent a report to Savary, Duke of Rovigo, the minister of police who, in turn, without even instituting further investigations, gave orders for the immediate arrest of the unfortunate Picaud. The wretched shoemaker, without so much as a judicial trial, was spirited away during the night, and completely vanished from view. His parents and his betrothed set inquiries afoot, but to no avail.

According to Peuchet's account, with the fall of Napoleon in 1814, Picaud, prematurely aged by his suffering and now almost unrecognisable, was released from the Château de Fenestrelle, in which he had been imprisoned for seven long years. During his captivity he had with great devotion cared for a fellow prisoner, an Italian prelate, condemned for life on political grounds. The old man had not long to live; on his death bed he bequeathed to Picaud by word of mouth a treasure hidden near Milan, which he had saved from the notorious Haller, Bonaparte's treasurer of the army of Italy. No sooner was Picaud released than he sought out this treasure, found it and removed it to a place of safety. Then under the name of Joseph Lucher, he returned to Paris. There he inquired what had become of a shoemaker named Pierre-François Picaud, who in 1807 had been about to marry Mlle Marguerite Vigoroux (Mercèdes in the novel). He was told that a carnival jest played on him by four practical jokers had resulted in the young man's disappearance. His betrothed had mourned him for two years and then, believing him dead, had agreed to marry the café owner, Loupian. Picaud asked the names of the other responsible parties and was told that he could obtain them from a man called Antoine Allut, who lived in Nîmes, the man who had disapproved of the practical joke.

Picaud, disguised as an Italian priest, with a quantity of gold and jewels sewn into his pockets, hastened to Nîmes. In return for a fine diamond, Antoine Allut gave him the names of the three practical jokers, whose 'joke' had had such a tragic sequel.

Picaud's vengeance was terrible. Now quite unrecognisable, he obtained himself a place as waiter, under the name of Prosper, in Loupian's café, which was still frequented by those responsible for his seven hideous years of imprisonment. One day, Chambard, one of the three, failed to arrive at his usual time. He was later found dead, stabbed in the back. The knife had been left in the wound, and on the handle was written 'Number One'.

Loupian, it will be remembered, had a son and a daughter. The girl, now sixteen years of age, was angelically beautiful. A dandy, claiming to be a marquis and a millionaire, seduced her. Finding herself pregnant, she confessed to Loupian, who far from scolding her, was delighted, since the elegant gentleman was prepared to marry her. A civil and religious ceremony took place, but between the nuptial blessing and the wedding breakfast the 'marquis' had disappeared. It was soon discovered that he was neither a marquis nor a millionaire, but a former convict wanted for murder.

On the following Sunday, Loupian's café, above which he and his family lived, was burnt to the ground. Loupian was ruined. Only his waiter, 'Prosper', and Solari, one of his regulars and one of the 'jokers' responsible for Picaud's imprisonment, remained faithful to him. As might be expected, Solari soon died, poisoned. On the black shroud covering his coffin was found pinned a piece of paper on which was written in bold letters 'Number Two'.

Loupian's son Eugène, always a weak character, was introduced, no one knew by whom, to some very shady characters. He was soon involved in a robbery and was sentenced to twenty years' imprisonment. Loupian had now lost everything – money, reputation and social status. The former well-to-do café proprietor sank lower and lower. His wealthy wife, Marguerite Vigoroux, died of grief, but her money reverted to her family, her legal heirs. 'Prosper' offered his savings to his destitute employer but on condition that his daughter became his mistress.

In order to save her father, she accepted. Loupian by this time was half crazy. One evening in a dark alley, a masked man approached him.

'Loupian, do you remember 1807?'

'Why should I?'

'Because it was the year of your crime.'

'What crime?'

'Have you forgotten that through jealousy, you had your old friend Picaud imprisoned?'

'Ah! God has punished me for that . . . punished me terribly!'

'There you are wrong. It was not God who punished you but Picaud, who to stake his vengeance stabbed Chambard, poisoned Solari, burned down your house, and gave your daughter a murderer as a husband, introduced your son to criminals . . . See now in Prosper the same Picaud at the very moment when he sets his mark on his third victim.'

Loupian fell to the ground murdered. But just as Picaud was about to leave, he felt himself held in a grip of steel, gagged and, under cover of darkness, carried off and thrown into a cellar. Here he found himself in the presence of a man whom he did not recognise.

'Well, Picaud,' said the unknown, 'for you, vengeance is no more a game. You have spent ten years of your life hunting down three wretches whom you could have spared . . . you have committed a series of horrible crimes, and in them I have been your accomplice, since it is I who sold you the secret of your misery . . . I am Antoine Allut!'

Vengeance for vengeance. Picaud was killed with the utmost savagery. His murderer escaped to England. In 1828, Allut, who had fallen desperately ill, sent for a priest and confessed to all these terrible events. He asked that after his death the whole story should be revealed to the French judicial authorities.

Allut's wishes were carried out; the document was housed in the police archives, where Peuchet found them.*

Here was a story ready-made for Dumas. He roughed out his novel and submitted it to Maquet. Maquet protested that he had left out the most interesting part of his hero's life – his love affair with Marguerite (Mercédès), the Catalan girl of the novel; the treachery of the café owner and his friends, and the years of imprisonment with the Italian prelate, the Abbé Faria, as Dumas calls him.

'I shall cover all that,' protested Dumas; '. . . come and dine with me tomorrow and we'll talk about it again.'

And so, together, Dumas and his collaborator completely revised the first draft. 'Maquet,' wrote Dumas, 'considered that he had done nothing more than give me friendly advice. But I insisted on his playing the part of collaborator.'

We now come to the vexed question of how much of *Monte-Cristo* was the work of Maquet and how much that of Dumas. Obviously it was quite impossible to make the hero, Edmond Dantès, a cruel, sadistic avenger like Peuget's Picaud. The real Picaud had pursued his vengeance in too ruthless a manner to become a popular hero. Picaud had assassinated his persecutors; he had taken vengeance into his own hands, whereas Dantès is *given* his vengeance. Loupian is divided into

* Jacques Peuchet, *Mémoires tirées des archives de la police de Paris.*

two and becomes both Fernand and Danglars of the novel. The magistrate, Villefort, is taken from a real police inspector, who saw promotion for himself in believing Loupian's slanderous denunciation. In the novel he goes mad. Fernand/Loupian marries Marguerite/Mercédès. Readers of the book will remember that Fernand commits suicide; Danglars is ruined. But to relieve the hideous darkness of the story, Dumas recreates the atmosphere of the *Arabian Nights* and presents Monte-Cristo with an oriental mistress, Haydée, the daughter of the Pasha of Janina.

In conclusion, far from having Dantès executed for horrible crimes of vengeance, Dumas's hero makes the noble gesture of providing the daughter of the police inspector, Mademoiselle de Villefort, with a dowry when she marries the son of his friend, Morrel. But when the couple wish to thank their benefactor, Monte-Cristo, and ask his sailor servant, 'Where is the Count? Where is Haydée?' the sailor points towards the horizon: 'They looked in the direction pointed out by the man, and on the dark blue water separating the Mediterranean from the sky, saw a sail no bigger than a seagull's wing . . .'

And so *The Count of Monte-Cristo* ends like a Hollywood film, with the scene of the hero riding alone out of the picture into the sunset.

CHAPTER TWENTY-ONE

Le Roi de Paris

What is really extraordinary is that both *The Three Musketeers* and *Monte-Cristo* should have been produced in the same year of 1844. With *Le Chevalier d'Harmental* and the 'modern novels' produced between 1842 and 1844, Dumas was already an outstanding figure with a personality of his own, but it was with the publication of *The Three Musketeers* and *Monte-Cristo* that he became a world-wide celebrity. No writer in his lifetime has ever enjoyed the same universal literary reputation as he. Neither Dickens nor Hugo had such European renown.

> The only approximation we can produce is in the films. Imagine a man as much discussed in the streets as the most popular 'star' of today – with the additional honour of meriting his celebrity; a man whose love affairs, *bons mots* and asides were windfalls for newsmongers and journalists; whose face and figure, prefacing the countless volumes of his works that were propogated from the antipodes to the poles, captured and caricatured by engravers and cartoonists of the time, were the most familiar to the thousands in Paris, the millions in all France.*

Dumas possessed as no other writer a charismatic quality which made him loved by all, from the highest to the lowest, with the exception of a few jealous literary rivals. Villemessant, the journalist, is probably the best of the many recorders of Dumas's triumphs. In his *Mémoires d'un journaliste* he describes a musical soirée to which Dumas (who, as we know, had no ear for music, but who enjoyed the company of musicians) had consented to come:

* A. C. Bell, *Alexandre Dumas.*

Well before the concert was due to begin, the room was filled to
overflowing ... It was not to the platform, however, that all eyes were
turned, but to the door; Alexandre Dumas was expected ... never has any
King making his entry ... produced such effect. In a moment everyone in
the room was standing up; everyone was turning to gaze on the great
romancer ... [who] could only make his way to his seat through a veritable
fusilade of greetings and handshakes ... When he spoke, famous
personages stopped talking to listen [to] the only man who in a hundred
years made himself the god to every class of society from the Boulevard
Saint-Germain to the Marais and the Batignolles.

Dumas's books, his travels, his manner of working, his loves,
multiplied until he became a legend in his lifetime. It was said that he
kept collaborators in his cellars while he went off on travels to
unknown places; that he had more mistresses and illegitimate children
than he could account for. His generosity was proverbial. Only when
savagely attacked for appropriating practically every *feuilleton* to the
exclusion of other writers − the fault of editors rather than Dumas −
did he show signs of impatience or short-lived anger. Towards the end
of 1843, Louis de Loménie, a young man who had written several
commendable works which had failed to attract attention, published
*The Gallery of Illustrious Contemporaries by a Man of no
Importance*, complaining of the 'overpowering chimes that prevented
his little sleigh bells from being heard'. Saint-Beuve had already
fulminated against 'industrialised literature'; now Loménie was
inveighing against Dumas's literary 'factory'. 'It is physically
impossible for M Dumas,' he wrote, 'to write or dictate all that pours
out under his signature.' This was true enough, but it did little to
harm our hero's popularity. He still remained the literary lion of
Paris.

Some two years later in 1845, the year after the incredible success of
The Three Musketeers and *Monte-Cristo*, a pamphleteer Eugène de
Mirecourt (his real name was Jean-Baptiste Jacquot), published a
brochure entitled *A Factory of Novels, The House of Alexandre
Dumas and Company*. It is worth pointing out that before his virulent
attack on Dumas, de Mirecourt had himself offered to work for the
great man and had even proposed the basis for a novel which Dumas
had turned down.

An amusing anecdote is told of Jacquot's first attack on Dumas. At
a meeting of the Société des Gens de Lettres, Jacquot's letter, which

was intended to condemn the practice of keeping 'literary workshops', was on the agenda. Jacquot called on the society, without, however, mentioning any particular name 'to brand this corrupt practice with its distinct condemnation'. The president of the society and many other prominent literati were present, including Maquet; all were a little hesitant to become embroiled with such a redoubtable adversary as Dumas. Suddenly the door opened and Dumas himself was announced. He strode in, poked the grave president facetiously in the stomach with a *'Comment ça va, mon vieux?'* ran over to Maquet and wrung him by the hand. 'How are you gentlemen? I see you are holding a meeting. Confound it, if I am in the way, say so. I just dropped in to see if my friend Pommier had a few écus to lend me. Any cash about you Pommier? By-the-bye – what's all this about? Talking about me, it seems!'

The president had risen from his seat. Dumas coolly assumed the vacant academic chair. Someone then handed him Jacquot's paper containing the charges against him. He glanced over them with a certain disdainful contempt and presently (for once) became angry. 'Accuse me of keeping a workshop – it's a lie, a calumny! Assistants in writing my stories! I deny it. I will take my oath on it.'

'There is no allusion to you,' said an obsequious member.

'No matter,' replied Dumas. 'It is transparent. Everyone will see who is intended. I can prove it to be false, for I can show the original manuscript of every one of the thirty-six volumes I have produced this year and all in my own handwriting.'

'That would be a fair test,' said another; 'so suppose we—'

'What is all thus humbug?' said Dumas. 'Am I in the witness box to be cross-examined in this style? Suppose I have done some stories in partnership. I don't deny it, but it is with only one man and there he is – Maquet!'

At this confession there were loud murmurs: 'Why, you denied it solemnly a moment ago.' Then the president interposed with a smile:

'It is merely the firm of Moiroud & Co,' alluding a well-known play.

The *société* passed a resolution to the effect that 'it was urgently necessary to regulate the principles of collaboration in literary works'. The meeting then broke up.

Since Dumas had refused Jacquot's offer of collaboration, his pamphlet therefore was inspired more by pique than honest indignation. In his letter to the Société des Gens de Lettres he had protested against methods 'that permitted a single writer to corner all the newspapers, furnish all the serials and deny the young any possibility of earning their livelihood'. Dissatisfied with the rulings of the *société*, Jacquot next wrote to Emile de Girardin, editor-in-chief of *La Presse*, asking him to 'close his portals on the shameful mercantilism of Alexandre Dumas' and open them to young people with talent, in other words himself. Girardin replied that it was Dumas whom his readers wanted and Dumas they would get.

It was then that Jacquot published his pamphlet. He was sufficiently well informed concerning Dumas's methods of work to present what he thought would be a really damning indictment. Several of Dumas's collaborators, feeling perhaps that their services had been underestimated and their genius deprived of legitimate fame, confided in him.

He pounced on Dumas's work, drama by drama, novel by novel, and turned the searchlight on those whom he termed 'the real authors' – Adolphe de Leuven, Anicet Bourgeois, Gaillardet, Gérard de Nerval, Théophile Gautier, Paul Meurice, and especially on Auguste Maquet. He did not mention that by no means all Dumas's collaborators were dissatisfied – on the contrary, some were perfectly happy to accept what they regarded as fair remuneration – nor did he mention that many would never have made a livelihood without the help of Dumas.

It is doubtful if Jacquot's attack would have every carried much weight; Dumas was far too popular, both as author and man, to be deeply affected. It was common knowledge that he had collaborators, but Jacquot's pamphlet was so scurrilous and in such bad taste that far from destroying Dumas's reputation, it rebounded on himself.

Even Balzac, jealous of Dumas's popularity, was outraged by de Mirecourt. In fact, far from doing Dumas harm, our hero triumphed. He brought an action for libel against de Mirecourt. The court found for Dumas and condemned his prosecutor to fifteen days imprisonment. The sentence aroused wide publicity and de Mirecourt was discredited in the world of letters.

Auguste Maquet, Dumas's principal collaborator, one of those whom de Mirecourt had cited as 'slave labour under the whip of a mulatto overseer', proved a truly loyal friend and wrote to Dumas on 4 March 1845:

210

Dear Friend,

Our collaboration has always done without figures and contracts. A true friendship and a word of honour have sufficed us so well that we have written half a million lines about the affairs of others without ever thinking about a word of our own.

Have you not paid me well for the books we worked on together . . .?

I hereby declare as of this date, I renounce all claims to all rights of ownership and reprints with regard to the following works which we did together – namely *Le Chevalier d'Harmental, Les Trois Mousquetaires, Vingt ans après, La Guerre des Femmes, La Reine Margot, Le Chevalier de Maison-Rouge* . . . considering myself once and for all generously and duly indemnified by you according to our verbal agreements.

Keep this letter dear friend in order to show it to some greedy heir, and tell him clearly that, during my lifetime, I regarded myself most happy and honoured to be the collaborator and friend of the most brilliant of French novelists.

Let him feel as I do!

Maquet*

For a long time a perfect friendship existed between Dumas and Maquet. Dumas was always prepared to recognise Maquet's share in his productions and always introduced him as 'Monsieur Auguste Maquet, my collaborator'. It is sad to mention that the friends in later years quarrelled and Maquet claimed paternity of the *Trois Mousquetaires*, but once Maquet tried to launch out on his own he achieved nothing, nor for that matter did Adolphe de Leuven, Gaillardet, Anicet Bourgeois, or any other collaborator. The master's touch was missing.

Dumas, far from denying that he used collaborators (which was no uncommon thing for French authors in the nineteenth century), would even make a joke of it, as he did at Bourg-en-Bresse, where he was obtaining local colour for his *Les Compagnons de Jéhu*, when a sarcastic magistrate addressed him:

'So you are really going to write a novel yourself!'

'Yes, really. I had the last one written by my valet, but as it had a great success the fellow demanded such an outrageous fee that to my great regret I had to dismiss him.'

He was a lovable man. Unlike de Musset or Hugo, he was incapable

---

* Letter published in Henri d'Alméras' *Alexandre Dumas et les Trois Mousquetaires*, cited by André Maurois.

of cynicism or pessimism. He loved life. Maxime de Camp wrote: 'Like a giant who knows his strength and fears to use it, he was gentle. I have never seen in him – I will not say [show] a sign of anger – but not even a moment of impatience. If ever a man was lovable . . . Dumas was that man.'

Théodore de Banville in his *Souvenirs* tells a story which illustrates Dumas's generosity. Once, when out duck-shooting with friends, he became separated from his companions. While splashing his way through some tall reeds, he suddenly came across a little ragged girl of about seven or eight years of age, lost and crying among the tall grasses. Immediately Alexandre slung his gun over his shoulder and gathered her in his powerful arms. Between sobs she explained that her mother had recently died, she was now an orphan and was lost. Without further ado, Dumas carried her back to his host's home, where with his own hands he prepared her a meal and after a good wash tucked her up in bed.

In the evening, when his friends returned, they inquired what had happened to him. He explained that he had taken the liberty of entertaining a little guest in his host's house. Later, after supper, Dumas's host proposed a toast – but to whom? Dumas had no hesitation in suggesting his little friend. All agreed. Then Dumas, searching in his pockets, flung a handful of gold coins onto a plate. 'Let us all contribute to help the poor child,' he declared. Most of his friends were wealthy men and it would have been difficult not to follow his example. The plate was soon overflowing with *louis d'or* and *écus* – enough to invest in the name of the little girl, who was able to receive a good education.

Dumas rarely refused anyone help, even when financially pressed himself. He invariably kept a cup filled with coins in his work room, which unlike the opulent splendour with which he liked to surround himself, consisted of nothing but a plain deal table, and piles of different coloured manuscript papers. Here he worked in his shirt sleeves, sometimes for fourteen hours a day. Interruptions were frequent, especially from spongers who knew their Dumas. 'Help yourself,' he would say, pointing to the glass filled with *louis d'or*. 'Pay me back when you can.' They seldom did.

Would-be collaborators frequently turned up to submit plots for stories. Of course it was those he turned down who were the most virulent of Dumas's detractors. Even de Mirecourt abused his munificence. De Banville tells us another story of his generosity. An actor, out of work and almost starving, called on Dumas, who immediately invited him to dinner, gave him some money, and said, 'Come and see me tomorrow'. For weeks this continued until, at last, the impoverished actor, ashamed of sponging, asked if there was nothing he could do in return for his benefactor's generosity. 'Yes,' replied Dumas. 'I would like you to take the temperature of the Seine at noon every day from the Pont Neuf. It would be most useful for me.'

The stories of his generosity, or, if you wish, his prodigality, are too numerous to mention. His prodigious output, his insatiable capacity for work, were not undertaken merely for love of money. He was a compulsive worker and expected his collaborators to work just as hard and long as he.

In England, collaboration was no innovation in the theatre. In the late sixteenth century and early Jacobean period, before the Puritans banned the theatre, the custom was for the manager of a players company to buy a play outright and then have it 'doctored' to his requirements by a team of hack writers. But not all hacks merely 'doctored' original scripts. They often collaborated to write by no means indifferent original plays. Marlowe and Thomas Nashe wrote *Dido* together; Ben Jonson, George Chapman and John Marston all had a hand in *Eastward Ho!*; Thomas Dekker, John Ford and Samuel Rowley wrote *The Witch of Edmonton*; the names of Beaumont and Fletcher are invariably linked. Fletcher also collaborated with the now almost forgotten Massinger, Rowley and Shirley. Fletcher almost certainly collaborated with Shakespeare on *The Two Noble Kinsmen*. As we know, Shakespeare borrowed freely for his plots from Holinshed, and in *Henry VI* lifted whole lines from a dull play written by a syndicate consisting of Greene, Thomas Lodge and George Peele, called *The Wounds of Civil War*. Molière 'borrowed' true stories for himself – even the absurd but delightful comedy the *Bourgeois Gentilhomme* was drawn from life.

Balzac, almost as prolific as Dumas, seems never to have come in for the same censure as Dumas, although he drew more than one of his great novels from sources suggested to him (*Beatrix* by George Sand, *Le Lys dans la Vallée* by Saint-Beuve, *La Muse du Département* by Caroline Marbouty). Even Stendhal owed *Lucien Leuwen* to the manuscript of an unknown woman. But it is preposterous to suggest that Dumas was without imagination. It was while engaged on *Ange*

Pitou, in which he records the atmosphere of Paris during the Terror so vividly, that he won the admiration of the historian Michelet, that Maquet deserted him, and Dumas found himself deprived of all the documents accumulated by his collaborator. Though this might have put off a lesser man, Dumas now endowed *Ange Pitou* with his own youth as a hunter and poacher in the forest of Villers-Cotterêts. So much confidence did he have in his own imagination that when he wrote *Le Collier de la Reine*, he did not even bother to visit Versailles, but invented the setting. When he announced to the newspapers that he was writing another book under the title of *Le Chevalier de Rougeville* (later to be entitled *Le Chevalier de Maison-Rouge*), a young Chevalier de Rougeville, a direct descendant of the authentic hero, committed suicide, leaving a great pile of papers dealing with the subject. Shortly before the young man committed suicide, he had written to Dumas protesting against the use of his name as the title for a novel. Only an hour before killing himself, however, de Rougeville had a note delivered to Dumas: 'Sir, call your novel what you will. I am the last of my line, and am blowing my brains out within the hour.'

The young nobleman kept his word. After Dumas's death, the pile of documents which de Rougeville bequeathed to him were found unopened. The great romancer's fiction was an even better story than the real-life tragedy.

Bibliothèque de l'Arsenal. Charles Nodier lived here in 1843. *By courtesy of the Victoria and Albert Museum.*

Boulevard des Italiens, Paris, by Edward Goodall. *By courtesy of the Victoria and Albert Museum.*

Villers-Cotterêts at noontime, from 'Bouquet de France', published by Gourmet Distributing Corporation, New York.

A quay on the Seine, Paris 1833. A drawing by Callow. *By courtesy of the Victoria and Albert Museum.*

CHAPTER TWENTY-TWO

The Success of *Monte-Cristo*

Never in the history of literature has there been anything comparable to the world-wide success achieved by the *feuilletons* of *Monte-Cristo* and *The Three Musketeers*. But the fame of these two books made work in Paris almost impossible for Dumas. The stream of visitors and admirers constantly calling at his door, and the piles of letters from hopeful writers and hopeful collaborators, not to mention spongers demanding his attention, made life intolerable. In a vain attempt to escape from these interruptions, he moved from rue de Richelieu to the rue de Mont Blanc (now rue de la Chaussée d'Antin).

The rue de Mont Blanc, however, provided him with no more privacy than his former residence. He had finished the original version of *The Three Musketeers*. The public, however, were clamouring for more. He now decided to look around for a place in the country, while maintaining his Paris residence. Eventually his choice fell on Saint-Germain-en-Laye. The railway, as today, ran between this little provincial town, once the seat of the royal court of France, and the capital, a mere half-hour's journey. At the end of May 1844 he took a day off from work, admired an old twelfth-century château, inspected the Pavillon Henri IV, which had lately been rebuilt (not altogether happily) and turned into a high-class restaurant (which it still is) with apartments to let. Here he rented a part of the building known as the Villa Medicis at a rental of 2000 francs. A few days later he and Ida were installed there. His existance for the next few years was devoted to work. It was here that he completed *La Reine Margot*, *La Dame de Monsoreau*, *Vingt ans après*, and goodness knows how much else. He also visited Spain and Algeria, of which more later.

When Dumas announced to his son that he was leaving Paris to seek peace and quiet in the country, his son laughingly told him that if he left Paris, Paris would come to him – and so it proved. Ida stayed with him for only a short while; life with Ida had become more and more impossible. She did not try to understand him. She was only interested in herself. Dumas could not tolerate any interruption of his work. She was continually inviting persons whom he did not particularly like to visit them. Shortly after installing himself in the Villa Medicis they had had a quarrel more violent than usual, and by mutual agreement Ida returned to Florence. Dumas never saw her again. Her hopes of being provided for by her princely lover, as she and Dumas had wished, seem not to have materialised; and although some biographers assert that he never failed, even when he himself was almost bankrupt, to pay her the 6,000 francs legally agreed upon, it is doubtful if he actually did so, since Ida later brought a court action against him for arrears of alimony. She died in 1859.

After his break with Ida, his relations with his son improved. Father and son now lived in comparative harmony. The young Alexandre had come to accept his father as he was. 'My father,' he wrote, 'is like a great big child whom I had when I was a little boy.' He was well aware, too, that after a while his father would get bored with life in the Villa Medicis. His father continued writing as hard as ever, one novel or serial overlapping another, but Saint-Germain-en-Laye was a dull place. Nothing ever happened there. After a while, as his son predicted, he found provincial existence intolerable. It was not long before he was inviting friends to visit him; Sunday was the great day for relaxation and entertaining. Among the celebrities who were habitual visitors were Hugo, Delacroix, Rachel, Duprez (the singer) and Boulanger. The most celebrated Parisian actors and actresses would come, and after a magnificent meal, prepared by Dumas himself, would give impromptu performances in the little local theatre in aid of some charity or other. The little town of Saint-Germain became transformed. On one occasion the whole town turned out at (for the respectable citizens of this quiet little *bourg*) the unearthly hour of ten o'clock, to watch a fireworks display from the terrace of the Villa Medicis, a display which was visible and audible in Paris and Versailles.

In his *Mémoires*, Dumas wrote: 'I carry about with me – I don't know how it is – an atmosphere of life and excitement that has become proverbial. I lived for three years at Saint-Germain . . . I infected the place with a life and animation which they took at first to be a species of endemic and contagious disease . . . the railway company confessed one day to an increase of 20,000 francs for each year I had been at Saint-Germain.'

Although he had complained that Ida was constantly interfering with his work, his own social life seriously interfered with his writing. Tired of living in rented apartments, he now decided to build a house to his own design. One day, while out walking, he came across what seemed to him an ideal situation for a retreat, a delightful spot on the road between Saint-Germain and Pecq; near Marcy. He chose a spot close to Port Marly, sent for the architect Plante, and showed him a draft sketch of the sort of retreat he required. He explained what he wanted – a neat little cottage with two or three rooms.

Before long both he and Plante had expanded their ideas. It would be absurd to go to expense and not have room in which to turn about and entertain a few friends, plus a room for his son. Thus the estimate gradually grew from a modest 1,600 francs to the sum of 15,000 francs. A second floor was to be added. As soon as the scheme was fairly started it filled Alexandre's mind. It became almost an obsession. The plans for a humble cottage began to assume palatial proportions. No sooner was the site selected than all the neighbouring peasants and landowners, knowing of the great man's prodigality, immediately offered him adjoining lands for sale at exhorbitant prices. Dumas, playing the role of Monte-Cristo, never haggled. He now saw himself as a landed proprietor. On 27 July 1844, he invited his friends to a picnic breakfast and made an engagement with them to come and enjoy the same meal three years hence in the new villa's dining room, which would occupy the very same site as that on which they had breakfasted. A promise he kept. Work was immediately put in hand. In addition to the services of the architect Plante, there were added those of Durand, a man with big ideas.

The 'château' grew in proportion to the land acquired. In digging the foundations it was discovered that the soil was no better than loam. The architects expressed doubts concerning the security of the foundations.

'Dig down to the rock and build on arches,' replied Dumas. 'We will have cellars.'

'But that will mean something like an additional 50,000 francs!'

'No doubt,' replied Dumas with a shrug of his shoulders.

Springs were discovered and, as the workmen dug deeper beneath the loam, a whole quarry was discovered which supplied stones to enclose the estate with a wall. The costs rose fantastically from 15,000 francs to 60,000, then to 120,000, and a short time later, to 150,000 and even more. The springs gave Dumas the idea of constructing a lake with an island and bridges. On the island was to be built his study where he would be cut off from the outside world and free from importunate visitors. The most famous designers were called in to execute sculptures, designs and friezes. Later, when, he visited Africa, he added oriental décor to this quite extraordinary building, which, not only from contemporary photographs, but from all descriptions, would have been to modern eyes a 'folly' in the worst taste.

At first, he had opened the grounds to the public, but so many people flocked to visit the magnificent grounds and watch the growth of the château, that a notice had to be posted: NOT OPEN TO THE PUBLIC.

The only thing lacking to the château was a name. All sorts of suggestions had been made – Villa d'Artagnan, Villa Palmière, Maison Dumas, and so on. It was not until one day when the actor Melingue and his wife, on arriving at Pecq, the nearest railway station, took a cab and facetiously ordered the coachman to drive them to MONTE-CRISTO, that the name became universally adopted.

In 1846, father and son were living together in conditions of disorder and mutual tolerance; sometimes even sharing mistresses. Later, Dumas *fils* was to become almost a paragon of virtue, but in 1846 he was the lover of an actress at the Vaudeville. At a supper party given by this young lady a violent quarrel arose between a young journalist, Dujarrier, who was on the staff of *La Presse*, in charge of the publication of serials, and a certain Rosemond de Beauvallon. A duel ensued in which Beauvallon killed his adversary on the instructions, it was said, of a number of rival newspapers. 'The war for subscribers had now gone to the length of murder.'

At first acquitted, Beauvallon, who was accused by Dujarrier's supporters of having killed his adversary by a foul blow, was ordered by the court of appeal to appear before the Rouen tribunal, by which he was sentenced to eight years' imprisonment. The two Dumas, *père et fils*, were present at the trial as witnesses, accompanied by their mistresses. Their behaviour was severely censured by the Rouennais.

As a witness, Alexandre *père* covered himself with ridicule. He discredited for ever the word "gentleman," ' wrote Nestor Roqueplan to his brother Camille.

On the whole, Rouen was one of the few places that appears not to have appreciated Dumas. When one of his plays was performed there, it was hissed. When a somewhat malicious critic remarked on the fact, Dumas retorted, 'I am not surprised. After all they burnt Joan of Arc there, didn't they?'

After the Beauvallon trial, Dumas was subjected to considerable adverse criticism, which upset his son. In 1846 both father and son gladly took advantage of a unique opportunity to leave France on a prolonged visit to Spain and Algiers.

Salvandy, the Minister of Public Instruction, after a visit to Algiers, had observed to his travelling companion, the writer Xavier Marmier, what a shame it was that such a beautiful country was so little known. How might it be popularised and colonised, he wondered. Marmier, with no hesitation, suggested that arrangements should be made for Dumas to make the identical trip as they and write two or three books about it. He had three million readers and would develop a taste for Algieria in perhaps fifty or sixty thousand of them.

Salvandy, himself a man of letters who had received Victor Hugo into the Academy, saw that Marmier had a very good point. On his return to Paris, he invited Dumas to dinner.

'*Mon cher poète*,' said Salvandy, 'you must do us a little favour.'

Dumas, intrigued, asked what could a poet do for a minister. Of course he would oblige if only for the rarity of the occasion. Salvandy explained his plan and offered him ten thousand francs for travel expenses.

Dumas, who after his enormous success with his *feuilletons* of *Monte-Cristo* was now almost indentifying himself with his own hero, replied grandly: 'I shall add forty thousand from my own pocket and will go on the voyage.' Salvandy seemed surprised at this munificence, and prompted Dumas to behave more like the Count of Monte-Cristo than ever. Our hero announced that, at his own expense, he would invite his son Alexandre, his collaborator Maquet (with whom he had not yet fallen out), and the artist Boulanger to accompany him. Certainly he would undertake the trip. All he demanded of Salvandy was a man-o'war to take him and his friends along the coast of Algeria.

The minister was certainly taken aback by this outrageous demand from the forty-four-year-old romancer. What he was demanding, he said, was only done for royal princes.

'Very good,' replied Dumas. 'If you were going to treat me as you do *ordinary people*, it was pointless to ask me. I have only to write to the officers of the *Messageries maritimes* and reserve my place on one of their ships.'

'All right,' replied Salvandy, 'you will have your battleship. When do you want to leave?'

'Well, I have two or three novels to finish first. Shall we say in about a fortnight?' (He was writing *Balsamo* among other things at the time).

On the day following this audience, Dumas dined with the Duc de Montpensier,* the fifth son of Louis-Philippe, who held Dumas in affection because, perhaps, of the writer's genuine friendship for the King's eldest son, the Duc d'Orléans, who it will be recollected was killed when falling from his carriage. The Duc de Montpensier on this occasion granted him permission to build a theatre, just as the Duc d'Orléans had once hoped to do. Dumas was delighted. He was, of course now not entirely dependent on the royal purse. He immediately decided to build a theatre. What should it be called? Le Théâtre Historique, Le Théâtre Européan or even Le Théâtre Montpensier? Here would be performed not only his own dramas, but also those of Shakespeare, Calderón, Goethe and Schiller. Naturally it would cost a great deal of money, but was he not now the Count of Monte-Cristo? Money was no object.

Over dinner he told the young royal duke of his conversation with Salvandy on the previous day.

'Capital idea,' said the Duke, 'especially if you come via Spain and attend my wedding.' (On 10 October 1846, the Duc de Montpensier was to marry the Infanta Luisa, the younger sister of Queen Isabella II, heir presumptive to the throne of Spain, a marriage which, since it might one day result in a Frenchman once again wearing the Spanish crown, gave some concern to the British government.)

Dumas naturally accepted the invitation without hesitation. The great republican could not resist royalty; besides, had not Montpensier given him a licence to build a theatre? Prospects had never looked better. He immediately sent out invitations to his son,

* Another version is that he met him in his box at the theatre.

Maquet and Boulanger. The caterer Chevet (he who had helped him with his famous banquet) recommended an Abyssinian Negro as his servant, a man with the delightful name of Eau de Benjoin, who added just the exotic touch which so appealed to Dumas.

There is some confusion here. Dumas, in his *Histoire de mes Bêtes*, writes of a little Negro boy, Alexis Benjoin, who was brought to him in a basket of flowers by the actress Dorval. The little Alexis stayed with Dumas for eight years. The Abyssian Negro was known as Paul.

Dumas started to write his travel diary as soon as the party started on their voyage: 'The locomotive snorts its acrid breathing, the immense machine shakes itself, the grating clash of iron is heard, lanterns flash past as swift as the firebrands of imps on the witch's sabbath,' etc.

The account of his trip to Spain has the real Dumas magic touch. Just as the account of his travels in Switzerland, written in 1832, is as lively as any novel, so now his *De Paris à Cadix* and *Le Véloce* possess that same magic touch, but the Spanish journey was even more fascinating than *Voyage en Suisse*, and its narration surpasses that of the earlier work. 'In Switzerland he had made his own company and his own adventures. In Spain they were made for him.'* Everywhere he went, he was acclaimed and fêted. Never again was he to taste quite so richly the fruit of universal recognition and adulation. His name was as familiar as that of Charlie Chaplin in our own day. His name acted as a magic talisman.

His real journey began at Bordeaux, where he exchanged the train for a coach; he detested trains and like all great travellers, like George Borrow, like Dickens, like Stevenson, did not count a train journey as travelling, any more than we today regard a journey by aeroplane as travelling, so much as a transition from one place to another. So it was by coach that they proceeded to Madrid at all possible speed to arrive in time for the royal wedding. Dumas and his friends reached Madrid in October 1846, our hero bringing with him three huge trunks bursting with new clothes, and six chests containing guns and pistols, which 'the customs passed in the most complimentary fashion'. Dumas would have us think that his name alone was sufficient for the customs officials to waive all formalities. There may be some truth in

* A. C. Bell, op cit.

this, but in fact it was Guizot, Louis-Philippe's chief adviser and Minister of Foreign Affairs (he did not become Prime Minister until 1847), who procured for Dumas what was virtually a diplomatic passport and described him as 'travelling on a mission from the Minister of Public Instruction'.

On arrival at Madrid, Dumas attended all the fêtes, and even witnessed the marriage contract. A year later when accused by the Chambre des Députés of abusing his fame as a world-famous literary figure to act as though he was an official ambassador, he told a crowded court: 'I went so completely in the capacity of guest, that I was the only Frenchman who assisted at this private marriage. Then I received the grand cordon of Charles III which was not given to me as a literary man, but to me—' and here he struck his chest '—to *me*, Alexandre Dumas Davy, Marquis de la Pailleterie, the friend of the Duc de Montpensier.'

Leaving Madrid behind, the party went to Toledo and on to Aranjuez. It was a journey full of incident, which Dumas recounts in his best vein. His coach was overturned, nearly sending the travellers over a precipice; they narrowly avoided an encounter with brigands. At Granada, a city which Dumas took to his heart, there was a fight with some disagreeable neighbours which nearly brought their visit to an unhappy conclusion. With the risk of facing a Spanish court of law, the party slipped out of the city in the grey dawn for Cordoba. The three days spent here were made memorable by a hunt in the Sierra Morena with mountain bandits.

From Cordoba they travelled to Seville. Dumas's account of 'the agonies and tribulations' of his journey by mail coach to the Andalusian capital is written with a verve and humour which perhaps no other author, with the exception of Dickens, could equal. Seville proved the crowning glory of the tour. Everywhere he was fêted. Balls, bullfights and even a play were put on in his honour, but it was the Spanish national dances that Dumas particularly loved.

By the middle of November he was at Cadiz to meet the vessel promised him by Salvandy which was to take him to Oran. Here he found the *Véloce*, a small gunboat, under one Captain Bérard, which plied between Oran and Tangier. Alexandre was enchanted with his welcome. He tells us how the captain welcomed him at the gangway, and how he was piped aboard. This great big child assumed that the ship and everything in it was to be his. He was handed a letter from the

224

secretary of Marshal Bugeaud, the military governor of Algeria, hoping that he would come with all speed to Algiers, where he would be treated with honour. Dumas describes his state cabin, with its gilding still fresh (for not long before, the vessel had been fitted out for a journey of the royal family). At Tangier he was rowed ashore in state in the ship's barge. He was enchanted with everything he saw. After a brief stay he visited Gibraltar where he was welcomed by the governor, Sir Robert Wilson, 'a charming old man'.

Their next port of call was Tetuan. The journey was delightful. Dumas and his party went ashore from time to time; they shot and hunted. They visited bazaars, where Alexandre loaded himself with costly ornaments and furniture for his new 'palace'.

At Tetuan, the captain spoke to him for the first time of the fate of a number of French officers and other ranks who had fallen into the hands of Abd-el-Kader.* Negotiations, it seems, had been going on for some time for the ransom of the prisoners who were to be released at Melissa; but the situation was still uncertain due to the temper of the Arabs.

When giving evidence at the later tribunal already referred to, Dumas said: 'These gentlemen [Gaillardet and Véron] wish to know what I was doing there. I will tell them. I know by prompt intervention, I saved twelve of my countrymen from execution. It was I who charged myself with the duty of rescuing Colonel Courby de Coignard . . .'

Unfortunately, there is not a word of truth in this statement. The *Véloce* had already been ordered to pick up the prisoners at Melissa, but because of the ship's late arrival, they had been moved to Djemar 'Azouat under the command of Colonel Macmahon, later marshal and President of the French Republic (1873).

Knowing his temperament, it is probable that Dumas believed every word he said. '*It was I,*' he declared, '*who had under my orders* the vessel that was to bring the prisoners away. This vessel *I* took to Melissa and brought the prisoners to Djemar 'Azouat, *where three thousand persons gave me dinner.* If you claim 2,000 livres from me for being in Africa, I saved twelve of my countrymen, which I regard is well worth the money.'

---

* The Arab leader Abd-el-Kader, a scholar and brilliant soldier, had from the very beginning opposed the French invasion of North Africa.

Never was there such a delusion. The dinner was not given for him but for the prisoners – he was merely a guest, though admittedly a guest of honour. It was only now that he sailed for Algiers, but on arriving there found that Marshal Bugeaud was absent and would not return for a fortnight.

Another version of the story is that he did in fact meet Bugeaud, who greeted him coldly with the remark: 'So here you are, *monsieur* the vessel-taker. *Diable!* you don't stand on ceremony! Ships of 280 horsepower for your cruises!'

'Monsieur le Maréchal,' Dumas is said to have replied, 'I have calculated that I have cost the government 11,000 francs in fuel since leaving Cadiz. Walter Scott on his voyage to Italy cost the English Admiralty 130,000 francs, so the French government still owes me 119,000 francs.'

The Marshal's reply is not recorded.*

He thereupon decided to visit Tunis, though the captain protested that the French government had given him no authority to exceed their present itinerary. Dumas, however, insisted that the *Véloce* was his to command, and spent a further three weeks' voyage at government expense. He enjoyed every moment of it; he saw Tunis and Carthage, and met with many adventures, which he published on his return to Paris. It was excellent reading but there were those in responsible positions who began to look more closely into the matter. A naval vessel, taken from its duty by order of the minister, and placed under the command of M Dumas, so that he might write his agreeable and profitable travelogues!

It was scandalous! On 10 February 1847, a most mortifying scene for Dumas took place in the Chambre des Députés. One of the deputies, the Comte de Castellane, rose to put a question to the ministry. 'Was it true that a well-known contractor for stories [laughter in the chamber] had been paid in this way with a sum charged on the budget for indigent men of letters for the purpose of making Algiers known to France and the Chamber? Had he been provided with a vessel at the expense of the State?'

The minister, Salvandy, did his best to defend his action, but he was not helped by Dumas, whose bombastic behaviour was not such as to influence the deputies in his favour, despite the fact that he insisted

* See A. C. Bell, op cit, who unfortunately provides no source for this account.

that he had largely contributed to the cost of the voyage out of his own pocket. Nor did it help matters that Marshal Bugeaud's invitation, sent by his secretary, was unsigned. Infinitely worse, however, was the fact that he had broken his contracts with Girardin and Véron to supply their newspapers with their daily *feuilletons*. Four volumes should have been delivered on 1 July 1845, but nothing had been delivered and by September only one was completed. Later, on receiving a court summons ordering him to fulfil his contracts, Dumas set to work to slaughter all his characters wholesale and brought the story to an abrupt conclusion. The arrears of 1845 were never cleared off and in 1846 he supplied nothing, although he had received most of the money in advance.

His treatment of *La Presse* was ludicrous. As already mentioned, he was engaged on writing *Joseph Balsamo* when the tempting invitation to attend the Duc de Montpensier's wedding was received. Dumas, with his story still unfinished, abruptly ended his last chapter with the words: 'After this, there was little left for the young man except to die. He closed his eyes and sank upon the ground.' And there, as the lawyer for the plaintiff said pleasantly, 'there he was left for six months, no one knowing what was to happen next, while M Dumas was shooting lions and tigers, exhibiting himself to the natives and displaying the order of Nitchan [bestowed on him by the Bey of Tunis] on his chest where there was little room for it.'

When the court met again, it was known that Dumas himself intended stating his own case. The court was crowded to overflowing. His defence was 'sophistical but scarcely intelligible'. Although obviously filled with untruths, the court listened to him with amused indulgence. He described in a truly dramatic style all his communications with Véron. Véron, he told the court, had demanded something 'bright and sparkling' to be supplied in eight days. 'Oh, that gives us plenty of time,' he had answered. A volume of his writing, he explained to the court, consisted of 135 folio pages and 6,000 lines. He brought the exact number of pages to Véron gravely numbered from 1 to 135, to show his loyalty, and engaged that they should be filled with copy within the appointed time. Much amusement was caused when our hero explained that the words 'Yes', 'No', or 'Damnation' constituted lines in themselves. The contract was for 30,000 lines. He explained his sudden departure by telling the court that after writing 15,800 lines – not *words*, please note – or the equivalent of eight volumes in eighteen months, he was tired and had been told, not only by his own physician, but by that of the Duc de Montpensier 'who was above suspicion', that he was grossly overworked; despite their advice, he had continued to write almost non-stop.

After three days of this entertainment, the court gave judgement. It decreed that within one month M Dumas must resume his interrupted *feuilleton* of *Joseph Balsamo* for the *Commerce* and for every day's delay he must pay a penalty – the equivalent of four pounds. Should the penalties reach twelve pounds, he was to be sent to prison for a year. Moreover, he was ordered to indemnify the other papers with whom he had failed to honour his contracts. Véron, 'who had the misfortune of being a millionaire', was less interested in receiving Dumas *feuilletons* than 'acting the harsh creditor'. Dumas was greatly piqued that his genius as a writer was not better appreciated.

The sentence was comparatively light. He had broken off the *Bâtard de Mauléon* for the *Commerce* at chapter forty-five; and since he was writing several other stories at once, these too were suddenly interrupted when his avid readers were looking forward to the next instalment. The circulation of the newspapers dropped, much to the annoyance of the editors, who had paid Alexandre in advance.

CHAPTER TWENTY-THREE

Decline and Fall (1847–56)

During his absence in Spain and Africa, the 'château' of Monte-Cristo and his theatre, now named the Historique, were completed.

Undeterred by the law suit, Dumas took up the thread of his interrupted work in his moated island retreat, his 'pavilion' which, apart from the one cell-like room in which he worked, was as lavishly decorated as the 'château' itself. The windows of the pavilion were of stained glass, every stone carved with the title of one of Dumas's works, and over the entrance was a dog carved in stone, modelled after the famous Milord, with the words *cave canem*. Approaching visitors might notice, inside, an azure ceiling bespangled with stars, cloth hangings on the walls, a chimney-piece decorated in red and gold, and a panoply bearing the arms of de la Pailleterie, and on the other side, three horses' heads in memory of the battle of Mantua, where, as Dumas explained, his father had had two horses killed under him and had won his objective on a third.

In this pavilion Dumas shut himself up in his cell and worked all day. The 'château' and grounds were open to his guests 'from cellar to attic'. Dumas *fils* and Maquet alone were allowed officially into his sanctum sanctorum. At his deal table, in his open-necked shirt and rolled-up sleeves, he continued the prodigious output interrupted by the Spanish and African journey. He finished 'those two or three novels' which, like a truant schoolboy, he had left uncompleted. Maquet was given the task of finishing the *Bâtard de Mauléon* while Alexandre devoted himself to finishing *Joseph Balsamo* and *Les Quarante-Cinq*.

At about the same time his Théâtre Historique, situated on the corner of the Boulevard du Temple and the faubourg of the same name, was completed to a novel design and decorated at a prohibitive cost. On 20 February 1847, Dumas saw one of his greatest ambitions realised with the performance of *La Reine Margot*, a Dumas–Maquet dramatization of the novel in five acts and fifteen tableaux. For months previously, rumours of the splendour and originality of the design, the lavishness of the decoration, the magnificence of its stage, had been circulating all over Paris. When, therefore, the opening date was announced, the Théâtre Historique was the sensation of the season. The theatre was packed. All the élite of France was present, including the Duc de Montpensier and all who had a claim to fame in the arts, music and literature.

For the opening night Dumas could not have made a better choice of play. Perhaps with the exception of *Monte-Cristo*, *La Reine Margot* is the most gripping of all Dumas's works. As adapted for the stage it lost none of its thrills. From the moment the red and gold curtain rose on the first scene at half-past six until it was lowered for the last time at three o'clock on the following morning, the audience of two thousand were spellbound. *Le Reine Margot* was later followed by a dramatised version of *Le Chevalier de Maison-Rouge*, which concluded with a rousing song, 'Mourir pour la Patrie'. This song became almost as popular as the 'Marseillaise' (which was only adopted officially as the national anthem at the outbreak of the Franco-Prussian War).

The immediate success of the Théâtre Historique was assured from the first night. Although Dumas regarded his theatre principally as a means of showing his own plays, he did put on several plays by his contemporaries – Balzac, de Musset, Dumas *fils*,* Hugo, Jules Verne, and a comedy in verse by his namesake Adolphe Dumas (*L'Ecole des Familles*), which had a great success. *Intrigue et Amour*, an adaptation from Schiller, took the Théâtre Historique into the summer. The total takings for the first season amounted to 707,905 francs. Dumas was able to leave the management of the theatre in the hands of a M Hostein, in whom he could not have found a more capable administrator, while he himself was able to devote his whole time to writing.

Despite the insidious campaign initiated by de Mirecourt and the sniping of jealous contemporaries, despite the undignified debate in

* *La Dame aux Camélias.*

230

the Chambre des Députés concerning his misuse of the gunboat *Véloce*, the year 1847 marked the summit of Dumas's popularity. With his own theatre, his own château, and writing simultaneously in four or five journals, he remained the most outstanding personality of his epoch.

Cham the caricaturist, in his cartoon depicting him astride Paris, with a host of malevolent critics and hostile minor writers crawling like ants between his legs, gave a true expression of public opinion, and the manner in which he had captured public opinion the world over. In the following years it is estimated that his writings made him an income of something between £90,000 and £96,000. His contract with Cadot was for 4,488 francs per volume, royalties apart. Between 1843 and 1852 he published 329 volumes for Cadot, making his earnings 1,476,552 francs from that source alone. It is impossible to know what his total earnings were, since he was too unbusinesslike to keep accounts.

Not only had the building of Monte-Cristo, with its grounds and pavilion, and his theatre cost him a fortune, but his household expenses must have been astronomical. His domestic staff included Mme Lamarque, a splendid cook, and the little Negro, Alexis, brought by Mlle Dorval in a basket of flowers (see page 223). There was also Paul, who seems to have been the original Eau de Benjoin, recommended by Chevet and described with no little humour in *De Paris à Cadix*, whose functions at Monte-Cristo were, like those of most of the inmates, undefined and often superfluous. In addition, two magnificent Arabs in splendid costumes greeted visitors at the entrance – they were in fact architectural sculptors by profession, formerly slaves of the Bey of Tunis, whom Dumas had acquired to decorate his Oriental *salon*. Among Dumas's many extravagances was his menagerie, which was entrusted to the care of an invaluable member of his staff, a peasant known as Michel who was also head gardener and handyman.

Michel, however, was much more than a gardener and keeper of animals. He kept bailiffs and creditors at bay. Should a bailiff prove utterly intractable, Michel, from an invisible point, worked movable bridges, to such effect that an overzealous representative of the law was precipitated into the moat.

The relationship between the illiterate peasant and Dumas was one of reciprocal admiration and attraction. It was a relationship of the

231

sort that had existed between the boy Alexandre and the poachers of the forests of Villers-Cotterêts. They were more like two friends with a mutual love of animals and sport than master and servant.

Not least among Dumas's retainers was Rusconi, an Italian, an ardent Bonapartist, and former secretary to General Dermoncourt, one-time aide-de-camp to Dumas's father. No sooner had Dumas learnt that Rusconi was now penniless and out of work than he engaged his services. But the difficulty was to find suitable enployment for the ex-secretary. When asked what was Rusconi's actual job on the household, Dumas invented a verb, *Rusconner*. This meant 'all and sundry'. He acted as gardener-secretary-valet-protector. In fact he did everything from looking after his master's wardrobe to describing to inquiring visitors the character and characteristics of his master's pets, as well as informing them of the names of plants and trees in his master's garden. *Le pauvre petit Rusconi*, as he described himself, worshipped his master. In a broad Italian accent he would tell visitors: 'I saw Napoleon Bonaparte at Elba when I was commissioner of police. I saw Madame la Duchesse de Berry arrested at Nantes when I was secretary to General Dermoncourt, and I see Monsieur Alexandre Dumas every day. So it is that I flatter myself that I have been close to the three greatest persons of this century.'

These were regular members of the household, but it is impossible to record the 'irregulars'. A register of the guests would be impossible. At Dumas's famous Sunday parties, when he invited friends 'just to vary the custom of the other six days when friends invited themselves', he often found himself host to thirty or more guests. Complete strangers came again and again.

There was, for example, the man who brought Dumas a mysterious parcel, and who somehow insinuated himself into the pavilion. Opening up the package, he displayed the skin of a boa constrictor which, he claimed, had been shot by Alexandre's father (the story is told by Blaze de Bury). On the strength of this lie, the ingenious rascal lived at Dumas's expense for the best part of three years.

When not being imposed on, Dumas managed to ruin himself. On one occasion he noticed a shabbily dressed woman, the wife of another impoverished out-of-work actor, sitting timidly on the lawn apart from the other brazen callers making free with his food and wine. She seemed exhausted by the heat. She was a complete stranger to him.

'Have you no sunshade, my poor woman?' asked Dumas.

'No, *monsieur*. I am afraid that is a luxury I cannot afford.'

'You must get yourself one,' he said, slipping some coins into her hand.

'But,' she stammered, 'you have given me far too much, Monsieur Dumas.'

'Never mind,' he replied, 'you will need an umbrella for rainy days.'

He rarely paid his bills, hence the bailiffs were always calling at his door. Not that he could not afford to pay but, *en grand seigneur*, such trifles seemed beneath him. One anecdote is typical of his attitude. One day his bootmaker arrived at the door to demand 250 francs which he was owed.

'You have come just at the right moment,' said Dumas. 'I want three more pairs of boots.'

'Certainly, Monsieur Dumas, but certainly, but what about my account?' said the bootmaker.

'Of course,' replied Dumas, 'we will talk of it over lunch. I am busy now. Make yourself at home. Go anywhere you like . . . Ask Michel to show you the menagerie . . .'

After lunch Dumas gave him flowers to take back to his wife, fruit for the man's children, and twenty francs for the railway fare. There was never any question of paying the account. After several such visits, the bootmaker had been paid his bill ten times over. Dumas still remained his debtor.

All these spongers, hangers-on, parasites of every sort, cost him thousands. And then there were the women. The reigning sultanas succeeded one another with great rapidity: Louise Beaudoin, known as Atala Beauchère; young actresses from the Théâtre Historique; women writers. The especial favourite of the year 1848 was the charming Céleste Scrivaneck, who although still very young, had understudied the famous Virgime Delazet, whose son had introduced Dumas *fils* to Marie Duplessis, the original 'Dame aux Camélias'. Mistress, friend and secretary, Céleste would also like to have been mother. Maurois quotes a letter from the Simone Maurois collection:

Céleste Scrivaneck to Dumas fils: My dear Alexandre, happiness could go no further; I shall not leave your father. He has agreed to let me help him with his work. I am to travel with you both *as a boy*. The tailor has just been to take my measurements. I feel wildly gay! Forgive me, my good, my excellent friend, for not having told you all this before now . . . I hope to see you again a month from now, but in the meanwhile, do send me a few friendly words.

I have done what you asked me. I am busy hemming your cravats. As soon as the tailor has finished your trousers everything shall be sent to you without delay . . . Adieu. Send me news of yourself soon.

Your affectionate little mother
C. Scrivaneck.

Dumas *père* revelled in this topsy-turvy household. He would have been divinely happy had his son consented to play the same role as Maquet and become a partner in 'Alexandre Dumas & Co'. He could, his father told him, easily make forty or fifty-thousand francs a year.

Despite the success of his novel, Dumas *fils* was short of money, and reluctantly consented to do some work for his father. Sometimes under pressure, he applied to Hippolyte Hostein, the businesslike young manager of the Théâtre Historique, who from time to time helped him out. Not that his father was unwilling to help, just as he would help any sponger; but somehow the young Alexandre, who knew his father only too well, hesitated to call on his purse, which, not surprisingly was very often empty.

Dumas *père* was at last beginning to feel the pinch – entirely through his own fault, though with his usual ebullient and optimistic character he refused to admit it. He continued to work night and day, but still piled up more and more debts.

CHAPTER TWENTY-FOUR

The 1848 Revolution

Although in its short life the Théâtre Historique had been remarkably successful, the end came more or less abruptly with the revolution of 1848, which swept Louis-Philippe from the throne. Although Dumas, the republican, wasted no regrets over King Louis-Philippe, he had lost valuable patrons in the royal princes.

The revolution of 1848 came as no surprise to many intelligent, thinking people. The revolutionary spirit in the middle of the nineteenth century was by no means confined to France, but was widespread over Europe. The monarchy of Louis-Philippe for a long time had been intolerable to most Frenchmen by reason of its dishonesty. The French could not be blamed for considering the Orléans rulers as Bourbons in disguise. The 'citizen king' certainly made every effort to make his government popular and national, but although the death of Louis, Duc d'Orléans (the young patron of Dumas), by a fall from his carriage, was genuinely mourned by the people as a whole (indeed, the princes were generally popular) sympathy for the royal family was not enough to produce any closer ties between the dynasty and the nation. Parliamentary life was restless and ministers were constantly changing. Majorities in the Chambre des Députés were secured by artificial means and bribery. Although Dumas makes little reference in his *Mémoires* to the historical events of his middle years, France was going through very troubled times. Conspiracies were discovered and suppressed, and plots for murder were made the occasion of the harshest measures against the radicals. But not one of the great social groups could be induced to link its future permanently with that of the House of Orléans. Unfortunately for himself, the King had reposed special

235

confidence in Guizot, who on the fall of Thiers in October 1840 became foreign minister, with practical control of the foreign and domestic policy of France. No more unpopular choice could have been made. Guizot's intellectual arrogance alienated the literary and political leaders of Parisian society; his initial liberal views had become increasingly reactionary.

The republican party had undergone many changes since the establishment of the July monarchy; it now exercised a greater power upon youthful talent. It is no part of our story to deal with all the political events that led to the bloody revolt in 1848. For our purpose it is enough to say that for some years past communist doctrines had been disseminating throughout France. A brilliant lawyer and orator named Rollin overshadowed all other politicians who had aroused any enthusiasm among Parisians. His newspaper, *La Reforme*, pointed consistently and unhesitatingly to republicanism as the only possible form of government.

The years 1847 and 1848 were notable for their particularly bad harvests. Food was scarce and prices soared; unemployment figures were the highest for years. There was widespread profiteering. The financial fabric of France was crumbling. The new railway systems were underfinanced and many projects were abandoned halfway through construction, throwing more men out of work.

'The ageing dotard', as Dumas referred to Louis-Philippe, under pressure, at last dismissed Guizot and began to confer with Comte Louis de Molé, a leader of the moderate liberals, on the formation of a new ministry.

On the evening of 23 February the crowds which thronged the boulevards gave loud expression to their delight in the dismissal of Guizot. Meanwhile republican agents were busily collecting the people of the suburbs, who had long been prepared for a rising, and sending them to the more excited quarters of the city. Probably nothing too serious would have occurred but for a completely fortuitous event. A crowd of people had gathered in front of Guizot's house which, although he had already been dismissed, was still guarded. Perhaps the crowd were unaware that the King was replacing him by Molé, since news, unlike today with hourly radio bulletins, travelled slowly. Unfortunately, some young firebrands began taunting the officer in command, and stones were thrown. A shot was heard. Immediately the troops opened fire. It is impossible to apportion the blame. A number of demonstrators were killed. Paris immediately rang with cries of 'Murder! To arms!' About midnight the alarm bells of Notre-Dame began to ring out the tocsin, and thousands flocked to raise the barricades. The morning of 24 February found Paris in revolt. There was some bloody fighting, the citizen King, who could rely neither on the National Guard nor the army, abdicated.

France was declared a republic on 25 February 1848.

The provisional government formed by Lamartine, however, was unable to set things to rights immediately, despite the reforms instituted including universal male sufferage. Unemployment was still critical and the working classes had expected an immediate amelioration of their circumstances. Rioting was by no means confined to Paris and continued in the provinces, particularly in Lyon. 'Mourir pour la patrie' had seized the public mind, and Dumas flattered himself that this strain had contributed materially to the success of the revolution. Although republican at heart and pleased to see the overthrow of Louis-Philippe, a spirit of chivalry prompted him to stand up for the exiled royal family, or rather the young Duc de Montpensier, to whom he wrote a letter seven days after the proclamation of France as a republic, which was published in *La Presse*:

> To Monseigneur le Duc de Montpensier,
> If I knew where to find your Royal Highness, I would in person hasten to offer the expression of my sorrow for the great calamity that has come upon your family.

Very strange words to publish openly from an ardent republican! His letter continues:

> I can never forget that during three years, in spite of politics, and even against the wishes of the King, you have received and treated me almost as a friend.
> Of this title of friend I used to boast when you were at the palace; now that you have left France I claim it.

As he himself admits, there was some danger in publishing such sentiments. It is indeed very odd that he should have done so, and in fact it did bring him into trouble on the very day following the publication of his letter. As he was returning from a fête, dressed in the uniform of commandant of the national guard of St Germain-en-Laye, he heard angry murmurs behind him, and turning round, saw a man leading a band of some fifty men. 'So it is you,' said the man, 'Citizen Alexandre Dumas, who addresses the Duc de Montpensier as *Monseigneur.*'

'*Monsieur,*' replied Dumas with the great politeness, 'I always make it a practice of calling an exile *Monseigneur*, a bad habit no doubt, but such is my way.'

'Then take this for your pains,' said the man, pointing a pistol at our hero's head.

A young man, a stranger to Dumas, knocked up the pistol which went off in the air. Dumas had half drawn his sword, intending to kill his opponent, but as he says, 'I thought the fellow not worth the trouble,' and returned home. Such is Dumas's version of the story. Another version was also circulated: The gallant commandant wished to harangue the crowd, but was hooted. 'Will you hold your tongue,' cried a heckler – 'you still have the butt end of Montpensier's cigar in your mouth.' Dumas was not, in this account, threatened by physical violence. But what a much better story he makes of the incident!

He now bought a share in the newspaper *La Liberté*, at a moment when its circulation was no more than twelve or thirteen thousand copies. According to Dumas, two months after his joining the staff, the circulation reached eighty thousand copies. He wished to insert a protest against the law exiling the Orléans princes, but the editor refused. His protest was finally published in *La Commerce*; he also pleaded for Prince Napoleon, but he had no more success with *La Commerce* than he had had with *La Liberté*. He therefore decided to found his own paper, *Le Mois*, in which he himself recorded daily political events, and of which he was editor-in-chief. His motto for the paper was, 'God dictates and I write.' *Le Mois* ran for only a few numbers and then expired. Undeterred, he made yet another excursion into the field of journalism, with *La France Nouvelle*, all at great expense, although he seldom paid his contributors. This also proved unsuccessful.

The eternal optimist, although heavily in debt, now had the quixotic idea of standing as a deputy for the newly formed provisional government. He made grandiose speeches in the clubs. He told his audiences that he was a workman, a workman of *thought*.

'Every day of my life,' he said, 'I am the means of supplying bread to hundreds of other workmen, my brothers, compositors, pressmen, etc, who work at my newspapers and books.' But his arguments had no effect and he was treated as unceremoniously as before. Next he decided to stand as a member for Auxerre. Three thousand people waited to meet him. On his way, his carriage broke down and he arrived late. The impatient crowd were in a very ill humour and as he rose to address them; one man hissed him. 'Sir,' said Dumas, 'I allow you to hiss my works, but not myself. Your name and address please?' This silenced the interrupter.

He was then challenged regarding his relationship with the Duc d'Orléans. He was delighted at this opportunity. 'I thank you for the question,' he said. 'In five minutes I'll have you all in tears.' Dumas then started off on a panegyric of the duke, the love the country bore him, and at the end of five minutes he had his audience deeply moved, even weeping. They rushed forward to embrace him. Nevertheless, he was not elected, because he did not belong to the district. He tried St Germain, the place which he had almost created, but even here he was not elected. For a while he even thought of standing for election in the Antilles. 'I'll send them a lock of my hair,' he said, 'to show that I am one of them.' But, once again, he had to abandon his project.

Thus, unsuccessful journalist, newspaper proprietor and politician, he returned once more to his plays and novels. It was high time he made some money. The takings of the Théâtre Historique had fallen to practically nothing. The enterprise was virtually bankrupt. From almost the very outset, Dumas's prodigality had terrified Hostein, who, exasperated, finally refused to be 'keeper to his great big baby' any longer and resigned in December 1849. From all sides, Dumas's creditors fell on him. There was a distraint on Monte-Cristo and the burden of mortgages amounted to 232,469 francs and six centimes. To add to his worries, Ida Ferrier or, as she now called herself in Florence, the Marquise Davy de la Pailleterie, claimed preferential treatment as a creditor. Her noble Italian lover had failed to support her in the manner which both she and Alexandre had anticipated, and she was now demanding 120,000 francs of her dowry, plus interest, plus alimony. Since August 1847 she had put her affairs in the hands of her lawyer, Maître Lacan.

In February 1848, the Tribunal of the Seine awarded damages against the estranged husband. He was ordered to make restitution of the dowry of 120,000 francs, which he had misappropriated and to pay alimony of 6,000 francs a year. Dumas appealed. The revolution, in addition to ruining him, had further complicated these family affairs. Monte-Cristo and its contents was put up for sale, but Dumas saw to it that this was only to be an artificial gesture. The 'château' was duly sold for the derisory sum of 30,000 francs to a certain Jacques-Antoine Doyen, who was obviously just a 'front', for he never took possession. Maquet was asked to borrow by hook or by crook enough money to buy the contents and remove them to Bougival, until Dumas was in a position to buy them back again. But it was already too late. One day Michel, the odd job man, came to see his master.

'I think I ought to tell you, *monsieur*, that there is no wine left for the staff. There is only Johannisberger and champagne.

'I have no money; drink the champagne,' replied Dumas – 'it will do you all good.'

It was not long, however, before the bailiff's men moved in. The furniture, pictures, books, carriages and even his menagerie were seized. Among the receipts left behind was: 'Received one vulture, estimated value fifteen frs.' This was the famous Jugurtha Diogenes which he had acquired from the brother of the Bey of Tunis and of which he was inordinately proud.

One day, when finally forced to quit the 'château', he offered two small plums to a friend, who took one. 'You have just eaten a hundred thousand francs,' said Dumas. 'Those two plums were all that I had left of Monte-Cristo ... and Monte-Cristo cost me two hundred thousand.'

Meanwhile Marie Dorval was dying. She had sent an appeal to her former lover, the novelist Jules Sandeau, and to her 'great pet', Alexandre Dumas. The former never replied; the 'gentle giant', Dumas, came running. To save her the humiliation of being buried in a pauper's grave, he was determined to raise the money to provide her with a proper burial.

Marie Dorval died. Dumas first went to see the Comte de Falloux, then Minister of Public Education, and asked him for help. The minister, however, could do nothing officially, but contributed one hundred francs from his own pocket. Dumas then hurried to a pawnshop and pledged his precious orders and medals for a further two hundred francs. This was indeed a touching sacrifice, for Dumas was passionately attached to his decorations.

Stripped of his 'château' of Monte-Cristo he was now almost penniless, living in Montmartre. His son no longer shared his apartment. They loved each other but constantly quarrelled. Alexandre *fils* now preached high-minded morality to his father. Since the death of Marie Duplessis, the son had become at least temporarily a reformed character. His novel, based on the life of his former love, had a remarkable success. With the popularity of his book, which he entitled *Camille*, the young dandy paid off all his own debts and settled down seriously to work. The subject of *Camille* was for the times singularly audacious. In a century of middle-class prudery, no writer had so far dared to describe beauty for sale, much less pity it, and then even maintain that his heroine La Dame aux Camélias, was not guilty of what she was doing. Persuaded by his friends, young Alexandre turned his novel into a play.

This was in 1848; at the time Dumas *père* still possessed the Théâtre Historique. Dumas *fils* spoke to his father of his play, but the latter showed little enthusiasm for the idea. His father's initial lack of enthusiasm, however, did not prevent the young man from carrying on with his project. His father, so sceptical at first, was enchanted by it and promised eventually to produce it at the Théâtre Historique. But, before this could ever be realised, there intervened the fall of the House of Orléans, and the Théâtre Historique closed.

Dumas's absorption in politics had had the effect of making the year 1848 the most unproductive of his whole life. True, some of his greatest works were under way – *Le Vicomte de Bragelonne* and *Mes Mémoires*. At the beginning of 1849 he fell back on the ever-popular *Trois Mousquetaires*, which Maquet dramatised under the title of *La Jeunesse des Mousquetaires*. *Twenty years after* was the swan song of the saga of the *Mousquetaires*. The *Mousquetaire* cycle is the saga of France, a world of epic loyalty, courage and devotion, chivalry and valour. The young Alexandre tells how one day, calling to see his father, he found him in his study in great distress, his face drawn and tears running down his cheeks. 'Porthos is dead,' Dumas *père* explained. 'I have just killed him. I can't help crying over him, poor Porthos.'

The death of Porthos, Dumas claimed, so prostrated him that feeling unable to continue with what he referred to as his 'epic poem', he revisited Villers-Cotterêts to find consolation amid old friends and the scenes of his childhood.

CHAPTER TWENTY-FIVE

The Debtor

It was quite true that Dumas needed to recuperate. The year 1850 saw 'the king of Paris' desperately trying to fight off his many creditors. Everything began to fail the gentle giant – politics, the theatre and even the *feuilletons*. On 16 October 1850, the Théâtre Historique finally closed its doors after three years and eight months. Dumas was in debt to the sum of 200,000 francs. Despite the huge sums he had earned, he was in debt everywhere, above all to Maquet.

The *coup d'état* of Louis-Napoleon came at the most opportune moment to provide Dumas with an excuse to avoid his creditors and lawsuits without loss of face. The unfortunate Maquet, to whom Dumas owed so much, was one of the worst to suffer. Relations between the two men had come to a breaking point. It was not that they quarrelled: on the contrary, the final separation was forced on Maquet by necessity. Dumas could not pay him for his work. Profiting by his apprenticeship with our hero, Maquet now branched out on his own. He was one of the few collaborators who, when left to his own devices, became a successful writer and made a fortune. But in spite of his success after leaving Dumas, his works today are less remembered than his name.

Like Hugo and others, Dumas went into voluntary exile in Belgium. The difference was that Hugo was fleeing from a tyrant, while Dumas, although he liked to give the impression that he too was a voluntary political exile, was fleeing the bailiffs.

In Brussels, Dumas, though ruined, somehow managed to live once more in luxury, all on credit. He rented a mansion, complete with a *porte cochère* and balcony, at 73 Boulevard de Waterloo and even employed a liveried servant to greet his guests. He was fortunate enough to engage the services of a banished deputy, Noël Parfait, a most reliable man with a wife and children. In exchange, Parfait copied novels, memoirs and comedies from morning to night, which Dumas turned out more rapidly than they could be reproduced – thirty-six volumes for Belgium, Germany, England and America. As Victor Hugo's son wrote: 'There was nobody else in the world who could write them but Dumas, and nobody else could copy them like Parfait.' In addition to his literary help, the appropriately named Parfait took charge of Dumas's finances and attempted to put some order into that house of extravagance. He claimed (successfully) royalties in arrears, arranged to have *La Tour du Nesle* revived, published what remained of *Travel Impressions* and even managed to scrape a few more louis out of the sale of the château of Monte-Cristo.

It would have been an impossibility for a man of Dumas's temperament to have lived the life of an anchorite. There were occasions when the house in the Boulevard de Waterloo was a scene of gaiety almost equivalent to the festive evenings at Monte-Cristo. A young friend of Dumas, Deschamel, has described such an evening, carrying with him a never-to-be-forgotten memory of Dumasian hospitality – of the *salon* 'with its gorgeous hangings, its oak frieze, its marvellous statuettes standing among vases of flowers, foliage and heathers'. He describes a supper for sixty guests or more in the winter-garden, set among foliage, tropical flowers, and candles; of the charming and lovely women; the magnificent dishes and wines; and afterwards the conversation that went on into the early hours, 'when the first light of daylight sent the last guests home for shame'.

After the arrival of Parfait such celebrations were the exception rather than the rule. A typical day was rather thus: after an early breakfast – about seven o'clock in winter, six in summer – Dumas would climb to his little room at the top of the house, a sort of attic on the third floor, just beneath the roof and lighted by one skylight, furnished with his usual plain deal table, covered with sheet upon sheet of blue paper.

All morning he would write. Between twelve and one he took lunch, then he returned to his cell to write until well into the night, oblivious to his guests below. By midnight, one, two or three in the morning, or even later, the last guest gone, he went to bed. If he felt very tired and his imagination jaded, he might read a little before falling asleep – for that was the only time he had for reading; if the mood were on him, should there be a chapter to finish, he would sit down once more at his table and complete it. If, as sometimes happened, the day had been wasted as far as writing was concerned by a visit to a friend or by a hunting party, when everyone else, dog-tired by exertion and fresh air, had gone home, he would throw himself on his bed, leaving orders to be called in three or four hours' time, and waking refreshed, work all night into the morning.

Courmeaux, who often dropped in to help Parfait copy and punctuate the master's works, might find thirty sheets of manuscript awaiting him.

Dumas's life, however, was not entirely devoted to work and playing host in his own house, as Deschanel and Courmeaux would have us believe, for he continued to see his fellow exiles, not only in his home, but sometimes in the house of the Belgian, Collard, where he would meet Hugo, Deschanel, Quinet and Arago. The Café des Milles Colonnes and the Café de l'Aigle too became favourite meeting places for these exiles. Moreover, from time to time he made clandestine visits to Paris. Nevertheless in the course of his three years' exile Dumas wrote more than most authors write in a lifetime, often writing two or three volumes simultaneously. He accepted more commissions for novels and articles than even he could accomplish. Although perhaps he did not meet all his obligations, he was able to settle accounts with the faithful Maquet, who insisted that his name should be always added to those of Dumas's as co-author on any book on which he had collaborated in any way.

Meanwhile in Paris, after some difficulty, Alexandre *fils* had found a theatre to stage his *Dame aux Camélias*. Since the *coup d'état* of 1851, the Duc de Morny, illegitimate half-brother to Napoleon III, now Minister of the Interior and the most powerful man in France, had persuaded the censors to lift the ban on the play, which formerly had been regarded as 'too immoral' to present to the public. Since the censors were unanimous in their opinion that the piece would not run for more than two or three nights at the most, they now raised little objection. But they were mistaken. The first evening (at the Vaudeville) was a tumultuous success. Instead of having supper with the actors after the performance, as was customary, young Dumas hurried home to his mother, Catharine Labay.

He telegraphed to his father in Brussels: 'Great success! So great that I thought I was attending a première of one of your own works.'

In Brussels where his fellow exiles were living in poverty, Dumas continued his life of luxury, despite the fact that he was still officially bankrupt. In the few leisure moments at his disposal (among other works, he was writing was his long and diffuse *Mémoires*) he still found time to conduct several love affairs, often simultaneously. He was never in the least bit ashamed of these liaisons and had no hesitation in writing to his daughter, Marie, to confess that a young married woman, Anna Bauer, whose husband was impotent (so she claimed), was soon to give birth to his child. To his son, too, he unashamedly admitted affairs with a Madame Guidi, Isabelle Constant, and others.

Thanks to Noël Parfait's control of his personal finances and the astute handling of his affairs in Paris by Hirschler, the former secretary of the Théâtre Historique, Dumas was able to come to an agreement with his creditors.* The official receiver wrote, 'Monsieur Alexandre Dumas has shown the greatest loyalty and zeal in carrying out his undertakings,' and in 1853 granted him his discharge as a bankrupt.

While Hugo had left Brussels for Jersey in voluntary exile in 1852, Dumas was beginning to hanker after Paris again. At the beginning of 1853, the agreement with his creditors was signed, and Dumas gave a sumptuous farewell dinner party to his friends. The house in Boulevard de Waterloo, which was leased to him until 1855, he offered to Noël Parfait. The latter asked for his final discharge as auditor. This Dumas gave to him by throwing all the accounts into the kitchen stove, and departed for Paris with a light heart, full of optimism.

---

* He proposed to surrender to his creditors one half share in the literary property of all his works, present and to come. Hirschler obtained for him slightly better terms.

CHAPTER TWENTY-SIX

Le Mousquetaire

On his return to Paris, Dumas embarked on a scheme which he had long had in mind – that of founding a newspaper of his own. This was to be an evening paper entitled *Le Mousquetaire*. Subscription: thirty-six francs in Paris, forty in the provinces. Offices at the Maison d'Or, number 1 rue Lafitte. The Maison d'Or was better known under the name of the Maison d'Orée, after a famous restaurant across the street, above which Dumas had an apartment. The title of the newspaper was well chosen – it immediately brought to mind the most famous of Dumas's novels.

The first issue announced fifty volumes of *Mémoires* by Alexandre Dumas. Fifty volumes! He had already begun writing these while in Brussels. Each day the proprietor and editor-in-chief, Dumas himself, promised to provide from his own pen 10,000 words! Friends and supporters welcomed the return of 'the irresponsible prodigal', while others regarded the whole venture as a thoughtless gamble. But these pessimists were wrong. Two reasons contributed to the immediate if ephemeral success of the venture. First, the still potent appeal of the very name – *Le Mousquetaire, journal de M Alexandre Dumas* – was a guarantee of good things worth paying for, especially as there was a lack of newspapers. Journal after journal had been suppressed for expressing anti-government views. Secondly, while old voices were either banished or silenced, the new had not yet made themselves effectively heard. Balzac was dead at the early age of fifty-six; Hugo and Michelet banished; Lamartine, Vigny, Gautier silenced. De Musset was finished; Flaubert, Verlaine, the brothers Goncourt, Baudelaire, Zola were yet to make their names. Romanticism was over – naturalism was not yet in force. 'The time was stagnant with the stagnation that heralds new events.'

Into this void, this lethargy, *Le Mousquetaire* brought a gust of fresh air. Lamarine, Michelet and Hugo all wrote to congratulate him. The very name of Hugo was anathema to the government – his letter, dated New Year's Day 1854, written from Jersey, reads: 'Dear Dumas, I am reading your journal here. You restore us Voltaire. Supreme consolation for humiliated and gagged France. *Vale et me ama*, Victor Hugo.' It was with the profoundest reluctance that Dumas withheld this letter from publication; its insertion would have at least involved a heavy fine for himself, or alternatively, imprisonment and the suppression of his newspaper.

On the front door of the Maison d'Or, Dumas had placed a small white placard on which was written *Le Mousquetaire. Tournez le poignet, s'il vous plaît.* (Please turn the knob.) The door would swing open to reveal a little ante-chamber, with the usual deal table and two or three receptionists, including Michel, the former gardener and handyman from the 'château' of Monte-Cristo, who ruled over the till.

'I put him in charge of the cash box,' explained Dumas, 'because he's just the man for the job. He can't count.'

There was, in fact, no necessity to count, since the cash box was perpetually empty. Yet the newspapers, miraculously appeared every evening. There were plenty of pens, ink and paper, but the contributors, who never received any financial remuneration for their work, were faithful to their posts.

Dumas worked tirelessly for *Le Mousquetaire* but knew nothing about the business of running a newspaper. He fondly imagined that he could pay himself fees equivalent to those he had received before his exile from long-established journals. In the beginning he had engaged the services of an administrator, a certain Martinet, who would come to see Dumas now and then to tell him: 'Monsieur Dumas, I have no more money,'

'How's that?' Dumas would exclaim. 'What about the subscriptions and what about the sales of single copies?'

'My dear sir, only ten minutes ago you took from me the three hundred francs that came in this morning.'

'But naturally I furnished a thousand francs' worth of copy yesterday.'

It is quite true that Dumas, installed on the third floor in a cell-like room, the sort of room he preferred, seated in his shirt sleeves, turned out ream after ream of memoirs, *Causeries*, plays and novels without respite – *El Salteador*, the beginnings of *Les Mohicans de Paris* and *Histoire de mes Bêtes*, the continuation of *Mes Mémoires*, *Les Grands Hommes en Robe de Chambre*, the plays *L'Orestie* and *Romulus*, *Une Vie d'Artiste*, memorial articles on Marie Dorval and Delphine Gay. In addition to which he wrote a host of dramatic and critical articles and other works published outside his own journal, three novels – *La Comtesse de Charny*, *Le Page du Duc de Savoie*, *Le Lièvre de mon Grand-père*, – and six plays, now all but forgotten.

In producing this vast output, how could he be expected to know what was happening below in the offices, how many staff were employed or even what salaries his employees were receiving? There were, also, constant calls on his generosity, which as usual he could never refuse. It was Hirschler, the former manager of the Théâtre Historique, who said that *Le Mousquetaire* was more of a charitable institution than a newspaper. Among Dumas's many acts of generosity was his interest in a charitable organisation for poor, ailing and deformed girls and the raising of subscriptions for the perpetual upkeep of the tombs of Hégesippe Moreau, Frédéric Soulié and Balzac, which were falling into ruin for lack of care. No wonder *Le Mousquetaire* was unable to show a profit.

All these acts of philanthropy, although a tribute to his heart, were a mistake in the policy of Dumas's editorship. It might not have been so had he not lost the services of Martinet and substituted Michel and Rusconi.

Audebrand, one of the twelve of the original staff (which grew to twenty-five), recounted how an observer of the ground floor of the Maison d'Or would have found 'the myth of the Tower of Babel made fact ... A stream, a river, a sea of people, surge, come and go, vociferate, gesticulate, chat, bring MSS, demand to see the editor, argue with Michel and Rusconi.'

The sight of these hordes of idlers exasperated Michel; he would rush up to Dumas's attic in impotent fury, complaining that 'while Monsieur works up here all day, down below there are a dozen writers who never write'.

With such a background, an editor who had not the slightest knowledge of editing, who sold articles intended for his own paper to other papers to raise the wind, a cashier who could not count, and a horde of writers who did not write, the paper was bound to fail. He promised sequels to *Les Quarante-Cinq, Monte-Cristo* and *Le Vicomte de Bragelonne*, which were never to see the light of day. Subscribers naturally complained. What sequels were contributed were by the pens of hack writers. The magic touch was lost. The circulation of the paper decreased, gradually at first, and then with increasing swiftness. The staff received no payment and, coming to the end of their patience, resigned in a body, only Michel and Rusoni remaining until the very end.

The last number of *Le Mousquetaire* appeared on 7 February 1857.

CHAPTER TWENTY-SEVEN

The Celebrated Traveller

Dumas had been restless for a year. Not that he ever ceased work. He visited Marseille to produce a play, revisited Belgium and the Rhine; visited Châlons and Varennes to gather material for a history of the flight of Louis XVI, paid a short visit to Guernsey* at the invitation of Victor Hugo.

Shortly after the closing down of *Le Mousquetaire* he paid two visits to England. Of the earlier of these two visits, when he stayed only a weekend, he has left no account. His second visit to England, judging by his *Causeries*, he seems to have enjoyed, although he shared Heine's view of the English in the 1850s at the height of Victorianism, as 'God's own comedians, too much like a prison to be enjoyed for long'. He was referring in particular to the English Sunday. Dumas wrote:

> I crossed the Channel, with the intention, or shall I say on the pretext, of seeing the Epsom races, and embarked on Monday, returning the following Saturday – thus making certain of missing the English Sabbath. In London, after having worked for six days of the week, you do not rest on the seventh – you bore yourself.

Dumas crossed the Channel on 25 May 1857 taking with him his son, and put up at the London coffee house of a Mr Young. He found the food monotonous and abominable. Their first call was at Daniel's of Bond Street to buy English china, for which Dumas had a passion. Next, they paid a visit to Madame Tussaud's whose famous waxworks so intrigued him that he devoted a separate *causerie* to the subject.

---

* Hugo had remained in Jersey only a short while.

250

Rotten Row delighted him. He was particularly struck by the predominance of unchaperoned young women. He visited the Crystal Palace, Greenwich Hospital and the largest and latest iron-clad ship *The Leviathan*, by which he was much impressed.

Derby Day left an ineffaceable impression on him. What Frith conveyed in paint, Dumas recorded faithfully with his pen.

Perhaps it was his visit to Hugo that inspired him to publish another newspaper. This was a weekly, produced 'without assistants' and named *Le Monte-Cristo*. Its career lasted from 23 April until 2 May 1860 and, after a break of eighteen months, from 1 January 1862, until October of the same year. This too, although *entirely edited and published by Alexandre Dumas*, as he himself advertised it, proved a failure. In the first few numbers he had recourse to his old practice, usually beginning an article: 'Dear Readers', followed by already familiar material, every sentence of which was a paragraph. Then followed some chapters of his romance *Monte-Cristo*, now already ten years old, and a short story, probably by some other hand but which the great man signed. By and by, even Dumas could not keep up the pace, and acquired assistants who were permitted to sign the copy themselves. As copy failed, recourse was had to the device of taking extracts, pages long, from de Musset or some other writer, introducing them with a few lines of his own and signing the whole, Alexandre Dumas. This *supercherie* was soon spotted. In extenuation Dumas wrote:

One of my readers complains that after I had announced that the whole journal was to be written by myself, I sometimes fill up the last page with an advertisement. I give a very simple answer. To finish exactly at the bottom of the last page, I must furnish every week *one hundred and fourteen thousand letters*. It must be admitted that when one has a *causerie*, or correspondence, and some eight or ten stories to finish all at once, it is difficult to finish *exactly* with the one hundred and fourteen thousandth letter. On the day I fall short by a couple of hundred letters, we have to fill up with an advertisement. Should the reader think that he has not got enough for his money, let him cancel his paper on the day of an advertisement.

It is quite obvious that Dumas was ingeniously avoiding the real charge, which was not that he was furnishing advertisements, but that little that he printed was his own. However exaggerated, and it is true that by Dumas's standards his output had considerably fallen off, he was at the time publishing the *Mohicans de Paris* and *Madame de Chamblay*, both of which the volatile editor left uncompleted when he suddenly decided to visit Russia, a country he had long wished to visit.

In 1839 Dumas had thought of presenting the Emperor Nicholas I with an ornately bound copy of his play *L'Alchimiste*. Not that he had any particular affection for the Emperor; but as he was such an ardent collector of decorations he thought that such a gesture might win him at least the Order of Saint Stanislas. After all, the painter Horace Vernet, who had recently made a triumphal tour of Russia, had not only obtained many commissions, but had received the decoration so coveted by the great romancer. The Russian embassy in Paris communicated this wish to Count Ouvaroff, the Czar's Minister of Foreign Affairs, adding that it might be good policy to grant it, since Dumas, the most popular writer in France, wielded great influence on public opinion, which at the time was very pro-Polish and anti-Russian. The book was forwarded to the Czar with a letter signed *Alexandre Dumas, Chevalier du Lion de Belgique, de la Légion d'honneur et d'Isabelle la Catholique*. The Czar was not impressed. 'A ring with a monogram will be sufficient,' he replied.

For Dumas this was by no means sufficient, but the Czar remained unmoved. Even when notified that the ring was being dispatched to him, it was not until he had lodged a complaint that he eventually received it – with very bad grace. Shortly afterwards he published in the *Revue de Paris* a novel entitled *Mémoires d'un Maître d'Armes*, which must have caused great offence to the Czar. It concerned the story of two members of the Decembrist conspiracy, an officer of the guards named Annenkoff and his young French wife, who shared with her husband his exile in Siberia. The story is put into the mouth of the *maître d'armes*, one Grisier, whose pupil Annenkoff had been. The novel was not unnaturally banned in Russia, but was nevertheless widely read by all who could obtain a smuggled copy, including the Empress.

Dumas was *person non grata* in Russia while the Emperor Nicholas was on the throne.

In 1851, Alexandre *fils* fell madly in love with the Countess Dimitri Nesselrode, wife of the Russian ambassador to France. This immensely wealthy and aristocratic lady so compromised herself with the young man that an imperial order recalled her and her husband to St Petersburg. The infatuated young Alexandre followed the couple on horseback, but was turned back at the Polish frontier by orders of the Czar. It was in this frontier town that the Countess Nesselrode discovered, in the possession of a high-ranking customs officer, love letters from George Sand to Chopin, who had died two years previously in 1849. These she confided to her best friend, Princess Narishkin, to convey to her lover. The Princess not only delivered the letters to 'young' Alexandre, but consoled him for the loss of the Countess, so effectively that she abandoned everything and became his mistress, to live with him in France at the Château Villeroy. In 1860 she presented him with a son, and finally married him thirteen years after they had first met.

When Dumas *père* met his son's Russian friends, he was enchanted. In 1858 he was introduced to a Count Kuschelev Besborodka and his family. They were doing the 'grand tour' of Europe in princely style worthy of Monte-Cristo himself, with unlimited funds at their disposal. Already in their entourage they had Daniel Dunglas Home, a famous Scottish spiritualist who at the invitation of the Empress Eugénie had made Paris his centre. It was in fact through Home that Dumas, always interested in the occult, met the Count and Countess. Dunglas Home could have been no ordinary charlatan, for he was frequently invited to court and had become engaged to the Countess Kuschelev's sister and was therefore almost one of the family.

Dumas frequently visited the Kuschelevs at the Hôtel de Trois Empereurs, where they lived when in Paris. One evening, as he was comfortably seated in the chair usually reserved for him, surrounded by the family, the Countess announced that the marriage between her sister and Dunglas Home was to take place in St Petersburg in about a month's time and that it had been decided that their new-found French friend, the celebrated M Dumas, was to travel home with them as their guest for the occasion.

Dumas protested. Of course he was grateful, but he could not entertain the idea – he had his newspaper to feed, he had a novel to finish, he had promised to write articles for this and that publisher . . . Besides, if he visited Russia he would like to write travel impressions on the same lines as *Voyage en Suisse*; a short visit to the city of Peter the Great would hardly provide him with enough material. 'I'd want to see Moscow, Nizhni-Novgorod, Astrakhan and return via the Danube,' he said.

'But that fits in excellently!' said the Countess. 'I have an estate near Moscow; the Count has some property near Nizhni, also at Kazan, and fisheries on the Caspian and a country home at Isatcha.'

Dumas asked for two days to think things over. He was given two minutes. He accepted.

The next eight months of Dumas's life, from June 1858 to February 1859, are recounted in his travel impressions entitled *En Russie* and *Le Caucase*. 'They were eight months of princely vagabondage ... One of the most splendid journeys I have ever undertaken,' he wrote.

He stayed six weeks with his Russian friends in St Petersburg. The grounds of his host's home measured more than thirty miles in circumference. Two thousand souls lived there. Three times weekly a military band came to play on the estate, which on these occasions was open to the public. Dumas was fascinated by the costumes of the children with their coloured shirts and baggy trousers tucked into boots, and the nurses with bonnets embroidered with gold brocade and flowered dresses.

He admired the droshkies and their drivers in their long gowns and caps which he likened to pots of *pâté de foie gras*. What seemed to astonish him most was how quiet were the Russian crowds. 'The Russians are spectres,' he wrote. 'Transport a Russian to the Boulevard des Capucines and he would go stark mad.' The Kuschelevs had promised to take him to the fair at Nizhni-Novgorod. They kept their promise. After six weeks of sight-seeing in St Petersburg, he travelled down the Volga for Moscow, stopping at Nizhni to soak himself in the atmosphere of the famous fair, where he met the original hero and heroine of *Le Maître d'Armes*. Moscow and the Kremlin were a dream to him.

Perhaps his greatest happiness during this journey was to notice that, among cultivated Russians, Lamartine, Victor Hugo, Balzac, de Musset, George Sand and himself were as well known as in Paris. Just as in Spain he found that everywhere he went grand dukes, governors of provinces, noblemen and high officials gave the 'great romancer' the warmest of welcomes, and he was flatteringly addressed as 'General' because he habitually wore one of the many decorations he had acquired. He tells us how in return for the hospitality he received, he offered his hosts cooking lessons and in return learnt recipes for seasoning sterlet and sturgeon and making preserves from roses with honey and cinnamon. But of the adventures he relates, it is difficult to distinguish truth from fiction, or more correctly accounts of events which of which he was not actually a witness, but which had been narrated to him. For example, did he really witness in the country of the Kalmuks a race in which ten thousand wild horses swam across the Volga? In the Caucasus, he tells us that a Persian deputation came to meet him, addressing him as 'Illustrious Traveller' and his host, Prince Bagration, allegedly explained: 'The fellow lecturing at you has read your books in Russian translation. All the people you see before you are admirers of the *Musketeers, Queen Margot* and *Monte-Cristo.*'

Did Dumas really expect his readers to believe that a group of illiterate Caucasian tribesmen could have heard of Dumas, much less have been in the least interested in French history?

At Tiflis, as it was then called, he enjoyed the 'voluptuous' pleasure of a 'Persian bath', explored the bazaars, and concluded his visit by emerging from a feast given in his honour, with the glory of having imbibed more wine than any other guest present and leaving the feast sober – a truly remarkable feat for a man who always drank in the greatest moderation and usually confined himself to water.

From Tiflis he journeyed to Poti on the eastern shore of the Black Sea.* Here, held up for several days, he wrote a good deal of his Russian 'impressions' in a room made stifling by the heat of the stove, freezing without it, and situated over a pigsty.

Leaving Poti, the official end of his Russian journey, Dumas travelled via Trebizond to Constantinople.

Dumas's accounts of his Russian and Caucasian adventures outshine even those of Monte-Cristo in the novel. How much was true, how much was false? But what did it matter? He told his stories so wittily and with such warmth and conviction, that everyone was convinced of their veracity, including Dumas himself.

Despite his success abroad, Paris once again disappointed him. Again he was almost penniless. A would-be novelist, Céleste Mogodor, formerly a super at the Bal Mabille and an equestrienne with the Franconi Circus, who had married a young sprig of the nobility and who now called herself the Comtesse de Chabrillan, came to call on Dumas in his house in the rue d'Amsterdam.

'His financial troubles,' she wrote, 'could be guessed from the broken windowpanes, dried-up and dusty plants and perches that

* Poti had only been part of the Russian empire since 1828.

swayed without their multicoloured birds.'

Céleste had come to show Dumas a novel she had written and to ask him to make any revisions he might think necessary, sign it with her, and share the profits.

'No,' he said. 'I only do that with beginners . . . Besides, you would do better to try your hand with dramas.' He went on to explain that in novels digressions are necessary, but boring to write. Plays are ten times easier; no settings to paint, no costumes to describe – that can be left to the stage designer.

He immediately proposed to help her register as a probationer at the association of dramatic authors. He even agreed to accompany her while she enrolled. As they walked down the rue d'Amsterdam, Céleste remarked that many passers-by greeted Dumas *père* respectfully.

'How happy they are to recognise you,' she said.

'They bow to me,' Dumas replied, 'but they admire you.'

At the corner of the rue Saint-Lazare he hailed a cab. The cabby took one look at the giant author and then at his emaciated horse, protesting that neither the springs of his cab nor his nag were capable of carrying such a load. Just at that moment a friend of Dumas happened to pass by. 'Ah, good morning, Dumas,' said his friend, 'I was just about to call on you.' At the sound of the famous name, the driver's attitude completely changed.

'Monsieur Dumas? Monsieur Alexandre Dumas? . . . Jump in, sir, I'll drive you wherever you like.'

This trivial incident is significant because Dumas, on his return from his Arabian Nights' adventures in Russia and the Caucasus, had lost some of his former popularity and was experiencing one of his few periods of pessimism. Parisian society of the Second Empire did not take so favourably to him as society under the Orléanists. He was regarded as something of a parvenu, and was no longer the cynosure of all eyes when he attended social functions as described by de Banville. The Princesse Mathilde was now in the habit of saying that he had grown quite impossible, adding that in the old days she invited him to her *salon* merely because he was 'an amusing piece of nonsense'. But nothing could stop him writing. He continued the work his Russian adventure had interrupted, proceeded with *Madame de Chamblay*, concluded the interminable *Les Mohicans de Paris*, wrote and published *Le Fils du Forçat*, *Le Père Ruine*, *L'Île du Feu* and *Les Mariages du père Olifus*. At this time he also wrote his third and last comic opera, *Le Roman d'Elvire*, an indifferent libretto with music by Ambroise Thomas (which was performed in the following year at the Opéra Comique), also a series of critical notes on the paintings exhibited at the *Salon*, published under the title *L'Art et les Artistes Contemporains au Salon de 1859*.

Although his social popularity may have declined, his readers remained faithful and he was soon able to recoup some of his fortune, although none of these last of his three hundred novels is comparable with his earlier works. His plays continued to be hits and his travel impressions, which he had published in several columns after the Russian trip, proved popular. Nevertheless he had fallen out of love with Paris, and with one hundred thousand francs to his credit he was seized with a desire to travel again and shake off the dust of an unappreciative city.

For some time he had been anxious to visit Syria and Palestine. Lamartine and Châteaubriand had travelled in the Orient – why shouldn't he follow in their footsteps? Furthermore he had fallen in love again, this time with another charming young actress, thirty-eight years younger than himself, whom he wished to transport far from Paris and gossip.

Emilie Cordier was of humble birth – her father was a manufacturer of buckets for water carriers. A delicate child, she had read much of Hugo, Balzac and Dumas, whom she worshipped. When she grew stronger her parents apprenticed her to a seamstress and then found her a position in the Halles. But Emilie had only one dream – to become an actress. A friend of her mother took her to visit Dumas in 1858 on the eve of his visit to Russia, in the hopes that he might find her a small role in one of his plays. It was an unpropitious moment, but Dumas never forgot the entrancing young girl. On his return in 1859 he wrote to her inviting her to visit him at his lodgings. She was nineteen, Dumas was fifty-seven. Her gifts as an actress were negligible; on the other hand her physical attractions were irresistible. She was a perfect lover and fulfilled all the desires of her elderly admirer.

In the spring of 1860, Dumas bought the *Emma*, often described by biographers as a yacht, in fact a simple little decked schooner. The cabin was so small that Dumas was for ever cracking his head against the ceiling. The voyage was to be a long one, for after visiting the East it was Dumas's intention to sail to America. He therefore selected his companions with care, the crew for their efficiency, the friends for their gaiety. The companions whom he gathered round him were all young, filled with the joy of living, and like their host, never wearying of themselves or of their own company. There was Legray, a celebrated Parisian photographer; Etienne Lockroy, the son of the well-known actor and dramatist; Paul Parfait, the son of Dumas's old secretary-friend; Théodore Canape, a Greek, whom Dumas had befriended and educated; Vasili, a Georgian peasant boy, whom Dumas had met in Tiflis and who, though knowing no language but his own, had pursued his idol all the way across Europe, and was now Dumas's trained servant; in addition there was a young doctor named Albanel and two Greeks, travelling only as far as Cyprus. Lastly there was 'the Admiral'. This was Emilie Cordier, dressed like a musical-comedy sailor and looking entrancing in her naval uniform, whom he naïvely tried to pass off now as his son, now as his nephew, and whom he addressed as Emile.

It was towards the end of April that Dumas left Paris, not to return for four years. He was both happy and sad; happy because he was about to embark on a long-projected venture; sad because he realised his heyday in Paris was over, pushed aside by the new generation of Second Empire writers, by Flaubert and Zola in particular. 'It is incredible how kind people become to me the further I am away from Paris' he wrote. 'Abroad it is even better.'

This was no exaggeration. A sincere proof of the affection held for him in his own country was given when he and his party arrived to embark at Marseille. Here the mayor and notables gave a farewell banquet in his honour. After healths were drunk and speeches made, the mayor presented him with the deeds of a strip of land in the Catalan area and the right to quarter the Château d'If on the arms of the Pailleteries – a privilege of which he never made use.

The warmth of the reception given to him by the citizens of Marseille did much to restore Dumas's spirits, and it was with a gay heart that he set sail on Wednesday 9 May 1860. But the great Odyssey was never to take place. When the *Emma* put in at Genoa, Dumas learnt that Garibaldi, champion of Italian independence, was about to start on his great adventure to wrest the Kingdom of the Two Sicilies from Bourbon rule and unite Italy. It is highly improbable that Dumas understood the extremely complicated political situation then existing in Italy, or the extent to which the peninsula was divided in opinion. How much did he know of the policies of Cavour and Mazzini, or the problem of incorporating the papal states, now defended by French zouaves, in one united Italy? Probably such thoughts never entered his head. It was enough for him to know that Garibaldi was planning to drive the Bourbons from their throne, the hated Bourbons of the Two Sicilies, who had so ill-treated his father. Dumas had met Garibaldi some time previously and had been captivated by the picturesque filibuster, who in return had taken to the famous swashbuckling novelist. No sooner had Dumas learnt of Garibaldi's presence than he hastened to meet him.

Dumas lost no time in offering his services to the liberator. Together they discussed plans of campaign. Three ships including the *Emma* were to carry troops to Marsala on the coast of Sicily on 11 May 1860. Less than a month after leaving Marseille, Dumas was in Palermo, meeting hardly any resistance. Garibaldi's 'Thousand' were welcomed by the Sicilians with the greatest enthusiasm.

A great banquet was held in Palermo at which Dumas scarcely stopped talking, but offended Garibaldi by bringing Emilie with him, dressed in her naval uniform.*

Following his almost bloodless conquest of Sicily, Garibaldi had to cross the Straits of Messina and march on Naples, but he lacked both guns and money. Dumas was still in possession of the *Emma* and, miraculously, had 50,000 francs at his disposal. Still in the role of the Count of Monte-Cristo, he offered everything to 'Italia una'. Garibaldi accepted. The crossing of the straits was effected without opposition. An English naval squadron standing by observed strict neutrality. The advance on Naples was accomplished. Many of the Bourbon generals who were sent against Garibaldi were unreliable, since their hearts were in the Italian cause. The soldiers who supported the Bourbons thought themselves betrayed, and murdered General Fileno Briganti after the latter had concluded terms of capitulation with Garibaldi. The mass of the people on the other hand welcomed Garibaldi as their liberator. The Bourbon king, Frances II, withdrew with his army of 60,000 men into a strong fortress on the Volturno.

On 7 September 1860, Dumas, dressed in a red shirt, marched into

* Giuseppe Bandi, *Les Mille: expedition de Garibaldi en Sicile*, quoted by André Maurois.

Naples at the head of Garibaldi's volunteers. What a superb revenge on those who had imprisoned and tortured his father! In exchange for his services, Garibaldi assigned him the Palazzo Chiatamone, the summer residence of the king. Now began a new life for him. He was appointed honorary director of antiques and supervisor of excavations at Pompeii. At Garibaldi's suggestion he also founded a newspaper, to be called *L'Independente*. The name of the journal was chosen by Garibaldi himself, who wrote: 'The journal which my friend Dumas is going to set up at Palermo will bear the noble title of *L'Independente*: and it will deserve its name all the more if it starts attacking me should I ever deviate from my duty to the people and from my humanitarian principles.'

When Garibaldi retired from the scene for the quiet of Caprera, the island of his birth, believing his destiny was fulfilled, Dumas, foreseeing the disintegration of all that Garibaldi had laboured for – and the internal strife, the lawlessness that would follow – protested with all the power at his disposal. He reminded Garibaldi of his own words: 'You shall attack me, you said, if ever I should turn aside from my duty as a child of the people and as a soldier of humanity. You have turned from it and I attack you . . . You have no right to desert your Southern Italy . . . What will become of Venice and Rome? What will become of your army? What will become of those to whom you were devoted if you leave?'

Despite the lawlessness that Dumas had foreseen, following Garibaldi's retirement, he continued to publish *L'Independente* (half in Italian, half in French).

Apart from supervising the excavations of Pompeii, the amount of work that Dumas accomplished for his paper was incredible. He wrote political editorials, news items, a 'Roman letter', long historical articles and, inevitably, a serial story. Among his other contributions are to be found proclamations and plans for military campaigns.

As if this was not enough, he was (without collaborators) writing a history of the Bourbons of Naples in eleven volumes, also *Mémoires* and the above-mentioned novel, *La San-Félice*. A pamphlet he wrote on 'The Origin of Brigandage, the reasons for its continuance and the means of getting rid of it,' makes it clear, as Benedetto Croce wrote, that this man, so often accused of being superficial, had analysed far better than the experts the solid basis on which agrarian reform in southern Italy must be built.

Alas! Ingratitude is universal. The narrow-minded Neapolitans complained that he was being housed at the expense of the municipality. A rival who coveted the merely honorary post of director of museums and excavations lodged a petition against this favouritism to a foreigner. The newspapers took up the cry, demanding his ejection from the *palazzo*. Forgetting the generous role Dumas had played, a crowd of two or three hundred brawlers demonstrated outside the palace, shouting insults and threats.

'Down with the foreigner! Into the sea with him!'

'I never expected ingratitude from Italy,' said Dumas, sadly. 'One might as well expect wolves to become vegetarians as to hope that fellow men will not show ingratitude.'

In October 1862, Dumas was tempted by another grandiose and adventurous project. He received a letter, posted from London, bearing the signature of a certain Prince Scanderbeg, self-appointed president of the so-called Hellenic-Albanian Junta, asking him to do for Athens and Constantinople what he had done for Palermo and Naples. It was, in short, simply a question of driving the Turks out of Europe! It was just the sort of adventure that was irresistible to our swashbuckling hero. He offered his schooner, *Emma,* and such money as he had left to this new crusade. In return for this generous gesture he was awarded the resounding title of 'Superintendent of the Military Establishments of the Christian Army of the Orient'. It proved to be as empty as that of 'Prince Scanderbeg', who turned out to be nothing but a common swindler.

Dumas's thoughts once again returned to France. In November 1860, Emilie Cordier had returned to France. For some time now it had been impossible for him to pass her off as a boy, for it was quite obvious that she was pregnant. On 24 December 1860 she gave birth to a daughter, baptised Micaëlla-Clélie-Josepha-Elizabeth. Now Dumas longed to see his baby daughter. He also wanted to leave Italy for the very reason which more than any other had kept him there – *L'Independente.* He and Garibaldi had considered that he could help the cause in no surer way than by running this journal and making it the mouthpiece for liberty and a united Italy. This he had done and given of his best but the paper was becoming more and more a burden to him, leaving him little time for original work. In the anarchy that followed Garibaldi's retirement, he found himself more and more embroiled in various Neapolitan factions. He had drifted away from

Garibaldi, who had departed entirely from the role that he, Dumas, considered he should take, nor had he hesitated to say so.

By 1864, Dumas felt that he could do no more. He had devoted four years of his life to the unification of Italy; he had done all that was humanly possible. Deserted by Garibaldi and unappreciated for his sacrifices, he flung *L'Independente* to the winds, sold the *Emma* to an explorer, and wrote to various friends of his decision to return to France. But the years he had devoted to 'The Cause', the money he had spent, the time and labour he had so ungrudgingly given, were never regretted. After relating the ingratitude of the Neapolitans, he concludes *Les Garibaldiens* with the following words: 'Nevertheless, may God protect Naples! And may I do for it all the good I dream of, and for the accomplishment of which I will risk my life again if necessary.'

In April of that year he was back in Paris, almost on the same day as Garibaldi paid a triumphal visit to London, where he was received by Queen Victoria.

CHAPTER TWENTY-EIGHT

The Last Years

If Dumas was not exactly given a State welcome on his return to Paris, his friends greeted him with enthusiasm, overjoyed at seeing him again after four years. Even his enemies and detractors felt a sneaking pleasure at seeing the familiar figure once more frequenting boulevard and *salon*. He was moved to say, 'I am never more popular than when I have been away.' Gabriel Ferry, who knew him well, wrote:

These four years' absence had not changed the appearance of the author of the *Les Trois Mousquetaires*. He was still the same man, big, strongly built, robust, so well proportioned that his stoutness was hardly noticeable ... His face, lit up by the animation of his eyes and the liveliness of his mouth, suggested perpetual good humour. Never was cordiality, joy of living and good nature so expressively printed on a human face as on that of Dumas ...

He had just seven more years to live; but for Dumas, growing old was out of the question. When he arrived in Paris after an eight-day train journey from Italy, he was met by his son. It was ten o'clock at night. His first request was to be driven to Neuilly to visit their old friend Théophile Gautier. Young Alexandre protested:
'It's late, papa, you've had a long journey and you must be tired.'
'I tired? I'm as fresh as a daisy!'
Gautier was asleep when they reached his house. Dumas shouted. Gautier appeared at a window.
'Everybody is in bed,' he called back.
'You lazy lot! Do *I* go to bed?'
So Gautier came down, unbolted the door and they talked until four in the morning, when young Alexandre at last succeeded in dragging

his irrepressible father back to his home in the Champs-Elysées. There were no *fiacres* at this early hour. They walked all the way down the Avenue de Neuilly and La Grande Armée, while Dumas *père* never stopped talking. They arrived home at six o'clock. Young Alexandre was tired out. Not so his father, who immediately asked for a lamp and began work.

Next day he installed himself temporarily at number 112 rue de Richelieu and life began anew. Here he wrote, simultaneously, *Les Garibaldiens*, a novel based on his Neapolitan adventures, and *La San-Félice*, a serial for Emile de Girardin, both of which he had begun in Italy.

Emilie Cordier slipped out of his life: she had talked too much about marriage. Dumas had had too much experience of that with Ida to think of it again, but he desperately wanted to acknowledge officially the little Micaëlla as his own. Emilie, however, wanted marriage or nothing. She did not want to see herself stripped of a mother's authority, just as Dumas had stripped Catharine Labay of her authority. By opposing Dumas's proposal she deprived little Micaëlla of the family inheritance, for the prodigal father once dead and his debts paid by the estate, his literary property would be of considerable value during the posthumous period of copyright.

After breaking with Emilie – 'the Admiral on half-pay', as he referred to her – he learnt that she had borne twins to a rich protector, named Edwards, now living in Le Havre. This did not alter his feelings for his *cher bébé* (Micaëlla), whom he showered with gifts, and later with money. The unfaithful lover made a good father.

Thanks to the success of *Les Garibaldiens* and *La San-Félice*, some money trickled back into his pocket. In 1864 he rented a villa at Enghien for the summer. Here, still confident that his pen would always supply him with ready cash, he continued to entertain – especially women.

Mistress followed mistress – Eugénie Doche (the original Camille); Aimée Desclée of the velvet eyes; the superb tragedienne Agar, born Léonide Charvin, and *demi-mondaines* such as Esther Guimont and Olympe Audouard.

When his son, now a respectably married man and author of lofty moral works, deplored his father's excesses, the elderly romancer protested: 'What do you expect? I need several mistresses. If I only had one she would be dead within a week.'

These more or less ephemeral love affairs were frequently interrupted by a more lasting liaison. For some time the reigning sultana was Fanny Gordosa, a passionate, jealous, Italian singer who had followed Dumas from Italy, and later in number 70 rue Saint-Lazare, where he had now installed himself, nothing could be heard but recitatives, trills and *bel canto*. Every other woman who asked to see Dumas was met with her violent abuse.

'Doomas? Doomas? What you want with Doomas? I tell you, leave Doomas solo!' 'Say her that Doomas him ill.'

But she proved to be as inconstant as she was jealous, and finally Dumas threw her out. She returned to Italy, taking with her what little money she could find in his drawer.

Many men also came to Enghien, including his old friends Parfait, Nestor Roquaplan, Roger de Beauvour and the usual spongers, but the cup which once contained *louis d'or* now only contained silver five-franc pieces. Tales of his generosity are numberless, despite the fact that during the last seven years of his life he only wrote seven novels – one novel a year was slow work for the giant who had often poured out four novels simultaneously. Although he probably made 40,000 francs in 1864, largely out of a stage production of *Les Mohicans de Paris*, he rarely had enough ready cash to meet day-to-day expenses.

Once again Dumas moved house. He now installed himself in the Boulevard Malesherbes with his daughter, Marie-Alexandrine, who had separated from her husband, Olinde Petel, who was suffering from a mental derangement. Marie-Alexandrine, too, seems to have been more than eccentric. After making a retreat at the Convent of the Assumption, she took to illuminating old missals. When she came to live with her father, it was ostensibly to keep house for him, but others said, more maliciously, it was to keep an eye on the ageing libidinous author, who had once boasted – 'I don't want to exaggerate, but I really believe that up and down the world I have more than five hundred children!'* When she came to live with her father she took to wearing the costume of a druidess with a wreath of mistletoe in her hair and a golden sickle at her belt. As for keeping an eye on her father, she was singularly unsuccessful. A succession of slightly clad ladies were continuously around the apartments.

Young Alexandre rarely came to see the old reprobate, although

* Mathilde Shaw, *Illustres et Inconnus: Souvenirs de ma vie.*

Dumas frequently visited his now successful son. He had acquired a fine mansion in the avenue de Villiers, the garden of which was so small that his father could not resist remarking: 'The house is excellent, Alexandre, really excellent – but you really ought to open the drawing room window just to give your garden a breath of air.'

Although the son rarely visited the father, Dumas was always present at his son's triumphs – *The Illegitimate Son* (1858), *The Prodigal Father* (1850), *The Friend of Women*. Seated in the centre of the balcony, Dumas, in a black frock-coat and white piqué waistcoat, with a bouquet of flowers in his hand, barely concealing his now enormous stomach, would rise to his feet and applaud furiously when the name of the author was mentioned, bowing left and right and blowing kisses to the ladies. He never complained that it was quite obvious to all that he was the model on which his son had based his plays. On the contrary, he seemed to draw attention to the fact with a certain pride. He was never jealous of his son's success. He was proud of him, as he was proud of Marie-Alexandrine when, in 1867, more and more preoccupied with theosophy and occultism, she published her first book, *On the Death Bed*. His boundless admiration for his children was all the more touching now that his own star was waning. Publishers and theatre managers hesitated to accept his novels, which scarcely sold any more, or his plays, which no longer had their former box office appeal. George Sand and other writers, however, maintained that his talent was as great as it had ever been. The Goncourt brothers, who met him at the table of Princesse Mathilde, wrote in their journal of 1 February 1865:

A sort of giant, with the hair of a Negro, now gone pepper-and-salt . . . With Dumas there is the indefinable something of both a side-show barker and of a merchant out of the Thousand and One Nights . . . the words still pour out, though they lack something of the old sparkle. With that husky voice, he draws only facts, *wonderful* facts from the vast treasure house of his memory. And always, always, he talks about himself, but with the vanity of a great child – yet he does not jar on one's nerves.'

Later in 1866, they wrote:

Just as we were conversing, in came Dumas *père*, white tie, white waistcoat, enormous, sweating, puffing, shouting with laughter . . . brimming over with a sort of boyish good nature and always sparkling with humour. 'What can you expect,' he said, 'when the only way the theatres can make money is to have plenty of tights – which split . . . That is what has happened to Hostein. He told his dancers never to wear anything but tights which would be sure to split . . . and always in the right place. That pleases the opera glass addicts. But the censor stepped in at last and the opera glass sellers are on their beam ends.'

In 1865 he had rented an old disused theatre which had been built under the arches of the Vincennes railway line – Le Grand Théâtre Parisien. Here Dumas had one of his best dramas – *Les Gardes Forestiers* – revived. It is pathetic to think that the great Alexandre Dumas should have been forced to such straits as to have one of his best works revived in a theatre which was shaken to the foundations by the trains passing overhead and where the whistles of the locomotives drowned the voices of the actors. The revival lasted but a few nights.

To help the members of the cast, Dumas arranged for a provincial tour in the neighbourhood of Paris, promising to accompany the actors as often as he was able. In the suburbs and provinces he retained his old popularity. The cast were to be known as the *Troupe dramatique d'Alexandre Dumas*. The venture proved a success. Whenever Dumas himself was present, repeat performances were called for. Laon and Villers-Cotterêt were the culmination of the tour. In the *département* of his birth he was received with all the enthusiasm he had enjoyed in his heyday. Dumas was delighted, but the success was ephemeral. More and more frequently he spent his time in the provinces and abroad. He gave lectures in Le Havre, Dieppe, Rouen and Caen. As already mentioned, at the beginning of 1866, Dumas had moved house for the last`time – to 107 Boulevard Malesherbes. Here on the fourth floor, like any impoverished student, he gathered around him his few remaining possessions.

Then, indefatigably, he began work again, plunging into project after project; but nothing succeeded for long. He proposed building another theatre, but since he had no money he tried to raise the necessary capital by subscription. The response to his appeal was disheartening. Paris was no longer interested in the type of play that had been popular twenty years previously. Now, under the Second Empire, a different generation had grown up. Light opera was all the rage – Offenbach, Hervé and Meilhac were the gods of the moment. *Bals masqués* and cabarets had taken the place of the theatre. Dumas, however, continued to work and produced two novels, the *Comte de*

Moret, of which no known copy is extant; *Parisiens and Provinciaux*, the last of his country tales, a pendant to *Conscience, Catherine Blum* and *Le Meneur de Loups*. He was to write other novels, but none has the imaginative energy and fervour that are to be found in his greater works. *Parisiens and Provinciaux*, as one critic put it, 'is the last corner stone in the vast edifice created by Dumas, his crowning work of fiction'.*

Dumas was now sixty-four years of age and was growing increasingly obese, probably due to dropsy, although this was unsuspected at the time. Sixty-four is not old, but Dumas was to age rapidly. He no longer rose every morning at seven o'clock. His pen no longer flew so rapidly over the pages, but, as we gather from the Goncourts' journal, he was still the irrepressible, ebullient Dumas of former days. He refused to admit that he was growing old. He still could not resist a pretty woman and, despite his obesity and somewhat grotesque appearance, such was his charm, his charisma, that women were still attracted by the ageing roué. It would be explicable if he were the millionaire of Monte-Cristo days, but he was now almost penniless, living hand to mouth, deserted by his former public; yet in 1866 he fell in love yet again.

He gained the affection of one of the most beautiful and attractive women, who was enchanting all Paris – Adah Isaacs Menken. Adah was already a legend in America and London, where she had taken the audiences by storm in *Mazeppa*, a drama inspired by Byron's poem. Breathlessly, the public watched her bound naked (though in fact she was wearing a flesh-coloured, skin-tight leotard) to a horse's back and carried up a 'mountainside' at the gallop. The final leap had more than once nearly cost her her life.

Adah Menken was born in Louisiana in 1831, or according to herself, in 1834. Before her début as a horsewoman, she had been a stage extra, an actress, a dancer, and had posed in the nude for a number of sculptors. For a time she had worked for a newspaper (the *Cincinnati Israelite*) and had toured the country lecturing on Edgar Alan Poe. This extraordinary woman, who knew English, French, German and Hebrew and was versed in both Greek and Latin, was

* A. C. Bell, op. cit.

268

mad about poetry. She herself wrote poems. As works of art they are crude, but this beautiful Jewess was forever burning with an unquenchable passion for fame. Walt Whitman, Mark Twain, Bret Harte and Joaquin Miller had all been her friends.

Three times divorced, she married her fourth husband, James P. Barkly, a professional pugilist, only because she wished to legitimise the child with which she was pregnant. Two days after her marriage she took ship for England. Here in London her success was no less extraordinary than in America. Dickens, Charles Reade, Rossetti and Swinburne all came under her spell. It is doubtful whether Swinburne was actually her lover, but his must be the credit for what is surely the loveliest epitaph to any woman ever: 'Lo! This is she that was the world's delight.'

But it was Paris, the gay Bohemian capital, which was the goal of Adah's ambition. 'Through the gateways of Paris, I shall reach the door of Paradise ... Paris is, after all, the heart of the world,' she declared. This ambition was not only because she wished to conquer the city as she had conquered America and London, but because she had an overwhelming desire to meet Dumas, whom above all French authors, she admired. To her great regret she had missed him in early 1865 when she had paid a brief visit.* Dumas was in the provinces lecturing, and when she returned to Paris in 1866, he was once more fleeing creditors and on his travels again. He revisited Naples, Florence and then Germany and Austria. From this short journey he brought back a novel – La Terreur Prussienne – in which once again he showed his clairvoyance and sensed the threat of impending war.

'Nobody who has not travelled in Prussia,' he wrote, 'can have any idea of the hatred felt for us by the Prussians. It amounts to monomania which clouds even calm and untroubled minds. No minister in Berlin can hope to be popular unless he makes it clear that sooner or later war with France is inevitable.'

Under the disguised name of Count von Boeswick, he had painted a premonitory portrait of Bismarck. The novel was quite up to Dumas's best style but, alas, Dumas was not taken seriously. The carefree, pleasure-loving Parisian public of the bel époque paid no attention to the warning of the former 'king of Paris'.

La Terreur neither enhanced Dumas's reputation nor did it

* Bernard Falk, *The Naked Lady.*

improve his financial position. The rent of his apartment had not been paid. Much of his furniture had been sold. The only precious mementoes from which he refused to be parted were the preliminary sketch which his friend Delacroix had made on the occasion of the famous ball he had given all those years ago (it is thanks to Mathilde Shaw, his friend but unreliable memorialist, that we know this. In his *Mémoires*, Dumas would have us believe that Delacroix painted his mural completely spontaneously without any previous preparation)*, and a towel spotted with the blood of the young Duc d'Orléans, some old-fashioned weapons, a portrait of his father and another of his son painted by Horace Vernet. His servants, with the exception of Vassili, his faithful Caucasian, had left him. According to Mathilde Shaw, he was even obliged on one occasion to borrow a few francs from his 'little rosebud', as he called her, in order to buy an evening shirt.

It was in 1866 that Dumaine, manager of the Gaiété, invited Adah to visit Paris. In December of that year, shortly after Dumas's return from his travels, she played in *Les Pirates de la Savane*. Before her début on 31 December, she wrote to Dumas assuring him of her 'respectful admiration', and in return he devoted an article in *Le Mousquetaire* to her career. In gratitude she sent him her photograph, a rare gift in those days. It was not until the following February that they actually met. He had decided to visit the Gaiété and see for himself this beauty over whom all Paris had grown rhapsodical. Knowing that he was to be in the theatre that night, Adah was all agog to meet the author whom she so admired. Seeing him in the wings, she immediately approached him and without any introduction started to converse with him. How fluent her French was we don't know; we can only assume that she had a good command of the language (she translated some Walt Whitman into French, no easy task), and Dumas must have found her conversation, let alone her undoubted physical charms, captivating. On leaving her, he kissed her 'in a half gallant, half paternal fashion on the cheek'. Thus began the last liaison of the elderly Don Juan. Another version of their meeting is that on first meeting him she threw her arms around his neck and kissed him on the lips. The affair is very elusive in its details. All that we know for certain is that from this moment Dumas became her lover.

It is hardly surprising that the ageing author should have fallen for

* See p. 154.

this captivating creature. Adah's veiled expression, long black hair and magnificent body, the adventurous life she had led – everything was calculated to please him. Of course Dumas was flattered. Every young man about town, all the *jeunesse dorée* of the time wished to possess her; and who should step in now, but an immensely stout and prematurely ageing bankrupt author?

Adah was an extremely intelligent young woman. She was not interested in money, as were the great courtesans of their epoch, the kept women of rich noblemen or financiers who displayed themselves in carriages drawn by thoroughbreds in the Bois de Boulogne, so admirably depicted in the drawings of Constantin Guys. She wished to be remembered because of her mind, not because of the notoriety won by her body. Doubtful of her own gifts as a poet, she made sure of posterity's attention by attaching herself to the great literati of her time. Whether she really loved Dumas it is difficult to say, but it is quite certain that she loved his company. For his part he was certainly infatuated by her, flattered that she should prefer his companionship to that of younger and wealthier men who sought her favours. He took her everywhere. He showed her old Paris, and from his inexhaustible memory would tell her, as only he could, anecdotes and the history of every building and street through which they wandered. He was delighted to be seen with her.

Throughout February and March of 1867 the affair went smoothly. He took her to Bougival, where forty years earlier he had taken Catharine Labay, and now in Adah's company he was able to recapture something of his youth. It was not only he who delighted her with his stories, but she delighted him with her own reminiscences. She was the perfect Scheherazade and entertained him with marvellous and completely fictitious stories of her past – how in Texas she had captivated the cowboys by successfully participating in hunting buffalo; how she had been taken prisoner by Indians, whom she had beguiled by her snake dance; how dressed as a young man she had become a captain of the National Guard of Dayton, Ohio. In fact, she had never been a dancer at the opera, nor had she been a tragedienne in California as she claimed. In seven years the only role she ever played was Mazeppa.

Sadly, it was Dumas's infatuation for this fascinating woman that drew more disapprobation and ridicule on him than any other affair in his life. In the 1860s photography was still something of a novelty.

Adah had a whim to pose before a camera with each great man in her life. It was more than a whim, it became almost a rite. She was proud to show photographs of herself in the company of Swinburne, Rossetti and others. Now she insisted that Dumas should pose with her. Dumas committed the imprudence of complying. This was in 1867. Liebert, the photographer, to whom Dumas owed a small sum of money, thought that a much publicised sale of photographs of La Menken perched on the author's knee or snuggling up against him in an affectionate pose would compensate him for unpaid bills. The prints were widely distributed and exhibited in shop windows all over Paris.

If Liebert wished for revenge, he certainly obtained it. The photographs made an unprecendented impact on the public. Talk of marriage, lampoons, caricatures, satires filled the journals. Young Paul Verlaine wrote a witty triolet, offensive to prudish ears, which was much quoted. Victor Koning, a journalist on the staff of *Vogue Parisienne*, wrote so scurrilous a satire that Dumas *père*, true son of his father the general, challenged him to a duel which, thanks to the intervention of Alexandre *fils*, came to nothing. But a lengthy and very much publicised law suit which Dumas *père* brought against Liebert the photographer (which he eventually won) only served to drag his name further into the mire. In an age of licence, when hardly any man of importance, including the Emperor and his illegitimate half-brother, the all-powerful Duc de Morny, did not possess a mistress or mistresses, the stir caused by the Dumas–Menken affair was quite absurd and the vituperative criticisms levelled at him were sheer hypocrisy and certainly occasioned by jealousy. Adah, being young and beautiful, could be excused, but by what right had the ageing Dumas, whose day was over, to step into the limelight as he invariably did?

It was all a storm in a teacup, one which weakened even more Dumas's already shaky position; but if anything it drew Adah closer to her sexagenarian lover. In June, she was obliged to visit Vienna to fulfil a contract (Mazeppa again), but the Viennese did not welcome her with the enthusiasm which her performance had evoked in London and Paris. She was soon back where her heart was. Two months later she was once again in London, seeking help from Swinburne in her search for a publisher prepared to accept her poems. The Idah Menken–Dumas affair was finished. There was no quarrel, no break. They met once again. In May 1868 Dumas was lecturing in

Le Havre; Menken was returning to Paris after a bad fall from her horse. Learning that her old lover was in the town, she broke her journey to see him again. The meeting was brief.* He was never to see her again. She left to take up an engagement at the Châtelet; he to complete *La Terreur Prussienne* and attempt to revive his newspaper *Le Mousquetaire*, but with no success. It was succeeded by *Le d'Artagnan*, with no better result. There had been some idea of writing a play for Adah, but Hostein thought it more economical to revive *Les Pirates de la Savane*, for which scenery and costumes already existed. During rehearsal Adah was taken seriously ill and died suddenly on 10 August 1868. Only her maid, her grooms and a few actors followed the hearse from her home in the rue Caumartin to the cemetery of Père-Lachaise.

News of Adah's death reached Dumas at Le Havre. For some time he was prostrated by grief, but bravely continued to write. His *Parisiens et Provinciaux* and his *Histoire de mes Bêtes* were little masterpieces, and although he knew that old age was creeping up on him, he still refused to recognise the fact, and was planning to write yet another historical novel. In public he maintained his former *bonhomie* and exercised his irrestible charm. The Princess Pauline Metternich wrote, in her autobiography, *Mes Années à Paris:*

> Dumas was enormously stout and looked like a mulatto, although his skin was far from black, but his hair curled tightly like that of a Negro. He gave the impression of a stout, good-natured old fellow, with no pretensions of any sort ... He always said the right thing and was perfectly natural. We liked him from the very first moment. During dinner he talked a great deal, and I never heard anyone express himself with such complete ease. He touched on every sort of subject. There was nothing he did not seem to know ... nothing on earth can even approximately give an idea of the wonderful vitality and versatility of this extraordinary man.
>
> After dinner I asked Dumas whether he was occupied with a new novel. He answered: 'Not yet, but I have the subject for one in my head, and one of these days I'll set to work on it.'
>
> 'And the title?'
>
> '*Création et Rédemption.*'
>
> Madame Marie Dumas was very much astonished at this piece of news. 'But, father,' she exclaimed, 'why have you never said a word about it to me? It is too bad of you to have kept me in the dark.'

---

* It was on this occasion that Dumas revived acquaintance with Emilie, 'the Admiral', and met again his darling daughter Micaëlla.

'Well, my child,' answered Dumas, 'if the Prince and Princess will allow me, I will tell them the story of my new novel, and then you will be among the first to hear it, and it will be a souvenir of the evening we have spent here.' And there and then Dumas began his narrative just as if he were reading it aloud: 'It was on a cold day in December,' etc. He went on and on never hesitating for a word, never making a mistake; every intonation appropriate to each character was correct.

How Dumas was able to remember all the events that took place in this remarkable story, and how he managed to keep all his numerous characters in sight, how he extricated them from the most complicated situations, and how he finally wound up the whole thing – all this passes my comprehension. When at last he ceased speaking there was a general cry of 'Bravo!' He had spoken uninterruptedly for two hours and a half, and not once had he been at a loss for a word.

'Tell me, M Dumas, when do you intend to publish *Création et Rédemption?*'

It was my husband who asked this question.

'Well, Prince,' he answered smiling, 'I doubt whether it will ever be published, since I concocted it this evening in honour of the Princess, and when I started it I had not the vaguest idea what was going to happen.

It is doubtful if Dumas was telling the truth when he claimed to have made up the story extempore. It will be recollected that once he had the germ of a plot in his head, he often recounted it to friends. *Création et Rédemption* (a story set in the time of the Revolution with a Pygmalian theme, in which a doctor befriends a mentally deficient girl, restores her to sanity and finally falls in love with her) was written during his declining years and was published posthumously in 1872, two years after the author's death.

Création et Rédemption is by no means a great work, but his *Causeries* and *Histoire de mes Bêtes*, together with *Souvenirs dramatiques* published during these last years are worth all the novels of the same time put together.

His financial situation was, as usual, chaotic. Although publishers and theatre managers no longer vied with each other to obtain his works, he was still earning sufficient for anyone less prodigal than himself to live in a comparatively comfortable style. But because of his own and Marie-Alexandrine's mismanagement of his affairs, he more often than not found himself penniless. The rent remained unpaid, his cook, servant and secretary thought themselves lucky to be paid at all. A dramatisation of *Madame de Chamblay*, staged at the Porte Saint-Martin, proved a failure. Profoundly discouraged, Dumas was happy to accept an invitation to lecture at the international marine exhibition held at Le Havre. This lecture was followed by personal appearances at Caen, Dieppe and Rouen. The success of these did much to restore his self-confidence. A second revival of *Madame de Chamblay* this time met with some approval, but in no way helped to alleviate the author's financial difficulties. He acquired a secretary, 'a small timid creature'. He stuffed her with sweets and poured into her ears from morning till night ideas for new plays and new novels, but came the day when ideas became confused and his stories mixed up.

It had been some time since Alexandre *fils* had visited his father; with the death of Adah it now occurred to him that this was a propitious moment for the old rake to settle down and marry Catharine Labay. When Alexandre visited his father in his small apartment in the Boulevard Malesherbes, he found him deep in a book.

'What are you reading?' he asked.

'The *Musketeers* . . . I always promised myself that when I was old, I would find out for myself what it was worth.'

'How far have you got?'

'I've finished it.'

'And what is your considered view?'

'It's good.'

When he read *Monte-Cristo*, he did not consider it a patch on the *Musketeers*.

When his son put forward his suggestion of bringing his parents together at long last, his father seemed tempted by the idea. At Neuilly he would have found a solid home and a thoroughly domesticated woman. He was beginning to feel a lack of security, a lack of confidence in his own writings. Would he be remembered by posterity? He was at last becoming aware that old age was creeping up on him and for the first time in his life was suffering moods of depression. But it was Catharine who gently refused to countenance the idea of marriage. 'I am over seventy,' she wrote to a friend; 'I am always ailing and live very simply with one servant. Monsieur Dumas would blow my small apartment to smithereens . . . It is forty years too late.' The story of Adah Menken made her smile. 'He's still the same,' she wrote, 'age has taught him nothing.'* It was indeed too late. She died

* A. Maurois, Simone André Maurois Collection.

on 22 October in that same year – 1868. She was seventy-four.

Dumas *père* spent the summer of 1869 at Roscoff in Brittany. He was looking for a quiet place in which to write his last great *chef d'oeuvre*, *Le grand Dictionnaire de la Cuisine*, commissioned by Ephonsetre Lemerre. He had begun the compilation of this monumental work years back. There is a reference to it as long ago as 1860 in *Les Garibaldiens* and in the *causerie Comment j'ai fait jouer à Marseille le Drame des 'Forestiers'*, where he speaks of it as being 'the pillow of my old age!' In his *De Paris à Cadix* he had written: 'Many readers, after perusing my books, have contested their merit, but there has never been a gourmet who, after having tested my dishes, has contested their merit.' He worked indefatigably on the dictionary, but he was growing daily more misanthropic.

'I keep thinking,' he said to his son, 'that I am a monument which is trembling, as if built of sand.'

'You have no need to worry,' his son replied. 'You have built the monument well: it will last as long as the French language, as long as our native land.'

It was hoped that with the spring his health and spirits would revive. But a painful abscess in the mouth only served to add to his mood of depression. Travel had always been the panacea for all his troubles, and so now with the assistance of his son, he once more journeyed to the Midi which he loved so well. But this time there were to be no more *Impressions de Voyage*. It was at Marseille that he learnt of the declaration of war against Prussia. His *Terreur Prussienne*, written 1867, had become a reality. In August he was back in Paris; his health none the better. The news of the first military defeats brought about an almost complete collapse. In September, partly paralysed by a stroke, Dumas dragged himself to Puys, near Dieppe, where his son had built a villa, which he now put at the disposal of his father and Marie-Alexandrine. Here, in a room overlooking the sea, the tired old writer was put to bed and fell asleep at once.

'My father was brought to me,' wrote his son, 'in a completely paralysed condition. It was pitiful sight, though not wholly unexpected.'

The sick man, from whom all news of the disastrous defeat at Sedan was kept secret, recovered sufficiently to move from his bed to an armchair and play dominoes with his grandchildren, whom he adored. But he was aware, as were all the household, that death was approaching. His moments of lucidity became less frequent, and as autumn approached he rarely left his bed. One day in November he rallied momentarily. His son was with him. Very weakly he began talking of his youth in Villers-Cotterêts, of his early days in Paris, of his first successes.

Close to his bed on a table where two golden louis, all that remained of the millions he had made. Now he took them between his fingers, gazed at them for a while and, once more turning to his son, said:

'Alexandre, everybody says I have been prodigal . . . Well you see how wrong people can be. When I arrived in Paris for the first time, I had two golden louis in my pocket . . . Look I have them still.'

Epilogue

Alexandre Dumas, the most prolific writer of all time died on the fifth of December, 1870.

His son wrote to a friend: 'My father died on Monday evening at ten o'clock, or rather, he fell asleep, for he suffered no pain. On the preceding Monday he had expressed a desire to go to bed at midday . . . He slept continuously. Nevertheless, when we spoke to him, he replied perfectly distinctly and always with a smile . . . it needed death to erase that smile you knew so well.'

Dumas was buried at Neuville les Pollet, less than a mile from Dieppe. He never knew that the Prussians had already occupied Puys. As soon as the war was over his son had his body exhumed and taken to Villers-Cotterêts to lie beside those of the General, his father, and his mother, Marie-Louise Labouret, in the simple country cemetery.

The ceremony was attended only by a few close friends and old acquaintances of his youth. In the words of his son: 'My father had always wished to be buried here, where he had so many memories and friendships. Those memories and friendships welcomed me yesterday evening, when so many arms were offered to assist the bearers in carrying my father's body to the church . . . It was my wish that this ceremony should be not so much one of mourning as of festival, less a burying than a resurrection.'

And so, this man, whose life had been so turbulent, was laid peacefully to rest beside the forest trees he had always loved.

Bibliography

The most important biographies, bibliographies, studies etc of Dumas and his works are, with three exceptions, French, the most interesting of these are:

Robin, Charles *Galerie des Gens de Lettres au 19ᵉ Siècle* (1848)

Chincholle, Charles *Alexandre Dumas aujourd'hui* (1867)

Ferry, Gabriel *Les dernières Années d'Alexandre Dumas* (1833)

Glinel, Charles *Alexandre Dumas et son Oeuvre* (1884)

—— *Le Théâtre inconnu d'Alexandre Dumas* (1899)

Blaze de Bury, Henri *Alexandre Dumas: sa Vie, son Temps, son Oeuvre* (1885)

Audegrand, Philibert *Alexandre Dumas à la Maison d'Or* (1888)

Lenôtre, Georges *Le vrai Chevalier de Maison-Rouge* (1894)

Parigot, Hippolyte *Le Drame d'Alexandre Dumas* (1899)

—— *Alexandre Dumas père* (1902)

Lecomte, Henri *Alexandre Dumas: sa Vie intime, ses Oeuvres* (1902)

Jaurgain, Jean de *Troisvilles, D'Artagnan et les Trois Mousquetaires* (1910)

Samaran, Charles *D'Artagnan* (1912)

Simon, Gustave *Histoire d'une Collaboration* (1919)

Gailly, Gérard *Mémoires de d'Artagnan* (1928)

Almeras, Henri d' *Alexandre Dumas et les Trois Mousquetaires* (1929)

Peslouan, Hervé de *Mesdames Dumas père* (1933)

Charpentier, John *Alexandre Dumas* (1947)

Maurois, André *Les Trois Dumas* (1956) well translated into English

English contributions include

Fitzgerald, Percy *Life and Adventures of Alexandre Dumas* (1873)

BIBLIOGRAPHY

Davidson, A. F. *Alexandre Dumas, his Life and Works* (1902)
Spurr, H. A. *The Life and Writings of Alexandre Dumas* (1902)
Gorman, Herbert *Dumas – The Incredible Marquis* (1929)
Gribble, Francis *Dumas: Father and Son* (1930)
Pearce, G. R. *Dumas Père* (1934)
Reed, F. W. *Bibliography of Alexandre Dumas* (1933)
Bell, A. Craig *Alexandre Dumas* (1945)
Hemming, E. W. J. *The King of Romance* (1979)

Appendix of Authentic Works

Alphabetical list of Dumas's authentic works, excluding poems and dramatisations of the novels.

B signifies Biography or Autobiography
D signifies Drama
F signifies Fiction
H signifies History
J signifies Journals
M signifies Miscellaneous
T signifies Travel
* signifies Unpublished
+ signifies Not reprinted, and therefore not to be found in the standard editions of Calmann-Lévy and Levasseur.

Alternative or secondary titles are given in brackets. The date given is, in the case of all works except the plays, that of the original edition, or, if unpublished, the year of composition. As regards the plays, the year is that of first performance, or, if unperformed, that in which they were written.

Abencerrages, Les,*	D	c.1821
Acté,	F	1838
Alchimiste, L',	D	1839
Alchimiste au dix-neuvième Siècle, Un,+	B	1843
Amaury,	F	1844
Ame à naître, Une, (Histoire d'une Ame)	F	1844
Ames vaillantes, Les,*	D	c.1852
Angèle,	D	1833
Ange Pitou,	F	1851
Année à Florence, Une,	T	1841
Antony,	D	1831
Armée française, L',+	M	1841–45
Art et les artistes contemporains au Salon de 1859, L',+	M	1859
Article nécrologique sur James Rousseau	M	1849
Article nécrologique sur Frédéric Soulié,+	M	1847

Article nécrologique sur Mme Emile de Girardin,+	M	1855
Article nécrologique sur Lamartine,+	M	1869
Ascanio,	F	1843
Aventure d'Amour, Une,	F	1860
Aventures de Lyderic,	F	1842
Bacchante, La*, (Thais)	D	1858
Bal masqué, Un, – See Souvenirs d'Antony		
Barrière de Clichy, La,	D	1851
Bâtard de Mauléon, Le,	F	1846
Black,	F	1858
Blanche de Beaulieu – See Nouvelles contemporaines and Souvenirs d'Antony		
Blancs et les Bleus, Les,	F	1867–68
Borboni di Napoli, I,+ (Les Bourbons de Naples)	H	1862–64
Bric-à-brac,	M	1861
Cachemire vert, Le,	D	1849
Caligula,	D	1837
Capitaine Aréna, Le,	T	1842
Capitaine Pamphile, Le,	F	1840
Capitaine Paul, Le,	F	1838
Capitaine Richard, Le,	F	1855
Catherine Blum,	F	1854
Catherine Howard,	D	1834
Catalina,	D	1848
Caucase, Le,	T	1859
Causeries,	M	1860
Causeries sur l'Italie à Mme Charlotte Dreyfus,+	M	1869
Cécile (La Robe de Noces)	F	1844
César – See Grands Hommes en Robe de Chambre	F	·1844
Charlemagne – See Hommes de Fer		
Charles le Téméraire,	F	1857
Charles VII chez ses grands Vassaux,	D	1831
Chasse au Chastre, La,	F	1841
Chasse et l'Amour, La,	D	1825
Chasseur de Sauvagine, Le,	F	1858
Château de Roche-Pot, Le,+	F	1835
Cherubino et Celestini (Les Enfants de la Madone) – See Souvenirs d'Antony		
Chevalier d'Harmental, Le,	F	1842
Chevalier de Maison-Rouge, Le,	F	1845

Christine,	D	1830
Cléopâtre,+	H	1858
Cocher de Cabriolet, Le, – See Souvenirs d'Antony		
Collier de la Reine, Le,	F	1849–50
Comment je devins Auteur dramatique,	M	1833
Compagnons de Jéhu, Les,	F	1857
Comte de Monte-Cristo, Le,	F	1844–45
Comte de Moret, Le,+	F	1866
Comte Hermann, Le,	D	1849
Comtesse de Charny, La,	F	1852–53
Comtesse de Salisbury, La,	F	1839
Conscience, La,	D	1854
Conscience l'Innocent,	F	1852
Corricolo, Le,	T	1843
Création et Rédemption (Le Docteur mystérieux; La Fille du Marquis)	F	1872
Curé Chambard, Le, – See Souvenirs d'Antony		
Dame de Monsoreau, La,	F	1846
'D'Artagnan', Le,	J	1868
Demoiselles de Saint-Cyr, Les,	D	1843
De Paris à Cadix,	T	1848
Dernier Roi des Français, Le, (Histoire de la Vie politique et privée de Louis-Philippe)	H	1852–53
Dieu dispose,	F	1850–51
Dîner chez Rossini, Un, (Les deux Étudiants de Bologne) – See Les Mille et un Fantômes		
Dîner d'Amis, Le,*	D c.1821	
Docteur mystérieux, Le, – See Création et Rédemption		
Dom Martins de Freytas,	F	1841
Don Juan de Marana,	D	1836
Drame de '93, Le,	H	1851–52
École des Beaux-Arts, L',+	M	1867
Écossais, L',*	D c.1836	
Edith aux longs Cheveux,*	D c.1830	
Emma Lyonna, – See La San-Felice		
En Russie,	T	1860
En Suisse,	T	1833–37
Envers d'une Conspiration, L', (Le Fils de Donald le Noir)	D	1860
Excursions sur les Bords du Rhin,	T	1841
Femme au Collier de Velours, La, – See Les		

Mille et un Fantômes

Femme Sans Amour, La,*	D	?
Fernande,	F	1844
Fiesque de Lavagna,*	D	1827
Fille du Marquis, La, – See Création et Rédemption		
Fille du Régent, Une,	F	1844
Filles, Lorettes et Courtisanes,	M	1843
Fils de l'Émigré, Le,*	D	1832
Fils du Forçat, Le,	F	1859
Fous du Docteur Miraglia, Les,	M	?
France Nouvelle, La,	J	1848
Frères Corses, Les,	F	1844
Gabriel Lambert,	F	1844
Garibaldiens, Les,	M	1861–62
Gaule et la France	H	1833
Gentilshommes de la Sierra-Morena, Les, (Dom Bernardo de Zuniga) – See Les Mille et un Fantômes		
Georges,	F	1843
Gracques, Les,*	D	c.1827
Grand Dictionnaire de la Cuisine, Le,+	M	1873
Grands Hommes en Robe de Chambre, Les, (comprises: Henri IV, Louis XIII et Richelieu, César, Octave Auguste,+ Néron*)	B	1856
Guelfes et Gibelins – See Hommes de Fer		
Guerre des Femmes, La,	F	1845
Gulliver,*	D	1850
Halifax,	D	1842
Henri III et sa Cour,	D	1829
Henri IV – See Grands Hommes en Robe de Chambre		
Herminie, (Une Amazone?)	F	1845
Histoire de mes Bêtes,	M	1868
Hommes de Fer, Les, (comprises: Pépin, Charlemagne, Guelfes et Gibelins, Le Sire de Giac)	F	1867
Honneur est satisfait, L',	D	1858
Horoscope, L',	F	1858
Huitième Croisade, L',	F	1868
Ile de Feu, L', (Le Médecin de Java)	F	1860
'Indipendente', L',	J	1860–64
Ingénue,	F	1854

Intrigue et Amour,	D	1847
Intrigues galantes à la Cour italienne+	F	1870
Invitation à la Valse, L',	D	1857
Invraisemblance (Histoire d'un Mort)	F	1844
Isaac Laquedem,	F	1852–53
Isabel Constant,+	M	1855
Isabelle de Bavière, (Scènes historiques)	H	1836
Italiens et Flamands, (Histoire des Peintres; La Peinture chez les Anciens; Trois Maîtres)	M	1845
Ivanhoe,*	D	c.1822
Jeanne d'Arc,+	H	1858
Jehanne la Pucelle,	F	1842
Jeunesse de Louis XIV, La,	D	1854
Jeunesse de Louis XV, La,*	D	1854
Joseph Balsamo (Mémoires d'un Médecin)	F	1846–48
'Journal du Jeudi',	J	1860
Journée à Fontenay-aux-Roses, Une, – See Les Mille et un Fantômes		
Joûte, Une,+	F	1833
Kean,	D	1836
Laird de Dumbicky, Le,	D	1843
Laurette – See Nouvelles contemporaines		
'Liberté,' La,	J	1848
Lièvre de mon Grand-père, Le,	F	1856
Lorenzino,	D	1842
Louis XIII et Richelieu – See Grands Hommes en Robe de Chambre		
Louis XIV et son Siècle,	H	1844–45
Louis XV et sa Cour,	H	1849
Louis XVI et la Révolution,	H	1850–51
Louise Barnard,	D	1843
Louves de Machecoul, Les,	F	1858
Madame de Chamblay (Ainsi soit-il!)	F	1857–58
Mademoiselle de Belle-Isle,	D	1839
Maître Adam le Calabrais,	F	1840
Maître d'Armes, Le,	F	1840
Major de Strasbourg, Le,*	D	c.1821
Marbrier, Le,	D	1854
Mariage sous Louis XV, Un,	D	1841
Mariages du père Olifus, Les, – See Les Mille et un Fantômes		
Mari de la Veuve, Le,	D	1832

Marie – See Nouvelles contemporaines

Masaniello+	H	1862
Médicis, Les, (Galerie de Florence)	H	1845
Mémoires de Garibaldi,	B	1860
Mémoires d'Horace,+	F	1860
Mémoires de Talma,+	B	1850
Mémoires d'un Médecin (Joseph Balsamo)	F	1846–48
Meneur de Loups, Le,	F	1857
Mes Infortunes de Garde nationale,+	M	1844
Mes Mémoires,	B	1852–55
Midi de la France, Le,	T	1841
Mille et un Fantômes, Les,	F	1849–50

> (comprises: Une Journée à Fontenay-aux-Roses, La Femme au Collier de Velours, Les Mariages du père Olifus, Le Testament de M. de Chauvelin, Un Dîner chez Rossini, Les Gentilshommes de la Sierra-Morena)

Mohicans de Paris, Les, (Salvator)	F	1854–59
'Mois', Le,	J	1848–50
Monseigneur Gaston Phoebus,	F	1839
'Monte-Cristo', Le,	J	1857–60
		1862
Montevideo, ou Une Nouvelle Troie,+	H	1850
Morts vont vite, Les,	M	1861
Mot sur la Poésie en Belgique, Un,+	M	1853
'Mousquetaire', Le,	J	1853–57
		1866–67
Moyen de reprimer le Brigandage en Belgique, Le,+	M	?

Murat – See La Salle d'Armes

Napoléon,	H	1839
Napoléon Bonaparte,	D	1831

Néron – See Grands Hommes en Robe de Chambre

Noce et l'Enterrement, La,	D	1826
Nouvelles contemporaines,+	F	1826

> (comprises: Laurette, Blanche de Beaulieu, Marie)

Nuit à Florence, Une,	F	1861

Octave Auguste – See Grands Hommes en Robe de Chambre

Oeuvre de Notre-Dame-des-sept-Douleurs, L',+	M	1854

Olympe de Clèves,	F	1851–52
Orestie, L',	D	1856
Othon L'Archer,	F	1840
Page du Duc de Savoie, Le, (Emmanuel Philibert)	F	1852
Pape devant les Evangiles, Le,+	M	1861
Parisiens et Provinciaux,	F	1868
Pascal Bruno – See La Salle d'Armes		
Pauline – See La Salle d'Armes		
Paul Jones,	D	1838
Pays Natal, Le,+	M	1864
Pêche aux Filets, La,	F	1845
Pèlerinage à Ermenonville,*	F	c.1821
Pépin – See Hommes de Fer		
Père la Ruine, Le,	F	1860
Petit Dictionnaire de Cuisine,+	M	1882
Phèdre,*	D	?
Pierre le Cruel,	F	1841
Piquillo,	D	1837
Praxède,	F	1841
Propos d'Art et de Cuisine,	M	1877
'Psyché', La,	J	1826–29
Puritains d'Ecosse, Les,*	D	c.1827
Quarante-Cinq, Les,	F	1848
Régence, La,	H	1849
Reine Caroline de Brunswick, La,+	H	1872
Reine Margot, La,	F	1845
Richard Darlington,	D	1831
Roman d'Elvire, Le,	D	1860
Romulus,	D	1854
Route de Varennes, La,	M	1860
Salle d'Armes, La,	F	1838
(comprises: Pauline, Pascal Bruno, Murat)		
Salteador, El, (Le Gentilhomme de la Montagne)	F	1854
Salvator – See Les Mohicans de Paris		
Samson,*	D	1856
San-Felice, La, (Emma Lyonna)	F	1864
Sapho,+	M	1858
Serpents, Les,	M	?
Simples Lettres sur l'Art dramatique,	M	1844
Sir de Giac, Le, – See Hommes de Fer		

Souvenirs d'Antony,	F	1835
(comprises: Cherubino et Celestini, Le Cocher de Cabriolet, Blanche de Beaulieu, Un Bal masqué, Le Curé Chambard)		
Souvenirs dramatiques,	M	1868
Souvenirs d'une Favorite	H	1865
Speronare, Le,	T	1842
Stuarts, Les,	H	1840
'Sylphe', Le,	J	1827–30
Sylvandire,	F	1844
Taureaux espagnols au Havre, Les,+	M	1868
Temple et Hospice du Mont-Carmel,+	M	1844
Teresa,	D	1832
Terreur Prussienne, La,	F	1867
Testament de M. de Chauvelin, Le, – See Les Mille et un Fantômes		
'Théâtre Journal',	J	1868–69
Tour de Nesle, La,	D	1832
Tour Saint-Jacques, La,	D	1856
Trois Entr'Actes pour "L'Amour Médecin",	D	1850
Trois Mousquetaires, Les,	F	1844
Trou de l'Enfer, Le,	F	1850–51
Tulipe Noire, La,	F	1850
Urbain Grandier,	D	1850
Vampire, Le,	D	1851
Véloce, Le,	T	1848–51
Vendée après le 29 juillet (1830), La,+	M	1831
Verrou de la Reine, Le,	D	1856
Vicomte de Bragelonne, Le,	F	1848–50
Vie d'Artiste, Une,	B	1854
Villa Palmieri, La,	T	1843
Vingt ans après,	F	1845
Vingt-quatre Fevrier, Le,	D	1850
Volontaire de '92, Le,+ (René d'Argonne)	F	1862

Index

INDEX

Rachel, 186, 218
Reine Margot, La, 196, 211, 217, 230
republicanism, Dumas's, 122-36, 143,
    165-9, 176, 181, 236-7
Revue des Deux Mondes, 135, 151, 157,
    172, 179
Richard Darlington, 145-6, 186
Rollin, Ledru-, 179, 195
Roman d'Elvire, Le, 256-7
Romulus, 188, 248
Roqueplan, Nestor, 95, 221, 265
Rossini, 152, 155, 173
Rousseau, James, 69-70, 101
Rusconi, 232, 248, 249
Russia, visit to, 254-5
Russie, En, 254

Saint-George, Chevalier de, 13, 53
Sainte-Beuve, 101, 144, 186, 187, 208,
    213
Salteador, El, 248
Salvandy, 221-2, 226
Samson, 89, 95
San Felice, 260, 264
Sand, George, 139, 147, 173, 213, 254,
    266
Sandeau, Jules, 240
Schiller, 48, 75-7, 93, 109, 111-14, 146
Scott, Walter, 51, 71, 75, 76, 80, 93,
    146, 152, 194, 196
Scrivaneck, Céleste, 233-4
Sebastiani, Marshal, 59-60
Shakespeare, 49, 50, 77, 78, 79, 115,
    186, 213
Shaw, Mathilde, 270
Smithson, Harriet, 79, 80
Soulié, Frédéric, 75-6, 80, 83, 90,
    109-10, 195, 248
Souvestre, Emile, 117
Spain, visit to, 221, 223-4
Sue, Eugène, 195
Switzerland, visit to, 167-70

Talma, 52-3, 55, 57, 71, 84, 114
Taylor, Baron, 85-6, 88, 89, 91, 95, 101,
    104

Térésa, 147-9, 177
Terreur Prussienne, La, 269, 273, 276
Théâtre Français/Royal, 52, 53, 71,
    84-5, 87-9, 95-6, 104, 138, 159, 186
Théâtre Historique, 222, 229-30, 234,
    235, 239, 241, 242, 245
Thibaut, Dr, 72-3
Thierry, 151-2, 171, 182
Thiers, 121, 132, 179, 236
Three Musketeers, The, 15, 27, 199, 202,
    207, 208, 211, 217, 241, 275
Tour de Nesle, La, 159-60, 162, 164, 170,
    175, 186, 243
travel, foreign, Dumas's, 134, 167-70,
    174-8, 185, 201, 221, 223-6, 250-1,
    254-5, 257-62, 269, 276

Véloce, Le, 223
Vendée après le 29 juillet, La, 135
Verdier, General, 60-1
Verlaine, Paul, 246, 272
Véron, 225, 227, 228
Vicomte de Bragelonne, Le, 196, 241, 249
Vie d'Artiste, Une, 171, 248
Viel-Castel, 189
Vigny, Alfred de, 98, 106, 108, 110, 112,
    138, 139, 150, 246
Villa Palmieri, La, 41
Villafranca, Prince of, 191
Villemessant, 207-8
Villenave, Charles de, 94-5
Vingt ans après, 27, 199, 211, 217, 241
Voyage en Suisse, 168, 171, 172, 186, 223,
    253
Voyage en Vendée, 151

Waldor, Mélanie, 94, 101, 106, 109,
    116-17, 120, 134, 140-1, 189
women, love affairs with, 43-6, 50, 70-1,
    91, 94-5, 109, 116-17, 140-1, 147, 148,
    167, 174, 188-92, 218, 233, 245, 257,
    264-5, 268-73, *see also under individual*
    headings

Zola, 245, 258

293